ITALIAN
CANADIAN
VOICES

ITALIAN CANADIAN VOICES

A Literary Anthology
1946 - 2004

Edited by
Caroline Morgan DiGiovanni

mosaic press

Co-Published with
Centro Scuola e Cultura Italiana
Toronto

Library and Archives Canada Cataloguing in Publication

Italian Canadian voices : a literary anthology, 1946-2004 / edited by
Caroline Morgan DiGiovanni.

Co-published by: Centro canadese scuola e cultura italiana.
Includes bibliographical references. In English; includes some text in Italian and French.

ISBN 0-88962-858-0
    1. Canadian literature--Italian-Canadian authors. 2. Italian Canadians--Literary collections. I. DiGiovanni, Caroline Morgan, 1947- II.
Centro canadese scuola e cultura italiana

PS8235.I8I83 2006   C810.8'0851071   C2006-903688-8

Published by Mosaic Press, offices and warehouse at 1252 Speers Rd.,
units 1 & 2, Oakville, On L6L 5N9, Canada and Mosaic Press, PMB
145, 4500 Witmer Industrial Estates, Niagara Falls, NY, 14305-1386,
U.S.A.

Copyright © Centro Scuola e Cultura Italiana 2006
info@mosaic-press.com
Printed and Bound in Canada
ISBN 0-88962-858-0
Published with assistance from Centro Scuola and
The Columbus Centre / Villa Charities Foundation

Mosaic Press in Canada:	Mosaic Press in U.S.A.:
1252 Speers Road, Units 1 & 2,	4500 Witmer Industrial Estates
Oakville, Ontario	PMB 145, Niagara Falls, NY
L6L 5N9	14305-1386
Phone/Fax: 905-825-2130	Phone/Fax: 1-800-387-8992
info@mosaic-press.com	info@mosaic-press.com
http://www.mosaic-press.com	http://www.mosaic-press.com

www.mosaic-press.com

For carlo, franca, and annamaria,
con amore.

Acknowledgements

Putting together an anthology means persuading many different people to contribute something of their own work to a common effort. For their enthusiastic participation in this revised edition of *Italian Canadian Voices* I must thank first and foremost the writers. Without fail they greeted our request for their works with spirit and generosity. I felt like a *zia* inviting all the relatives to a family wedding. Everyone accepted the invitation. This is a very vibrant *famiglia*.

I must thank in particular our poet priest Pier Giorgio Di Cicco who has been a creative force in Canadian poetry since the 1970's. Pier Giorgio was of great assistance to me by bringing to my attention some of the new names included in this edition.

The most energetic thanks must go to Centro Scuola e Cultura Italiana and Villa Charities for the financial assistance provided to make this volume a reality. Most of all, for his vision of the great potential within the Italian Canadian community, his leadership in creating opportunities for development, and his dedication to asserting the Italian presence in the Canadian mosaic, I thank Alberto Di Giovanni, my husband and lifelong companion.

Caroline Morgan Di Giovanni
Toronto, Ontario
2006

Table of Contents

Voices Table of Contents (cont).

III. Short Stories

IV. Excerpts

V. Poems

Voices Table of Contents (cont).

Afterword

Sources

Introduction

Twenty years ago, in 1984, the first edition of *Italian Canadian Voices* came into existence, bringing a collection of writers and their poetry and prose to the attention of the Canadian reading public. The book was supported by a federal government grant within the rubric of Multiculturalism. Poetry selections were made to build on the excellent 1978 collection entitled *Roman Candles*, edited by Pier Giorgio Di Cicco. The first prose selection, Mario Duliani's account of internment during the Second World War, surprised the younger generation, who had not been made aware of this chapter in Italian Canadian history. Other selections were made by ranging across the country, making contact with individual writers or, in some cases, locating their work in journals. It was a voyage of discovery, finding the "voices" that described for others the experience of immigration, up-rootedness, and settlement in a new environment very different from their familiar past.

As background, reference was made to the lives of the "sojourners," workers from Italy who came to Canada to work in the forests and on railroad construction. These early migrants generally maintained the pattern of moving back to Italy after earning enough in the New World to assist their families in their hometown. Prof. Robert Harney's studies of migration history contributed this picture of the Italians in Canada in the first part of the 20th Century. In fact, Prof. Harney's academic work on immigration influenced a generation of Canadian historians. He set out to record the impact of this change in people's lives, and demonstrated how significantly the arrival of new populations affected the social development of North America. Kings and Generals make their mark, but the movement of thousands of newcomers into cities and towns provides the opportunity for an energetic new culture to develop.

After the Second World War, Italian immigrant families from small towns affected by the conflict and post-war conditions chose Canada to start a new life. This generation set their sights on opportunities for their children. In the first version of this anthology, the majority of the writers were the offspring of this vigorous, hard-working population.

Their children went to university the way their parents had crossed the ocean-- to seek a new life.

Preparing the revised anthology, in 2004, became an exploration of ideas about identity within the context of Canadian literature at the start of the 21st century. A visual image of the Canadian population was created by artist Robin Pacific for a public library in a downtown Toronto neighbourhood. On a map of the world the artist arranged photos of local storekeepers, library staff, and neighbourhood personalities. Each individual is linked to a country on the map. The result is a network of red lines reaching to every continent in every hemisphere, all leading back to the tiny spot that is the library's location. Contemporary Canadian writers could be placed on a similar spread. The population provides the artists, and the Canadian population is one of the most diverse in the world. Italian Canadians draw upon the cultural roots of many centuries, notwithstanding the experience of transplanting their lives to the North American geography.

The objective of *Italian Canadian Voices* is to provide students and the general reader with a sample of Italian Canadian poetry and prose from the second half of the 20th Century and the first years of the 21st Century. These 60 years comprise a rich and dynamic period of Canadian cultural development. The variety of work presented here gives witness to the contributions Italian Canadian writers have made and continue to make to this flourishing literary scene.

Mario Duliani, whose work is the first piece in this anthology, was an established journalist in Montreal. Publishing *La ville sans femmes* in 1945 was an act of courage. It appeared first in French, an indication that it was intended for the general public. In 1946, the author published his Italian language translation of the book. In 1983, Antonino Mazza made the English translation of the portion that appears here.

Among the workers in the post-war railroad construction gangs in Northern Ontario was Gianni Angelo Grohovaz, a young journalist from Fiume. In 1953, while he lived the rough life on the track sites, he kept a daily journal of his impressions and experiences. Grohovaz went on to become the editor of an Italian language newspaper, Il Giornale di Toronto. Included here is his poem in memory of Bruno Mesaglio, the founder and director of the Italian language theatre company, Il Piccolo Teatro. Both the newspaper and the theatre company flourished as necessary cultural connections during the 1950's and 60's while the newly-arrived Italian families settled into their lives in a country of cold and snow, long hours and low wages.

The work ethic which motivated so many newcomers gave rise to a number of entrepreneurs within the Italian community who built new lives in Canada while still respecting their heritage. Giuseppe Ricci, founder of a successful pasta company, recorded his life story in a volume called *L'Orfano di Padre* (The Orphan). The chapter included here describes his decision to become a Canadian citizen. Thus, the First Voices section consists of memoirs of personal experience.

The appearance of *Roman Candles* in 1978 marked the coming of age of the children of the post-war immigration. Edited by Pier Giorgio Di Cicco, already a noted young poet at that time, this collection of the work of 17 Italian-Canadian writers reflected the lives of thousands of other members of their generation. Through their words, the reading public begins to know about their adolescence in two worlds, the family home and the outside community. The normal tensions between generations here also include differences in language, social acceptance, and personal identity. The selections in this anthology are a tribute to the original *Roman Candles* collection.

The third section contains short stories gathered from across Canada. Alexandre Amprimoz writes academic essays as well as poetry and short stories. Preludes evokes a child's point of view of the mystery of the adults who run his world. The story, Assimilation, by Edmonton writer Caterina Edwards, describes the gradual self-awareness of a young immigrant coming to grips with his new society. Vivi's Florentine Scarf is about a young woman who comes to a turning point during a trip to Florence. It is from Darlene Madott's second collection of stories, *Joy, Joy, Why Do I Sing?* (2004). Poets Len Gasparini and Antonino Mazza both began publishing prose writing in the 1990's. Antonino Mazza has provided Urban Harvest, from his recent work. This piece draws attention to the basic stuff of life interrupted by immigration. Len Gasparini has written and published a children's book and numerous short stories. Laura is one of them.

The fourth section of this anthology contains excerpts from novels that were published in the 1980's and 1990. Included is a portion of the novella *A Whiter Shade of Pale* (1989), by Caterina Edwards, a member of the Italian Canadian Writers Association. This piece references the main character's memory and experience in terms of an Etruscan archeological dig. The three other selections concern the impact of immigration decisions on the lives of women. Matilda Torres used her novel *La Dottoressa di Cappadocia* (The Doctor from Cappadocia) (1982) to document her own experience in choosing to leave her homeland and start a new life in Canada.

Frank Paci wrote a trilogy of novels that deserve closer attention now that Italian Canadian writing is recognized as a genre within Canadian literature. *The Italians* (1978), *Black Madonna* (1982) and *The Father* (1984) follow three families as they adjust to life in Sault Sainte Marie and Toronto, Ontario. Each story describes the conflicts and the deep connections between the immigrant parents and their Canadian-born children. The excerpt selected here comes from the middle volume, *Black Madonna*. The title character, a recently-widowed mother, remains isolated and enigmatic throughout the novel until the final ambiguity of her accidental death removes her from a life that was confined to her own household. The chapter in this anthology probes the daughter's search for identity and reconciliation as she examines her late mother's trousseau trunk, her few personal possessions.

Included here is an excerpt from Nino Ricci's first novel, *Lives of the Saints* (1990; 21st printing, 2004). This book won several prizes, including the Governor General's Award for Fiction in 1990. Nino Ricci completed his trilogy with *In a Glass House* (1993) and *Where She Has Gone* (1997). All three books centre on the character of Vittorio from his early childhood in Italy to youth and young manhood in Ontario. *Lives of the Saints* remained a Canadian best seller for many months; it has never been out of print, and it has been adapted as a film for television with Sophia Loren. The section reprinted here captures the complex dilemma of a young Italian woman in a small village while her husband is working overseas.

The final section contains a sample of the poetry now being written by contemporary Italian Canadian writers. Some of the poems here appeared in the in 1984 edition of *Voices*. New selections have been added. No collection can really do justice to the many books in circulation thanks to the small press industry, the dedicated poets, and the support of the Canada Council and an ardent public. A previous agreement with one of the publishers was not renewed for this revised anthology. Interested readers will find numerous titles and catalogues available in print and online.

George Amabile gave permission to use "Generation Gap" as long as we also included "Ancestors", harking back to the very beginning, "a mind squeezing light out of nothing at all."

Alexandre Amprimoz's poems in both English and French show his versatility. Celestino De Iuliis' poignant reflection "In My Backyard" captures the pain of tensions between generations.

Mary Di Michele's first volumes of poetry in the 1980's established her reputation as a writer to be noticed. The triptych of dramatic monologues included here articulates the emotional experiences of family members in the aftermath of emigration and resettlement. They appear in the collection *Mimosa and Other Poems* (1981). Len Gasparini published several books of poetry in the 1980's while he lived in Toronto. His tribute "To My Father" marks that era. Antonino Mazza is a gifted poet himself and a brilliant translator of the Italian poet Eugenio Montale. The selections here demonstrate Mazza's Mediterranean sensibility through his language, inspiration, and imagery. The poetry of Romano Perticarini from Vancouver exhibits a West Coast perspective.

Pier Giorgio Di Cicco's work has evolved in two segments. Between 1975 and 1986 he published 14 books of poems, including *Roman Candles* (1978), the first anthology of Italian Canadian writing. Then there was a long pause, during which time Di Cicco entered a monastery, undertook theological studies, and was ordained a Roman Catholic priest. Finally, in 2001, he was persuaded to resume writing poetry for publication. Included here are poems from both major periods. Fr. Di Cicco's poems on immigration themes influenced two generations of writers in their articulation of their heritage. His work since ordination describes a different kind of journey, internal and spiritual but still very dynamic.

Six other contemporary poets have been added to this revised edition of Italian Canadian Voices. In the selections here from his book *Credo* (2000), Carmine Starnino deals with family ties. Starnino is known also for his perceptive literary essays and reviews. Matt Santateresa's collection, *Icarus Redux* (2003) explores, among other themes, the critical father-son relationship. His portrayal of Ovid in exile captures the longing of displacement. Isabella Colalillo Katz provides the anthology with poems about motherhood. Her feminist perspective articulates coming to terms with both tradition and intelligent independence. Bruna Di Giuseppi-Bertoni reflects on the grief of departure. Joseph Maviglia is a singer as well as a writer and a worker. The poems here are chosen from his book, *freakin' Palomino Blue* (2004). Corrado Paina observes the life of new Canadians in Toronto and the suburbs, from his volume, *Hoarse Legend* (2000).

Pier Giorgio Di Cicco was the Goggio Visiting Professor of Italian Canadian Writing at the University of Toronto in the spring of 2004. He called his series of lectures "Mediterranea: Poetry and Poetics in Italian/Canadian Culture." His general thesis in the three presentations held that writers from the Italian peninsula bring a specific metaphysical ethos that derives from the heat, the light, the bio-cultural ecology and passion of their Greco-Latin heritage. Moreover, this sensibility translates into a new and unique vocal canon, inferring a connection to a spiritual quest in nearly every example. Such a theory brings to Canadian letters a view that contests and amends Margaret Atwood's thesis that Canadian literature is about survival in the wilderness. The Goggio lectures revision the analysis of the impact Italian Canadian writers have had on Canadian artistic expression after a half century of peaceful immigration.

There is no single approach to Italian Canadian writing. However, as time passes and as more and more Canadian writers emerge from backgrounds of global diversity, it is useful to take a closer look at the vocabulary and imagery they use. Can the readers find distinctions that identify writers with Italian heritage? Students taking courses in Canadian literature have the world at their fingertips. They can locate information about writers across the continent and around the world. Endless research is available. But memoirs, stories, novels, and poetry go beyond facts to the heart of human experience. The writers collected in this anthology share a common inheritance which they express in different ways, in an engaging conversation of Italian Canadian Voices.

An Added Word:
When the first edition of this anthology came out, Italian Canadian writers had stories to tell in every part of the country, but they had yet to create a network linking with each other. A conference in Rome, in 1984, brought together some of the writers to reflect on the history and origins of Italian immigration to Canada. Two years later, in September, 1986, a group of Italian Canadian writers gathered in Vancouver for the first formal conference organized by the writers themselves headed by C.D. Minni, Pier Giorgio Di Cicco, Joseph Pivato, Antonio D'Alfonso, and Pasquale Verdicchio. They formed an association, and met to share their insights, experiences, trials and triumphs. The Association of Italian Canadian Writers brings together a community of writers, critics, academics, artists, and others who promote the writing and artistic expressions of Italian Canadians.

Caroline Morgan Di Giovanni
Toronto, Ontario
2006

About the Authors

George Amabile

Poet, short-story writer and editor George Amabile was born in Jersey City, New Jersey in 1936, and studied at the University of Conneticut, earning a Ph.D. in1969. His poems have appeared in numerous magazines and literary reviews in Canada, the USA, Australia, South America and the UK. He has published eight books, of which *The Presence of Fire* (1982) won the CAA Silver Medal for Poetry. After a teaching career at the University of Manitoba, he retired and in 2000 took a position as poetry editor for Signature Editions, in Winnipeg.

Alexandre Amprimoz

A scholar, writer, and university professor, Alexandre Amprimoz teaches in the Department of Modern Languages, Literatures, and Cultures at Brock University, St. Catherine's, Ontario. He has published extensively in French and English, with additional poetry in Italian and Spanish. His work includes literary translations from English, French, Italian, Spanish, and Portuguese.
He was born in Rome in1948 and educated in Italy and France, before coming to Canada.

Isabella Colalillo Katz

Italian born, Isabella Colalillo Katz is a poet, writer, editor, holistic educator, translator and storyteller based in Toronto. She holds a Doctorate in Education from the Ontario Institute for Studies in Education at University of Toronto. Her poetry has appeared in magazines, journals, and in anthologies, including *Pillars of Lace* (l999). Isabella has contributed diverse articles to journals and magazines on creativity, holistic education, new paradigms and culture. As a translator, Isabella is currently translating into English E. Vittorini's *Conversazioni in Sicilia*. She is a co-editor of a collection of essays on holistic education, *Holistic Learning: Breaking New Ground* (SUNY, 2004). Isabella is co-creator and producer of the award winning children's audiotape: *Crocket,*

Carob and Crystals: The C3 Trilogy. She is the author of three books of poetry *Tasting Fire* (l999), *Light Remains* (in press), and *The Uses of Thorns* (2004)

Saro D'Agostino (1948-2000)

Born in Calabria in 1948, Saro D'Agostino came to Canada with his family in 1953. He studied with Irving Layton at York University. His poetry appeared in numerous magazines, including *Antigonish Review*, *Descant*, *Northern Journey*, and *Impulse*. In Toronto, he worked as an Italian teacher in the Heritage Languages program.

Celestino De Iuliis

From Campotosto, Abruzzo, where he was born in 1948, Celestino De Iuliis came to Toronto in the post WWII wave of immigration. He obtained a B.A. and a Master's degree from the University of Toronto. He is active in the Italian community in Toronto. His first book of poems, *Love's Sinning Song*, was published in 1981. His latest work is a translation of Dante's *Divine Comedy* into English verse in *terza rima.*

Pier Giorgio Di Cicco

Pier Giorgio Di Cicco is one of the most versatile poets in Canada today and has remained the central figure in Italo-Canadian "poesis" His work has evolved in two segments. Between 1975 and 1986 he published 14 books of poems, including *Roman Candles* (1978), the first anthology of Italian-Canadian writing. He was one of the founding members of the Association of Italian Canadian Writers, in 1986.
Then there was a long pause, during which time Di Cicco entered a monastery, undertook theological studies, and was ordained a Roman Catholic priest. Finally, in 2001, he resumed writing poetry for publication. The result was the collection, *Living in Paradise* (2001), followed by *The Honeymoon Wilderness* (2002), *The Dark Time of Angels* (2003) and *Dead Men of the Fifties* (2004). He continues to write new poems, reflections, and commentary in print media and the internet. In 2004, Fr. Di Cicco was appointed Poet Laureate of the City of

Toronto. In this capacity he has written and lectured widely on the place of culture and creativity in contemporary urban life.

Bruna Di Giuseppe-Bertoni

Bruna G. Di Giuseppe-Bertoni was born in 1951, and emigrated with her family to Scarborough, Ontario in 1964. Creative writing has been her passion since childhood. Her award-winning poetry has been published in magazines, in both English and Italian. In 2002, the poem 'I remember... Pier 21' was selected by the Pier 21 Society for publication as part of a promotion on Pier 21 History Museum's 'Are your foot prints on Pier 21' project. Her writing now includes fiction and non-fiction. She also paints on porcelain, and on canvas with acrylic and watercolours.

Mary Di Michele

Poet and novelist Mary Di Michele arrived in Canada in 1955. She graduated from the University of Toronto with a B.A. in 1972, and earned an M.A. from the University of Windsor, where she studied with Joyce Carol Oates. She has published eight books of poetry, and the novels *Under My Skin* (1994) and *Tenor of Love* (2004). Her literary work has won several awards, including First Prize in the CBC competition, 1980, and the Air Canada Writing Award, 1983. In the 1980's she worked as a freelance writer and editor for *Toronto Life*, *Poetry Toronto*, and the *Toronto Star* prior to moving to Montreal to take up her current position as a full professor in the English Department of Concordia University, teaching in the creative writing program. Her work has been widely anthologized, and is the subject of interviews and essays in Italy, Canada, and the US.

Mario Duliani (1885-1964)

Born in Istria in 1885, he began his writing career in Milan in 1906. By 1907 he had moved to Paris, where he worked as a foreign correspondent for *Il Messaggero* of Rome. At the same time, he wrote, directed, and produced plays in the Parisian theatre world. Duliani arrived in Montreal in 1936, sponsored by the Canadian Consul General in Paris and the editor of the Montreal daily *La Presse*. He was interned in Petawawa, Ontario then transferred to Fredericton, N.B. , from 1940 to 1943. He died in Montreal in 1964.

Caterina Edwards

Caterina Edwards was born in England in 1948, came to Canada with her family, and grew up in Calgary, Alberta. Her collection of short stories, *The Island of the Nightingales*, won the 2000 Writers Guild of Alberta Award for Short Fiction. Her novel, *The Lion's Mouth* (1982) received critical and academic attention. Guernica Editons reprinted it in 1993, and published a French translation in 1999. Her work includes the novellas *A Whiter Shade of Pale/ Becoming Emma* (1992) and the play *Terra Straniera* produced professionally in Edmonton and published by Guernica Editions under the title *Homeground*. Caterina has also co-edited two books of life writing by women: *Eating Apples: Knowing Women's Lives* (1994) and *Wrestling with the Angel: Women Reclaiming their Lives* (2000).

Len Gasparini

Len Gasparini is the author of ten volumes of poetry, including *Ink from an Octopus,* which was awarded the F.G. Bressani Prize in 1990. He has also published two story collections: *Blind Spot* and *A Demon in my View*; a children's book, *A Christmas for Carol ;* and a work of non-fiction, *Erase Me*, with photographs by Leslie Thompson. His one-act play *Enough Rope* premiered in Montreal in 1976. He edited *The Collected Poems of Bertram Warr* in 1970. He lives in Toronto.

Vera F. Golini

Vera F. Golini teaches at St. Jerome's University in Kitchener, Ontario. She has been actively engaged in teaching about Italian Canadian writers for more than 20 years. In addition to Italian studies, her teaching career has included university courses in Women's Studies as well as significant involvement with Italian classes for the Heritage Languages Program in

Ontario. Prof. Golini has served as President of the Canadian Society for Italian Studies, and as editor of the Society's journal. She gave one of the Iacobucci Lectures at the University of Toronto, 2006.

Gianni Grohovaz (1926 – 1983)

Born in Fiume in 1926, Gianni Grohovaz came to Canada in 1950 where he took a job with the construction crew of CP Rail in northern Ontario. He recorded this experience in his novel, *La Strada Bianca,* which was published posthumously in 1989. He became well known in the Italian Canadian community during his many years as a journalist and editor of *La Settimana,* the *Corriere Canadese, Il Giornale di Toronto, La Voce della Domenica,* and *Panorama.* His poetry in Italian won international awards, with special recognition for his book, *Per ricordar le cose che ricordo* (1974), a collection of poems in his native dialect. He also published the transcripts of radio talks he gave between 1980 and 1982.

Darlene Madott

Darlene Madott is a Toronto-born lawyer and writer. Prior to entering law school, she worked on the editorial staffs of *Saturday Night* and *Toronto Life* magazines, and did occasional book reviews for the Toronto Globe & Mail. Her call to the Ontario Bar in 1985 coincided with the publication of a collection of short stories, *Bottled Roses.* Her short stories have appeared in a variety of literary periodicals and anthologies, including *The Anthology of Italian-Canadian Writing* (1998), *Curaggia* (1998), and *Pillars of Lace* (1998). She has published in small magazines across Canada, including *Aurora: New Canadian Writing 1978, Canadian Forum, Canadian Ethnic Studies, Wave, Grain, Quarry, Wascana Review, The Capilano Review, Fiddlehead, Dandelion, ACCENTi.* She wrote a film script, *Mazzilli's Shoes,* in 1999. Her books include: *Song and Silence* (1977). *Bottled Roses* (1985). And *Joy, Joy, Why Do I Sing?* (2004).

Joseph Maviglia

A poet and musician, Joseph Maviglia's song "Father, It's Time" appeared on the Juno award- winning compilation *The Gathering* in 1992. His poetry has been published in a variety of journals and magazines in both Canada and the United States. His books of poetry include: *Movietown* (1990), *A God Hangs Upside Down* (1994), *Winter Jazz* (1998) and *freakin' Palomino Blue* (2003). His short opera *Binoculars* was presented by Tapestry New Opera Works in March, 2006, in the Opera to Go series.

Antonino Mazza

Born in Italy and proud of his Calabrese roots, Antonino Mazza came to Canada in 1961, where he studied at Carleton University and the University of Toronto, and taught at the University of Ottawa. His poems have appeared in numerous literary magazines and anthologies in Canada, the US, and Australia. His acclaimed work as a translator includes Eugenio Montale's *Ossi di sepia-The Bones of Cuttlefish* (1983); Pier Paolo Pasolini's *Poetry* (1991) and Mario Duliani's *La Ville sans femmes- The City Without Women* (1994). His recording of original poems, with music by Aldo Mazza, *The Way I Remember It* (1988) appeared in book form in 1992. Antonino Mazza lives in Ottawa.

Frank G. Paci

F.G. Paci was born in Italy and grew up in Sault Ste. Marie. He was educated at the University of Toronto (B.A., B.Ed.), and Carleton, where he received his M.A. in English Literature. He was writer-in-residence at York University for a year and has received an honorary degree from Laurentian (Algoma University). Since 1978, when *The Italians* came out, he has published 10 novels. *Black Madonna* (1982) is considered his most acclaimed novel. Since 1990 he has been working on a series of novels (The Black Blood series) that deals with the development of consciousness and religious search of a protagonist that closely parallels his own life. *Italian Shoes* (2002) is the fifth in the series. It won the F.G. Bressani Literary Prize in 2004, awarded by the Italian Cultural Centre in Vancouver. Other novels include *Icelands* (1999), *Losers* (2002), and *Hard*

Edge, (2004). F.G. Paci lives and teaches in Toronto.
A book of essays on his work , *F.G. Paci: Essays on His Work*, ed. J. Pivato, came out in 2003.

Corrado Paina

Corrado Paina was born in Milan in 1954, and emigrated to Canada in 1987. He has published poetry in Italian and in English, including *Hoarse Legend* (2000) and *the dowry of education* (2004). Corrado Paina has worked for many years in public relations and high tech consulting with the Italian Trade Commission in Toronto, and has travelled extensively in South America, Africa, Europe and the United States. He is co-editor, with Denis De Klerck, of a collection of essays, *College Street – Little Italy, Toronto's Renaissance Strip* published by Mansfield Press in 2006.

Romano Perticarini

Born in Fermo in the region of the Marches, in 1934, Romano Perticarini came to Canada with his family in 1967. He wrote for *L'Eco d'Italia*, an Italian language newspaper in Vancouver, and for *Il Cittadino Canadese* in Montreal. He has won a number of poetry awards in Italy, among them the City of Pompeii prize in 1977. His poetry has appeared in anthologies in Italy. *Il mio quaderno di novembre/ My November Record Book* (1983) was published in Vancouver.

Tony Pignataro

Tony Pignataro came to Canada as a child in 1953. His family settled in Toronto, where he studied and became a teacher in the Catholic school system. He wrote poetry, music, and songs. After retiring from his teaching career in 2002, he undertook full time studies at Regis College, working on a Diploma of Spiritual Direction. He has been a deacon since 1992, and an assistant at St. Mark's Parish in Etobicoke. He continues to write poetry,and also reflections, some of a spiritual nature, others simply remembrances.

Giuseppe Ricci (1901-1981)

From the Abruzzi region of Italy, Giuseppe Ricci emigrated to Canada
in 1925, where he began with modest means and established the
Lancia-Bravo Company, supplying the Canadian market with locally
manufactured pastas and Italian food products. He was an active member
of the Italian community in Toronto, and a generous supporter of its
cultural aspirations. *L'Orfano di Padre, Le Memorie di Giuseppe Ricci,*
remains one of the few personal documents of Italian immigration to
Canada before 1940.

Nino Ricci

Nino Ricci was born in 1959 in Leamington, Ontario. He earned a B.A.
from York University in 1981, and a M.A. from Concordia in 1987. He
spent two years teaching in Nigeria with CUSO, and one year studying
in Florence. He served as one of the directors of PEN Canada from 1990-
96, and as President during 1995-96. His novels include the trilogy *Lives
of the Saints*(1990), *In a Glass House* (1993), *Where She Has Gone* (1997)
as well as *Testament* (2002). Awards for *Lives of the Saints* include the
Governor General's Award for Fiction, the F.G. Bressani Prize for Prose,
and the W.H. Smith/Books in Canada First Novel Award. He currently
lives in Toronto, where he writes full-time.

Matt Santateresa

Matt Santateresa has published in numerous magazines and journals.
He has written three volumes of poetry : *Combustible Light* (1999), *A
Beggar's Loom* (2001), and *Icarus Redux* (2003) as well as two chapbooks:
Traveller and *The Other Side of Komodo Island*. He was born in Montréal
and was educated at the University of Toronto and Concordia University.
He presently works and teaches at Concordia University, Montréal.

Carmine Starnino

Carmine Starnino is a poet, essayist, critic and editor of Signal Editions (an imprint of Véhicule Press). His first poetry collection *The New World* was nominated for the 1997 QSPELL A.M. Klein Prize for Poetry and the 1997 Gerald Lampert Memorial Award. His second collection *Credo* won the 2001 Canadian Authors Association Prize for Poetry and the 2001 David McKeen Award for Poetry. His third book, *With English Subtitles,* was published in 2004. *Lover's Quarrel* (2004) is a collection of his literary criticism of Canadian poetry. Starnino is also the associate editor of Maisonneuve magazine and an editor of Books in Canada. He lives in Montréal.

Matilde Gentile Torres

Italian born and educated, Matilde Gentile Torres graduated from the University of Rome in 1975, with a degree in medicine. She served as the medical and health officer for the town of Cappadocia until 1977, when she emigrated to Canada with her husband. They reside with their family in Toronto. Her novel *La Dottoressa di Cappadocia* was published in Rome in 1982.

I
FIRST VOICES

MARIO DULIANI

NOCTURNE *Montréal, 1940*

C'est aujourd'hui le 29 juin, l'avant-dernier jour de ce mois de juin qui avait commence en suscitant une vive apprehension chez tous les Italiens du Canada. L'attitude du Gouvernement de Rome à l'égard de Paris et de Londres devenait de plus en plus menaçante. Les Italiens s'abordaient dans la rue avec une mine préoccupée.

— Croyez-vous que Mussolini déclarera la guerre?

— A qui?

— A la France et à l'Angleterre... à cause du pacte de l'Axe...

— Jamais de la vie! A l'époque de l'assassinat du chancelier Dolfuss, Mussolini a mobiisé deux armees contre l'Allemagne. En 14, il faut un partisan ardent de l'intervention italienne contre l'Allemagne et l'Autriche. Ii n'y a pas longtemps encore, il disait que...

— Oui, oui, oui, tout cela est très beau, mais les indices deviennent de plus en plus alarmants. On vient de suspendre le départ de paquebots faisant le service entre Naples et New-York. La presse fasciste, qui obéit à un mot d'ordre, devient de plus en plus violente contre la France... il n'est bruit que de mobilisation partielle, prelude de la mobilisation générale... Pensez donc! l'Italie dispose de huit millions de baïonnettes, de milliers d'avions, de plusieurs divisions cuirassées...

— Mais vous voyez bien que l'Allemagne et la Russie sont unies par un traité secret... Hitler peut s'entendre avec Staline. Mussolini ne le suivra jamais!

Et ainsi, pendant des heures et des heures, toutes les éventualités étaient pesées, supputées, examinés, faisant alterner dans le coeur de ces Italiens le doute et l'espoir, la crainte et un fugace sentiment de sécurité, car aucun d'entre eux n'aurait vraiment voulu que l'Italie changêat sa politique traditionnelle, la politique d'union à la France et à l'Angleterre, qui avait permis à un peuple divisé et dominé par l'étranger de reconstituer sa propre unité et decreér chez lui une vie prospère en l'espace d'à peine un demi-siècle. Mais on avait beau raisonner, discuter, questionner, les nouvelles de Rome devenaient de plus en plus mauvaises.

***

Alors ils n'osaient plus formuler leur pensée, exprimer leurs inquiétudes.

En tout cas, ce serait une «sale histoire» pour tous ceux qui, habitant le Canada, avaient manifesté une sympathie idéologique ou platonique envers le fascisme, car ils se trouveraient à devenir ipso facto des ennemis!

— Que deviendrons-nous? se demandaient ces Italiens, auxquels, évidemment, on ne pouvait faire grief de ce que déciderait le Gouvernement de Rome.

Des amis, gens bien intentionnés ou bien renseignés, avaient pris le soin de les prévenir:

— Prenez garde à vous! Si Mussolini déclare la guerre, vous courrez le risque d'être internés.

Les Italiens répondaient:

—Pourquoi le serions-nous, puisque nous n'avons rien fait contre le Canada, que nous avons créé une famille ici, dans le pays...

— N'importe! retorquait-on; les lois de la guerre sont les lois de la guerre! Des Canadiens seront internés en Italie. Il est naturel qu'il y ait des Italiens internés au Canada. Et Ie dialogue se poursuivait ainsi.

L'Italien avait beau faire valoir l'innocence de ses intentions, protester qu'il n'avait jamais été ni espion, ni chargé de mission, ni investi d'un mandat quelconque par le Gouvernement italien, la réplique inflexiblement logique était celle de l'ami «Les lois de la guerre sont les lois de la guerre! Il y aura des Canadiens internés en Italic. Il est naturel qu'il y ait des Italiens internés au Canada!>>

***

Dans un geste de folie, le Gouvernement de Rome venait de déclarer la guerre à la France et à la Grande-Bretagne. Le sort en était jeté.

A Montréal, commença la râfle...

Ceux qui étaient désignés devaient être arrêtés. Et ils le furent tous.

Après avoir été détenus pendant deux nuits et un jour dans les grandes cellules de la prison de la Sûreté provinciale, le mercredi 12, nous fûmes transportés dans des autobus escortés d'hommes armés à quelques milles de Montréal. Pendant dix-huit jours, nous restâmes là, soigneusement surveillés et bien nourris. Enfin, hier matin, on nous divisa en deux groupes. Le premier fut envoyé à une prison et l'autre, celui dont je faisais partie, fut placé dans un train spécial qui se dirigea à toute vitesse vers une destination inconnue.

***

En effet, vers quatre heures du soir, notre train s'arrêtait au milieu d'un camp militaire. Des camions recouverts de bâches nous attendaient. On nous y fit montre. Puis le long cortège des véhicules se mit en marche, dans une route percée à travers la forêt. Plus on avançait, plus on s'enfonçait au milieu des arbres... Puis, un camp en vue. Des baraques dressées. Des fils de fer barbelés. Des sentinelles. D'autres internés, des Allemandcs, qui y longeaient depuis september 1939, semblaient guetter notre arrivée.

Enfin, nous voici dans la baraque, en pleine nuit, avec cette atroce impression d'être enfermés pour on ne sait pas combien de temps encore, ignorant tout de ceux qui nous touchent de prés, sachant que ceux-ci n'apprendront que dans plusieurs jours que nous ne sommes plus prés d'eux, que nous ne pourrons pas les revoir avant longtemps.

La sensation d'égarement s'accentue, s'aiguise, torture.

Je me trouve tout à coup, haletant, les mains accrochés au petit cadre de la fenêtre voilée de toile métallique, et je pense ne jamais pouvoir surmonter mon désespoir. Puis, au zénith, le ciel se tinte d'une lueur lègére. La masse sombre de la nuit se recompose en un soupçon de forme. Graduellement, cette forme se précise, prend des contours. Les cîmes des arbres dessinent de nouveau leur broderie verte sur l'immense métier de la voûte céleste.

***

Le jour est venu, clair, net, frais, pur! Et avec lui la fin du cauchemar nocturne auquel peu d'entré nous ont pu se sourtraire. Alors, je me reprends à croire en moi, en l'avenir et en la réalité des choses qui m'environnent. Ce que je vis n'est qu'une parenthèse, une courte mais bien pénible parenthèse dans mon existence, épreuve qu'il faut accepter avec sérénité, fermeté et, surtout, avec une patience résignée.

"La loi fatale qui règle les choses de ce monde veut qu'à chaque action corresponde une réaction et qu'a tout événement contraire fasse pendant une événement favorable. La minute où tout sera rétabli dans le monde pour que reprenne le jeu normal des evenément, ce sera, pour nous aussi, le rantrée dans l'ordre.".

D'ici là, patience, patience.

Un coup de clairon, au loin, sonne le réveil.

De tous les lits de la chambrée surgissent les hommes. Les interpellations suivent. Chacun ravale sa peine intime, ne voulant pas, par une sorte de pudeur, paraître souffrir. Des mots, des plaisanteries mille fois ressassées, se colportent de bouche en bouche et, chose étonnante, font rire! Des vulgarités méme. N'importe quoi. Pourvu qu'on ait l'air de <<tenir le coup>>.

Seul ou en groupe, on sort pour se débarbouiller, chacun tenant à la main la serviette, le savon, le dentifrice. L'action bienfaisante, énergique, de l'eau fraîche se fait sentir. On songe peut-être, au fond de soi-même, au réveil habituel, chez soi... mais personne n'en souffle mot. On serre les mâchoires et l'on feint d'être gai. Gai, même dans ces uniformes bleus aux larges disques blanc ou rouges tracés dans le dos dont tons les internés, dans tous les pays du monde, sont vêtus et qui donnent l'aspect de masques de carnaval où le bouffon frise le sinistre.

L'activité de la journée est déjà toute fixée, distribuée, partagée. Ceux-ci, formant une équipe, iront dans la forêt couper des arbres. Ceux-là, aussi par équipes, s'en iront dans des camions à une quinzaine de milles d'ici pour travailler à la réfection d'un pont. D'autres se contenteront de besognes plus modestes. Les hommes de santé faible ou delicate iront éplucher les légumes dans la cuisine. Quelques-uns seront de service au réfectoire. Il y a aussi ceux qui auront la charge, relativement aisée, de balayer et delayer la chambrée.

Six cents hommes, insensiblement réadaptés à une nouvelle condition, à un nouveau milieu, reprendront un semblant de rythme de vie. Je regarde chacun s'acheminer vers sa besogne. Et je me dis:

—Courage! Il faut toujours accepter la vie comme elle vient...

Chap. I, La Ville sans Femmes (Montréal, 1945)

NOCTURNE   *Montreal, 1940*

It is today the 29th, the penultimate day of this month of June that began with manifest apprehension among all Italians in Canada. The attitude taken by the Government of Rome with regard to Paris and London was becoming more threatening every day. The Italians approached each other on the street with anxious looks.

— Do you think that Mussolini will declare war?
— Against whom?
— Against France and England... because of the Axis Pact...

— That could never be! At the time of the assassination of Chancellor Dollfuss, Mussolini mobilized two armies against Germany. In '14, he was an ardent supporter of the Italian intervention against Germany and Austria. Not long ago he was saying...

— Yes, yes, that's all well and good, but all indications become increasingly alarming. They have already suspended liner service between Naples and New York. The fascist press, that follows party orders, is becoming more and more aggressive toward France... We hear nothing but talk of partial mobilization, no doubt a prelude to general mobilization... Look! Italy counts eight million infantrymen, thousands of planes, numerous armoured divisions...

— But don't you see that Germany and Russia are united by a secret treaty... Hitler may come to an agreement with Stalin. Mussolini will never comply with him!

And so it went, for hours and hours, as all eventualities were considered, weighed, reckoned, while the hearts of those Italians swung back and forth, from doubt to hope, from fear to a fleeting sense of safety, since each in himself would not have really wanted Italy to change its traditional politics that bound it to France and England, the politics that had permitted a divided people, dominated by foreign powers, to conceive a unity all their own and to fashion a life of prosperity in their own country, in the span of a mere half a century. But despite the arguing, questioning, reasoning, the news from Rome kept getting worse.

***

Soon they no longer dared voice their thoughts or express their fears. Whatever the outcome, this whole thing was sure to turn into a "dirty affair" for all who, while living in Canada, had shown some ideological or platonic sympathy toward Fascism, since they would become ipso facto enemies!

— What will happen to us? those Italians kept wondering; clearly the decisions of the Government of Rome could not be held as a grievance against them!

Friends, well intentioned or well informed persons, had taken the trouble to warn them:

— Beware! If Mussolini declares war, you run the risk of being interned.

The Italians would answer:

— Why should we be, when we've never done anything against Canada, when our children were born and raised in this country...

— It doesn't matter! they would reply; the laws of war are the laws of war! There'll be Canadians interned in Italy. It is natural that there should be Italians interned in Canada. And so the dialogue pursued.

Even when the Italian insisted on the innocence of his intentions, protesting that he'd never been a spy, nor been in charge of any mission, nor been invested with mandates by the Italian government, still, the inflexibly logical reply of the friend came back: "The laws of war are the laws of war! There will be Canadians interned in Italy. It is natural that there should be Italians interned in Canada!"

We reached thus, Monday, the tenth of June.

***

In an act of folly, the Government of Rome declared war against France and Great Britain. The die was cast.

In Montreal, the round ups began...

Those who had been pointed out, had to be arrested. And none was spared.

After being detained for two nights and one day in the prison ward of the Provincial Detention Centre, on Wednesday the 12th, we were transported, with armed escort, in buses, to a place a few miles outside Montreal. Here we remained for eighteen days, carefully guarded and well nourished. Finally, yesterday morning, we were broken up into two groups. The first was sent off to a prison and the other, the one to which I belong, boarded a special train that sped toward a destination undisclosed to us.

***

In fact, at about four o'clock in the evening, our train stopped in the middle of a military camp. Tarpaulin-covered trucks were waiting for us. They made us climb into them. Then the long file of vehicles started to move, along a road cut through the forest. The more we advanced the more we sank into the trees... Then, a camp in sight. A few improvised barracks. Barbed wire. Guards. Some other prisoners, Germans, who'd been kept there since September 1939, seemed to be on the lookout for our arrival.

At last, here we are in the barracks, in the middle of the night, with this atrocious feeling of being prisoners who knows for how much longer, not knowing what our loved ones might be going through, aware that they will not learn for several days that we're no longer near them, that we will not be able to see them again for some time to come.

This sensation of being astray intensifies, sharpens, tortures.

I find myself suddenly out of breath, my hands clinging to the small frame of the window veiled by a metal grid, and I think that I may never be able to overcome my despair... Then, at the zenith, the sky becomes coloured with a faint glimmer. The thick shadow of the night recomposes itself into a suspicion of forms. Gradually, these forms gather details, take precise shapes. The tree tops draw anew their green embroidery on the immense loom of the celestial vault.

Day has come, clear, clean, cool, pure! And with it the end of the nightmare which few among us were able to elude. And so I try once more to believe in myself, in the future and in the reality of the things that surround me. What I endure is nothing but a parenthesis in my existence, a trial that must be accepted with serenity, firmness, and above all, with resigned patience.

The fatal law that governs the things of this world determines that to each action there corresponds a reaction and that to each adverse event there corresponds a favourable one. The moment when all things will be restored in this world so that the normal course of events may return, will be, for us too, our return to order.

Till then, only patience, patience.

The sound of a bugle, in the distance, calls the reveille.

From all the beds in the cell the men emerge. The interpellations follow. Each one swallows his intimate anguish, not wishing, by a kind of reserve, to appear to be suffering. Words, the pleasantries we sift through a thousand times over, pass from mouth to mouth and surprising as it may seem, make us laugh! Even vulgarities. Whatever it may be. So long as we give the impression of holding on.

Alone or in groups, we go out to wash, each holding the towel, the soap, the toothpaste. We feel the salutary action of the cold water. We dream perhaps, inside ourselves, of having woken up as usual, in our own homes... but no one utters a single word. Everyone keeps his jaw locked and feigns to being cheerful. Cheerful, even in these blue uniforms with the large red or white discs drawn on the back, worn by all prisoners, in all the countries of the world, that look like carnival costumes where the clownishness grazes the sinister.

The activities of the day are already planned, assigned, distributed. These men, as a team, will go into the forest to fell trees. Those others, also as a team, will be transported in trucks, to a place fifteen miles from here, to work at the repairs of a bridge. Others will be satisfied by more modest chores. The men of feeble or poor health will go to peel vegetables in the kitchen. A few will do work in the refectory. There are also those who will be in charge, a relatively easy task, of sweeping and washing the barrack-room.

Six hundred men, insensibly readapted to a new condition, to a new environment, will resume a seeming rhythm of life. I watch each one moving toward his burden. And I tell myself:

— Courage! Life must be accepted always as it comes...

Translated by Antonino Mazza, The City Without Women
The translator wishes to express his gratitude to Francine, for her collaboration and assistance in the translation of this text.

GIANNI GROHOVAZ

A BRUNO...*

Non posso smorzare il sole
per far sapere al mondo
cosa mi dice
il tristo verdetto
che ti vede ormai prono
davanti all'uscio
dell'ultimo casolare,
là, in fondo al villaggio
di questo breve mondo....

Né posso darti
risposta alcuna
ai fin troppi quesiti

che hai chiesto alla vita
senza saper
che solo la morte
potea illuminar
la tua dubbiosa mente....

Mentre cento cavalli
col crine al vento
irrompon nella valle
dei tuoi pensieri
lascia che ti parli,
Bruno,
cosí, per esserti accanto
in quest'istante
sí denso d'emotivo sprezzo
pel misero speme
che non ha "chance" alcuna,
e arrendersi deve
quando non c'è più
neanche un granello
di sabbia nel vetro
della clessidra...

Vorrei morir con te,
almeno un poco,
per scoprir insieme
il grande mistero...
là dove si ferma
il brusio del mondo
e dove inizia invece
il loquente silenzio
del maestoso nulla....

Lasciami scender con te
la spirale via
che conduce
al luminoso buio
del vuoto
che non conosco,

ma tu intravvedi già
oltre la Baia
dove non c'è Caron che attende
ma i volti asceti
di chi ci amò in passato
oppur ci ha odiato
senza pensar che un giorno
anche il sole
si sarebbe spento,
e il mare
mai più avrebbe cantato,
con la risacca,
il canto che sembrava eterno....

Lasciami morir con te,
amico mio,
almeno un poco
per esserti banal conforto
quando il tuo sguardo
darà l'addio
a tutte le illusioni della vita...
e un nuovo dì, senz'ore,
sorgerà sul sempre
della tua vera pace....

L'uomo "della buca", ricordi?
nulla avrà da suggerir
sul nuovo palco
d'attori sempre veri...
né inventiva di scenario...
o dizione... o grazia nel cantar
le tante gesta,
finte e vere
della commedia d'ogni giorno,
avran timor d'un fischio
o trepida attesa
per un applauso...
né pubblico...
e forse neanche il brindar

prima dell'atto,
per darsi contegno
oppur coraggio...
Ricordi?

Chissà cos'è
l'eterno domani...
Tu già lo sai,
almeno in breve,
e geloso sei del tuo saper
ma tu non parli
perche cosi, come sul palco,
ognun deve imparare la sua parte....

Eppure, nel pien degli anni,
quando il tuo genio
imprimeva sul papiro
feconde armonie di colori
...non eri avaro... anzi...
Con gioia donavi
agli occhi avidi
paesaggi veritieri
che solo l'arte
può veder tra la foschia
dell'assurdo mondo
che ci accoglie
cosi tremendamente
in breve...

...Tre donne
cercan di sorrider
mentre ti appresti
per il grande viaggio...
Non vogliono mostrarti
l'amarezza
del grande vuoto
che si profila già d'intorno...
Forse dovrebbero piangere,
ora,

e con le calde lacrime
frettar la primavera...
da nuova linfa
alla terra
che attende...

La nuova vita?
davanti alla morte che aspetta
per farti veder
l'ultimo tramonto?
o farti sentir,
per una volta ancora,
il dolce cinguettar
dell'usignolo?

Vita... morte, vita, morte...
il dilemma non dà pace,
equivocar non vale
e... a che serve?
Curiosi si nasce.
Prodighi si vive.
Avari si muore.
...E forse è menzogna
e l'uno o l'altro
non fan specie alcuna....

...Ecco, mentre ti parlo
hai chiuso gli occhi...
Col soliloquio
t'ho fatto addormentar;
sei quieto
e sereno è il tuo volto...
Non ho fatto nulla per te,
ma ho vuotato il sacco
e mi sento più vicino a te,
Bruno....

E anche più appresso
alle tue donne

che mentre dormi
posson lacrimar
senza timor di farti male...

Addio Bruno, amico mio,
verrà il mio giorno
e ti vedrò ancora.
E sarà un giorno lungo,
senza fine...

Quando Elena, con occhi di pianto,
mi disse che tutto era vano...
3 aprile 1977

From Parole, parole e granelli di sabbia (Toronto, 1980)
* Bruno Mesaglio, un caro amico dell'autore, fu il fondatore e direttore
del Piccolo Teatro Italiano. Dal 1950 fino alla sua morte avvenuta nel
1977 Bruno partecipò attivamente in tutti gli aspetti della vita del
teatro italiano in Canada. Fu un energico esponente del Circolo Italiano
dell'Università di Toronto dirigendo molte delle loro presentazioni
all'Hart House Theatre.

TO BRUNO...

Could I eclipse the sun
the world might know
what this unhappy verdict
means to me.
Prostrate, alas,
before the threshhold
of your last retreat
there, at the village outskirts
of this brief domain...

Nor can I offer
any answer
to the countless questions
you asked of life
without imagining
that only death could illuminate
your doubting mind...

As a hundred horses,
manes to the wind,
burst into the valley
of your thoughts
let me
speak to you
Bruno,
be with you for this instant
so laden-down with stirring scorn
for our afflicted seed
that has no chance at all
and must surrender all
when not a grain of sand
remains
in the hourglass

I want to die with you,
at least a little,
uncovering together
the great enigma...
there, where the buzzing of the world
ends,
where the eloquent silence
of majestic emptiness
begins...

Let me descend with you
the spiral path
to the glowing shadows
of the abyss
that I know not,

but you have glanced
beyond the Bay
and Charon does not wait
but ashen faces
of those who loved,
or hated us
thinking not the day would come
when even the sun
would be extinguished,
and the sea
never more would sing
to the beating of the surf,
the song that seemed eternal....

Let me die with you,
my friend,
at least a little
to be some simple comfort
when your glance
will say farewell
to all of life's illusions....
and a new day, hourless,
will dawn
on your forever
on your true peace....

The man "in the box" remember?
will have nothing to prompt
the new stage
of actors ever-true...
no fantasy in staging...
or delivery.., or grace in singing
the many feats
contrived and real
of life's persistent comedy,
neither will they fear a taunting hiss
or timidly
await applause
neither a full house...

nor even the toast, perhaps,
before curtain time,
will give them bearing
or even courage...
Remember?

What can it be
the eternal tomorrow...
You know already,
at least a hint,
and guard your knowledge
but do not speak
thus it is, as on the stage
each one must learn his part...

And even in your prime
when your genius
engraved on parchment
fruitful harmonies of colour
...you were not chary... hardly...
With joy you gave
to thirsty eyes
landscapes true-to-life
which only art distinguishes amid the mist
that welcomes us
but briefly
to this preposterous world...

...Three women
attempt a smile
while you prepare
for your great journey,
not wishing to display
distress
before the boundlessness
contoured 'round about...
Perhaps it would be best
they cry,
now,

and hasten spring
with their warm tears...
donate new living fluids
to the waiting earth...
A life renewed?
Does death attend
to let you view
your final sunset?
or will you hear
once more
the nightingale's sweet song?

Life... death, life, death...
dilemma unrelenting,
what use... conjecturing?
Born to discover.
Lavishly to live.
...to die a miser's death.
Perhaps it's all a myth
and everything
is grossly overstated.

...Alas, while still I speak
you close your eyes
lulled to sleep
by my soliloquy;
and quiet now
your look serene...
Nothing have I done for you,
but purged myself
and closer now I feel to you,
Bruno...

And able now
your women to ensue
who while you sleep
can weep
without the fear of hurting you...

Addio Bruno, dearest friend,
my day will come
and seeing you again...
a day as long as we shall wish...
a dawning
without end...

> *When Elena, with tearful eyes,*
> *told me that all was in vain...*

Translated by Vilma Ricci
* Bruno Mesaglio, a close friend of the author, was founder and director of the Piccolo Teatro Italiano. From the early 1950s to his death in 1977 Bruno was active in all aspects of Italian theatre life. He was an active supporter of the Italian Club of the University of Toronto directing many of their presentations in the Hart House Theatre.

GIUSEPPE RICCI

LUGLIO 1930

Avevo già compiuto cinque anni di residenza in Canada e per me tutto era cambiato. Mi sentivo di essere nel mio paese perché avevo imparato la lingua. Inoltre avevo molti amici italiani con cui potevo divertirmi. Volevo diventare cittadino canadese per avere più diritti e partecipare in tutte le attività di questo grande paese, come avere diritto al voto, avere un passaporto canadese con cui poter viaggiare all'estero, ed essere riconosciuto dalle autorità sia locali, sia provinciali e sia federali.

Pur avendo questo desiderio, non avevo cambiato nulla delle abitudini italiane: come tradizioni, valori morali e materiali e più di ogni altra cosa come il mangiare all'italiana. L'Italia era sempre la mia madre patria.

Per ottenere la cittadinanza canadese era necessario fare una domanda presso l'ufficio d'emigrazione e cittadinanza e per questo mi recai in uno di questi uffici e dovetti riempire un modulo e rispondere a tutte le domande scritte nello stesso, firmare e inoltrare all'ufficio della cittadinanza.

Passarono più di tre mesi. Una sera, appena dopo cena, un uomo bussò alla porta. Era un ispettore dell'emigrazione. Fu il caso che io stesso aprissi la porta e gli domandai in inglese che cosa desiderava ben sapendo che era stato mandato dall'ufficio dell'emigrazione. Lo feci entrare in casa e, sedutosi, subito mi domandò perché volevo diventare cittadino e se potevo essere identificato da un vecchio residente e cittadino canadese. Per caso quella sera si trovava in casa Michele Trisi, lo zio di Maria, e lui gli disse che mi conosceva da tanto tempo e che io volevo la cittadinanza perché era mia intenzione rimanere in Canada il resto della mia vita. L'ispettore fu completamente soddisfatto e mi disse che in seguito avrei ricevuto una chiamata dall'ufficio d'emigrazione per andare a fare il giuramento e dopo il giuramento avrei avuto la cittadinanza canadese. Se ne andò ringraziandoci per le informazioni ricevute.

Io pensavo che in pochi giorni avrei ricevuto la chiamata per il giuramento. Invece passarono più di due mesi ed era la fine di novembre quando ebbi la chiamata di presentarmi al vecchio municipio di Toronto dove un giudice esaminava tutti gli aspiranti alla cittadinanza. Io a quel tempo lavoravo nel nuovo pastificio e pur essendo occupatissimo dovetti lasciare il lavoro per mezza giornata per trovarmi davanti al giudice alle dieci di mattina.

Eravamo più di cinquanta persone in maggioranza italiani, e dovemmo fare la fila perché c'era un solo giudice ad esaminare e a far prestare giuramento. Tutto procedeva lento e silenzioso. Io fui uno dei primi a trovarmi davanti al guidice, un uomo anziano di grande statura, dai capelli bianchi con una voce soffice che dava l'impressione di un grande consigliere affabile.

Dopo le formalità del giuramento, il giudice mi domandò quale lavoro svolgevo per vivere, e quando gli risposi che avevo già cominciato la manifattura di maccheroni rimase un po' sorpreso. Incuriosito, mi domandò come e con che cosa si facessero i maccheroni. Io gli spiegai in breve il processo e il procedimento della manifattura della pasta. Egli ascoltava con grande interesse ed appena finii di parlare, con un leggero sorriso, mi disse: "If you can make macaroni you are a good citizen, and now you can go."

Rimasi soddisfatto perché ero sicuro di ricevere la cittadinanza in breve tempo. Passarono poco più di due settimane ed erano i primi giorni di dicembre del 1930 quando ricevetti la carta cittadina che io ancora conservo.

From L'orfano di padre (Toronto, 1981)

JULY 1930

I had already been living in Canada for five years and everything had changed for me. I felt as though I were living in my own country because I now knew the language. Moreover, I had made many Italian friends with whom I spent my leisure time. I wanted to become a Canadian citizen so that I would be entitled to all the rights under the law and to fully participate in the life of this great land. I wanted to be able to vote and to hold a Canadian passport so I could travel. I wished to be recognized by the local, provincial and federal governments.

Even though I wanted to become a citizen I hadn't changed any of my Italian ways, neither my traditions, nor my moral or material values. Above all, I continued eating "all'italiana". Italy would always be my mother country.

To obtain Canadian citizenship it was necessary to apply to the Department of Immigration and Citizenship. I went to one of their branch offices where I had to fill out a form, answer all the questions on it, sign it, and forward it to the Citizenship Department.

More than three months passed. One evening, after dinner, a man knocked at my door. It was an immigration inspector. It so happened that I answered the door and asked the caller in English if I could help him, knowing full well that he had probably been sent by the Immigration Department. I invited him in and as soon as he was seated he immediately asked me why I wanted to become a citizen. He also asked if I knew an established Canadian citizen who could vouch for me. Fortunately, Maria's* uncle, Michele Trisi, was visiting that evening and he assured the officer that he had known me a long while and knew also that I wanted to become a citizen because I intended to live in Canada for the rest of my life. The inspector was completely satisfied and said that I would be receiving a call soon from the Immigration Department to go and swear an oath after which I would receive my Canadian citizenship. He thanked us for the information and left.

I imagined that I would receive the call to be sworn-in within a few days. Instead more than two months passed and it was already the end of November when I was called and instructed to present myself at the Old City Hall in Toronto where a judge was examining all the citizenship candidates. At that time I was working in the new pasta factory and even though I was extremely busy I had to leave work for half a day so that I could stand before the judge at ten in the morning.

There were more than fifty candidates, for the most part Italian, and I had to queue up because there was only one magistrate to both examine and administer the oath of allegiance. The proceedings were slow and silent. I was one of the first before the judge, a tall and elderly gentleman with white hair and a soft voice. He gave the impression of being an important, but friendly, counsellor. After the swearing-in formalities the judge asked me what I did for a living, and when I answered that I had already started my own macaroni factory he was quite surprised. His interest having been aroused, he asked me how, and with what, did one make macaroni. I briefly explained the process of manufacturing. He listened with great interest and as soon as I had finished speaking, smiling slightly, he said: "If you can make macaroni, you are a good citizen, and now you can go."

I felt pleased because I was certain that I would receive my citizenship papers in a short time. A little more than two weeks passed when during the first part of December 1930, I received my citizenship papers which I cherish to this day.

* Giuseppe Ricci's wife

Translated by Vilma Ricci

II
ROMAN CANDLES

ALEXANDRE AMPRIMOZ

ROMAN RETURN

A sky where falcons fly and fall
    where lights change and die,
A sky where the sunrise is a sodden sunset
Welcomes my Roman return.

Over there stands Castel Sant'Angelo.
Like the loose teeth of a tortured pope
The bricks are chattering with strident sounds of long ago.

Sometimes in the ancient air
The Parthian perfume of a gone life returns
And in that balm I meet
The lovers who tailored my aching skull.

Sometimes in the weary water
The Thyrsus-like taste of a distant wine returns
And in that liquid I meet
The lovers who tailored my aching bones.

Over there dreams il Colosseo.
Like the trembling hands of Roman Emperors
The walls are sleeping, holy in their pagan nightmare.

A land where water sobs and suffers
    where seeds are stranded and rare,
A land where the sun saws secular stones
Welcomes my Roman return.

SARO D'AGOSTINO

WAKE

The women are in one room, the men
in another. Zio Crescenzo died
three hours ago. The women line
the walls of the living room, the
only light comes from a candle
in front of his picture on top
of the television set. The women
wear only black, only their hands
and faces are visible. Some
of them have been wearing black
for more than twenty years, Zio
Crescenzo was the second youngest
of seven children. My mother
is the youngest.

           I have been taught
death is the mother of beauty, but
my family takes death less seriously.

The men are sitting in rows of chairs
lining the walls of the kitchen.
The sons are crying with their heads
buried in their arms. My mother and
father and I kiss each one, their faces
are covered with tears.

In the living room the women have begun
to wail and scream as though possessed
by demons or death itself. Later on,
 in the middle of the night, it will
become a chanting.

           Another brother dead,
and she still stays up all night
to cry the pain of his life, learning

nothing more than ageing from all
the others:

>Salvatore,
found in a ditch in Argentina
with a knife in his back, Stefano
killed with an axe over some Calabrian
point of honour, Tommasino
who made it big in America and died
a lonely American death, Saro
who was born in a bad year and died
simply because half the babies
of the village died that winter.

The women will cry until the chant
is broken and one of them collapses.
Then some of the men will enter
and try to help them, but the cries
and chants soon begin again.

>In the
middle of the night cousins will drive
down from the suburbs with hot coffee
which they will serve in demi-tasses.

PIER GIORGIO DI CICCO

THE MAN CALLED BEPPINO

When a man loses his barbershop during
the war, as well as an only son, and his wife and
daughter sing the blues of starvation, the man

believes in the great white hope, now the red white
and blue. The man ventures overseas, and lands finally
in Baltimore, Maryland, usa,—destined to be the
finest barber at eastpoint shopping plaza.

the man works for nothing, because his english
is less than fine; the customers like him,
and the man is easily duped, he believes in the
honest dollar, and is offered peanuts in return.

This while the general manager runs to Las Vegas,
to take porno pictures of himself between
tall whores.

The man who loses his barbershop during the war,
loves great white roses at the back of a house beside
a highway. The roses dream with him,
of being understood in clear english, or of a large
Italian sun, or of walking forever on a
sunday afternoon.

Never mind the family. It is this man, whose
hospital checks are being spent in Las Vegas,
it is this man whose hair will shine like
olive leaves at noon; it is this man who will sit
on his front lawn, after the fifth haemorrhage, having
his last picture taken,
because he drank too much.

it is this man who will sit under his mimosa
by the highway, fifty pounds underweight, with no
hospital, and look

there are great white roses in his eyes.

ITALY, 1974

—nella campagna—couched between two hills
in the circular dark I lay in the summer cool.
Not two steps from the house the stars were
wincing like sun on wet shoals.
I heard the wind go down the garden
and fumble in the dark green and come back, its
hands in everything.

In far orchards I heard crickets measure out
the dark earth.
The landscape flowed from me,
spilled over where I touched it.
The earth was mine as it was to antaeus
when the bole of his wrist touched his mother;
balanced on one hand, his limbs spread like an olive tree
and the ends of his fingers dwindled in far orchards.

In daylight, old men wear the sun like lovers; eyes
bright, the good years brimming.
Their feet never leave their earth; they grow ancient
in their fields, and go in their sleep.

MARY DI MICHELE

TREE OF AUGUST

Summer's long tongue, a sun setting, licks the hills carmine.

The light makes a deep bow,
drops a bloody rose
into a spinster's vocabulary,
as she sits in an enclosed garden

filled with the voices of mother.

You have broken the bread of loneliness,
experience a burnt crust, hard chewing
a char life has consumed
all my city mouse knowledge
breathing the vapours of rat's sewers.

Reading your country notes
with an ear to the heart's
cornucopia, our language
speaks for itself.

I have seen your despair in an unblinking
gaze, the pupil like a pool of muddied rain
with the sun breaking wafer cloud,
staining a rainbow in its dark glass.
Woman you live for books
and the keeping of your mother's house,
mummied in the ease of time's
unwinding the dressings of old wounds.
A monument of patience, you smile
at the pebble that sang
to your window, some years ago,
late in the musk of an april night,
a brief courtship for a plain girl.
Now your toe caresses (the hand that touched)
you imagine, hearing again
that mocking tender mouth.

Looking into my sister's eye
I see Italia behind my shoulders.

Under the tree of August,
thirty and unwed,
purple figs mature
like mulatto suns
overhead bursting.

ENIGMATICO

His limpid skin is green gold as he reclines
in a shade that crowns him with the leaves of vines.
As smooth as the golden skinned grapes his firm
thighs are about to burst their denim husks,
the golden thighs of a man of bronze.

Eyes of pale amber, with the bite of brandy.
Lips that kiss her lady's shoe, her knee,
the liquid outward curve of her hip,
lips that call her madonna,
his dream of a bright aproned jewel for his
kitchen,
he polishes it there in the long grass of August
until he rips her leisurely as a silk,

and she cries out caught
with one bare foot in a village in the Abruzzi,
the other busy with cramped English speaking toes in Toronto,
she strides the Atlantic legs spread
like a Colossus.

Photograph of a girl dressed as a gypsy,
child waist pinched by a red girdle,
for Carnevale,

in another world, wearing the black academic gown,
a rabbit skin about her shoulders,
she hangs on the wall of a suburban bungalow.

LEN GASPARINI

I WAS A POET FOR THE MAFIA

It pays to have relatives in Cicero
who mean business in Chicago,
and connections in Detroit
who make book for the big publishers
in New York and Toronto.

My typewriter was steely black
and deadly portable.
Its hair trigger inspired my finger.
I forget the actual number of editors
slumped over desks,
pumped full of poems.
Rejection slips were their death warrants.
They didn't understand
poetry was a front
for the back of my hand.

I collaborated with torpedoes
who were the avant-garde
in their profession;
attended literary parleys
in sunny hiding places
like Palermo, Las Vegas, and Rio.
I lived high and fine
and never had a deadline.
My books made the WANTED list.
I was quoted on police line-ups
by suspects who knew my poems by heart.

The critics tried to convict me,
but my agent happened to be
a syndicate lawyer with pull.
I became as infamous as Capone
with the power of the poem.

Alas! I learned too late
that vice paid worse than verse
when a bullet obliterated my poetry.
I was a poet for the Mafia.
Bury me in Sicily.

IL SANGUE
for Pier Giorgio Di Cicco

The blood that moves through your language
moves through mine.
The heart that gives it utterance
is ours alone.

Come away from that cancer of neon
with its running sores of money.
The city's iron skyline
bends before the structure of a poem.

Our people work in the Tuscan fields,
where the rain walks barefoot,
and the fragrance of the breathing earth
rustles like the body of a woman
reaching out to you in sleep.

Let us play our mandolins and sing
O Sole Mio! The joy is ours.

Strangled by a spaghetti stereotype,
an Italian is supposed to lay bricks.
You build poems with the stars.

Revised, 2005

ANTONINO MAZZA

OUR HOUSE IS IN A COSMIC EAR

In a cosmic ear of sharp peaks and stepped hills
        where broom and cyclamen bloom
            side by side with the lemon trees
is the house where I was born.
This house... let's look at it from a childish
                point of view.

A village of bells crowded in the velvet street,
        no sidewalks. Sunday morning, no Monday.
How is it? I was running home, there were cherries
in my pockets, my mother had a nightingale
                between her lips?

And the afternoon? Siesta!
                The sun
        was a magnet at the summit of a transparent planet.
But the cloud? The blazing breath of the Sahara whirled
a single cloud, over the sea
                over Sicily,
until, nearing the harsh Aspromonte, fragile with humidity,
            it was... ready to burst.
And Blasted!
        reaching, violently, for the stubborn stubbles,
            for earth.
After the first splatter on the baked roof,
        the lean torrents, clay snakes,
            wound their course, out from the birch forests,
                    down the steep volcanic slopes,
                                slowly,
as if to admire the grace of the stern landscapes: the yellow
and pink weeds glowing on the violet crags
                        and on the steppes
the white blanket of orange flowers.
Before the rain would stop, I'd retire
                in my mother's ear, sound asleep.

For four years I dreamt of my father coming back.
    It was a childish dream.
He was aboard a little purple ship, returning
to our beautiful Calabria.
        Phoenician's and Etruscan's land, bathed
  by the sea of Ulysses.
For four years I waited for him on the stony beach.
From there I could see the almonds mingling with the olive trees,
           in the hills,
     and the house where he was born.
  He had gone to bring gifts to the world.
He would return, soon.

I'd wake up to the melody of nightingales.
And the dream? It is evening, but never dark. The bells die
    in the deep blue street. The sky is a paradise
       of fireflies. The scent of lilacs, of lemons,
   flood the warmth, the breeze. The sea is a mirror
 of purple stars. We're having supper on the terrace tonight,
in the crystal air the moon is abundant light.
I keep remembering this cosmic gift
      in my sleep.
If the dream doesn't stop, if the word,
    if the house
  is in the word and we, by chance, should meet,
my house is your house, take it.

CANADESE

Because life for him
has been labour and struggle,
Canadese, remember your father.
Don't try to stifle your mother tongue,
in our cage, it is wrong;
do canaries smother their private song?

Be patient, don't rage,
Canadese, in time we'll belong;
we'll acquire our own sense of this land;
we'll record life and death of our million births;
we'll have families,
above and below the earth.

Canadese, you must never forget
what you are... never!
because when you do, they'll remind you

TONY PIGNATARO

THE IMMIGRANT

On holidays the men would spend their time
at the cantina (where he was known as "il caporale")
playing cards or pitching pennies against the walls.
The women slept.
The deepest rivers run through quiet canyons,
the loudest often flow on shallow beds.
The order of their lives was simple.
The meaning of their existence profound.
Events cyclical. Birth and death; for one there

was a reason, for the other a necessity.
    These were the seasons:
the seed (truth is what is seen as evident).
Months of labour. Mud baked onto their boots
like a second skin.
    The harvest. (Moulded bread or bread that fell
was not discarded but kissed and then consumed.)
The stench of fermenting wine,
the bitter chill beneath the blankets,
these were the seasons: this was their understanding.
    They were a people wanting understanding.
They had faith and strength. God had stretched
His Hand outward over them, He had uncovered His
Face in the face of all creation. He had spoken to
them in the noise and confusion of all their activities.
Nothing was silent. To wander into the mountains was
to intrude on the conversation of rocks earth and air.
In the fields a murmur, an echo
of a tiller's plough in the distance.
    They washed their eyelids in water.
They drenched their hands in blood. Joy and sorrow
were dipped in the same cup. Everything emerged
from the same primordial centre.
    A man's work, the seed pouch girdled to his waist. A
pointed stick to open earth. And after the harvest the feel of
hands like tree bark or eroded stones. This is legacy; a man's
years at the plough. This you can leave to your children with
pride, renewal, lambs in the spring, seasonal toil.
    At the airport in Rome he felt invaded.
His sister's face whom he had not seen since '51
was a silent crypt to all that he once knew.
    Folklore was being recorded on tape by anthropologists;
it no longer served as oral tradition. Young men
migrated to the cities; had left the land
searching for jobs.
    The olive groves had flourished into tall apartment
buildings; machines had crushed the vineyards;
covered them with tar.
    He saw huge slabs of black reflecting glass

on subway walls like the ones in Toronto.
   He was told that the old village shoemaker had died;
that his grey cat sought constant solace
at the cold heels of death.
   His homecoming had sprouted a tree in his heart
with boughs of steel that wedges
could not fell.
   Life was a long distance telephone call
across the Atlantic. He thought of his wife
as he walked through the old sectors of the town;
there was little there that he wanted to renew.
He wished to wander through it and yet having left
it once he did not want to learn to leave it again.
   Change affirmed its omnipotence; he had not
forgotten what other men forget the most.

III

SHORT STORIES

ALEXANDRE AMPRIMOZ

PRELUDES

In the child's mind the idea of war was equal to the smell of garlic. For a long time he believed war was a spice like oregano that pushed men to kill. Everything the adults said was important: he spent his time letting their words marinate in his head, basting them with his own voice. "The tomatoes are back in the marketplace!" his mother had exclaimed. Nestor didn't understand why such things were so important, but he kept repeating them, trying to imitate his mother's intonation.

Nonno had told him that flies and beetles live only a few days. Nestor was four years old. He wondered if the insects considered him a Methuselah.

They told him that Nonno was the father of his mother. He didn't know what to think of that, but he knew that Nonno was nice to him, yes, much nicer than the women of the house. Nonna, the mother of his mother, wasn't so nice. She forced him to eat rice and *bacala* every Friday. *Bacala* was dried, salted fish that Nonna would put into a blue bowl every Thursday night. Once he asked, "When you put *bacala* in water does it become alive again?" Everyone laughed. Nobody liked fish, but they all ate it on Fridays because the priest told them to. He often wondered why they kept feeding the goldfish since no one ever ate them.

Nonna didn't say anything when Nestor talked to Tara, but he wasn't allowed to speak to the maid. Tara was the cat. Bigger animals lived longer than insects. His father had run away to Algeria with the French army. In a war, men are killed. The dead didn't move anymore, just like the flies that he captured and squeezed against the windowpane of the balcony. Algeria was a mysterious place with many flies and a few flying carpets. How many men had his father killed?

Nonno was his friend. "Are the stars distant fireflies?" Nonno always answered this type of question with a smile. The old man never laughed at him as the women did. It was easy in the afternoon after the siesta to run to the vestibule and choose one of Nonno's canes for the daily walk.

So many houses were, like the Forum, open to the wind, the wallgrass, and the cats. The Forum was beautiful because it was made with the ruins of old wars. The new houses were only fresh ruins. Only old things were beautifuL

They had been back in Rome for a week.

"So you returned with the child," Nonno smiled at Nestor. Affecting a more rigid expression, he asked Mamma, "Where is the brave soldier?"

"Are you going to start stories at this time of night?" interjected Nonna.

"I am still the head of this household and my daughter owes me respect."

The old man caressed his grey moustache and repeated, "Where is the brave soldier?"

"The same song again. Have you been drinking?" Nonna demanded. Making one of those strange gestures peculiar to the Italian race, she added, "Do you want to wake up the maid and the neighbours to let everybody know our business? You should be ashamed of yourself. I can smell it from here."

Ignoring his wife's complaints, Nonno repeated, "Where's the brave soldier?"

Mamma, who all this time had been staring at her white shoes, answered with a very tiny voice, "He is not a soldier; he's an officer."

Nestor jumped into his grandfather's arms, "Nonno, Nonno, Nonno," he screamed. "I'm back!"

The old man took the child and, holding him in the air with his large hands, said, "This child is tired, get his bed ready, women, instead of causing problems at this time of night!"

When Nonno kissed Nestor, a strange smell filled the child's nose. He looked at the old man and whispered, "Nonno, you smell like a French soldier tonight."

A smile passed over the old man's face as he asked, "Did you take the boat?"

"No, Nonno, we took the plane."

"Wait a minute."

"Aren't you going to keep me company?"

"One minute, I'll be back, don't worry."

Nonno went into the bedroom and Nestor heard him ask, "So we are modern now?"

"What do you mean?" asked Nonna.

"I mean that she took the plane with a child of that age, and her husband didn't say anything."

Nonna looked at her daughter with inquisitive eyes.

"I did," Mamma humbly confessed.

Nonno left the room triumphantly and, with a big smile on his face, returned to Nestor.

"Go to sleep now.., don't worry, you're okay."

He was falling asleep thinking of the white stucco houses and the dusty streets of Oran under the midday African sun. Suddenly voices in the hall woke him up.

"She had to return because of the child."

"What do you mean?"

"The doctor said that Algeria wasn't good for his health."

"She married a French soldier... I am a fascist and I have in my house the wife of a French soldier!"

"Be quiet! Mussolini is dead... do you want to get us into trouble?"

When you had a moustache and grey hair, you were old. When you were old enough they let you smoke cigars.

Nestor had developed many strategies to obtain whatever he wanted from his grandfather.

"Please, let go of my hand.., you don't have to hold it... I am old enough to walk by myself."

Generally, Nonno would give in. Then the child would run to the closest café, sit at a table and call the waiter. Usually by the time Nonno reached the table the waiter had already asked, "What would you like, Sir?"

Nonno had to sit down and order a drink while Nestor enjoyed his *granita al caffè*.

Nestor saw again in his mind the picture of the Kasbah in flames. He went to sleep dreaming of the smell of ashes.

In the morning there were always some dead beetles lying on the kitchen floor, and Nonna would whisper, "They come from the house next door. Those people are dirty."

"Sicilians," Nestor's mother would answer, nodding her head in agreement.

He was four years old and so many things had already happened. When he threw a marble against the bedroom mirror, he was almost two. "He does everything I do." That was the explanation he had given Nonna for his action. A severe spanking followed, but that had happened a long time ago: Tara wasn't born yet and he had seen generations of flies and maids leave the house.

"Who was the boy in the mirror?"

"Oh, Nonno, I was a child then..."

Nonno smiled and his eyes looked strange because it was morning and

he didn't have his glasses on yet. Then he left the room singing:
Il Piave mormorava
Non passa lo staniero...

It was a song in which the river was whispering: how was that possible? Perhaps rivers did whisper but only for great occasions. The song of the wind, the ears of the walls, and the holy communion were for Nestor miracles of equal importance. Often he dreamt of Christ walking across the water. In his sleep Nestor would try to follow the Lord, but he usually woke up thinking that he was going to drown.

Beetles were black and when dead they looked like coffee beans. He didn't fear coffee beans because they didn't move. But beetles, that was a different question. He often wondered if once dead they could not live again. Huge beetles made him scream at night, but he never saw them when he was awake.

He watched Nonna prepare the breakfast. When he was in Oran, his father would always be gone by the time he was awake. The smell of espresso coffee was the nicest smell he knew. Back in Algeria, his mother couldn't make espresso. "This French coffee is so light it's like sock juice," was her favourite expression. When the maid washed socks, the water turned the colour of French coffee. He remembered one morning after a sandstorm, they had to eat terrible food. Mamma ordered him, "Drink your coffee." He tried but the image of the sock juice came back to his mind and made him sick for the rest of the day. "All that happened a long time ago, before they operated on me for appendicitis."

A father, what was that?

His eyes turned again towards the dead beetle and he wondered if that insect had a father.

"You're not saying much this morning," said his mother while spreading the tablecloth.

"Leave him alone," answered Nonno's voice from the hall

When he was three years old, they explained to him that the appendix was a blind bowel which was totally useless. He remembered the pain and his mother's telling him, "I told you not to eat the orange seeds." It had happened so long ago that he couldn't remember everything clearly. There were images of his father driving in the jeep to the airport while his mother was holding him in a green blanket. Then he remembered the plane, the clinic of Montpelliers, the nasty nurses, and the good Soeur Agnès.

In Oran, their balcony was above the Arabian cemetery. In the evenings, he liked to stand above the dry field and listen to the mourners' prayers. Sometimes he felt as if someone was pulling his hair. His father would tell him that it was time to go to bed because the ghosts were getting up. He didn't remember the features of his Papa. "My father was a ghost."

The tablecloth was white and clean, the hall was dark and dangerous, and Nonno's voice was something safe.

A father, what was that?

Maybe somebody like a priest? When he asked questions of adults, they always laughed. It was much better to talk to coffee beans or to beetles: at least they didn't laugh.

The white and green of the tablecloth were constantly fighting for territory, but their war never changed the aspect of the tablecloth. The real invasion was accomplished by coffee, spaghetti sauce, red wine, and olive oil.

In a war men were wounded and you could see the scars for a very long time. He liked to look at the scar left by his operation. Was his appendix alive? He had been told that organs die when they are cut off from the rest of the body. His blind bowel was dead; therefore, he himself was not quite alive anymore. At the clinic, he had seen soldiers without arms or legs. They were far more dead than he. Did the doctors keep all those things? Could one have a funeral for an arm or a leg? He imagined himself praying and bringing flowers to the tomb of his appendix.

He looked down at his white socks and thought that soon they would turn grey and good enough to make French coffee. Nothing remained white and even the clouds sometimes looked dirty.

His father had written a letter to *le Directéur du Service de Sante* at the hospital of Montpelliers because a young doctor had been very careless in performing the operation: complications had arisen and Nonno had said, "The poor child will have troubles for the rest of his life... French doctors are butchers!"

Nonna opened wide the half-closed shutters. Nestor shut his eyes to shelter them from the vivid morning light and his mind returned to his first idea. The priests had their own father — that was what they meant by "In nomine patris." In his young mind, he tried to imagine the Sunday father who was "invisible," as the adults said. He saw him above the rare clouds of the cerulean sky with a beard longer than Via Appia Antica, a beard that couldn't hide his endless smile. Remembering what had happened the day before, he felt like running away from them. While he was walking between Nonna and his mother, he had proclaimed, "Look, there, above the clouds... I see my father." "This child is evil," Mamma had whispered to Nonna. If he wasn't talking to them that morning, it was because he had been punished.

Nestor had never killed a beetle because he was afraid of them. When he played with Tara, he always lost and cried because of the scratches on his hands. One day, he decided to kill Tara. He brought the cat to the fountain and tried to throw it into the water. Alas, Tara ran away, making a great deal of noise. Since that day, he only killed plants and flowers.

There was a Roman Genesis, then a scriptural void followed by a French New Testament.

There were strange stories about his family, and for Nestor they were a complicated system of different tales that he was trying to rearrange in a logical order.

A Medici had poisoned her husband in order to run away to Rome with her German lover, Kauman. A cardinal had left all his money to his mistress who was a member of one of the richest families in the Eternal City. How much of that was true? How did they lose their money? "All that wasn't so important," Nonno used to answer whenever Nestor asked about the family history.

A father, what was that?

The earliest memory of the too often absent *pater familias* was a clear picture that Nestor used to contemplate in time of solitude. He remembered a man holding a suitcase in his left hand and kissing his mother. The expression on the face looked so much like his own and was hard to recapture. It was just a moment and Nestor was absorbing an eternity to meditate on that moment.

Usually he couldn't think because an overabundance of ideas came to his mind, pushing each other out of his head: books were a consolation... money was something that you could pay the maid with... planes were more common but not as nice as flying carpets... an image was something like a statue, something that you could make to remember the dead... respect was something that children could pay their parents with.., what for? never be a soldier... never... wine was something that women didn't like... wine had a smell that stayed with people... when you light a match you set the Kasbah on fire....

Once he dreamed that Mozart was giving him a music lesson. He rushed out of his room screaming, "Nonno, Nonno... Mozart gave me a music lesson!"

"What did he tell you?" asked Nonno, amused.

"'A cenar con teco',,. he kept saying 'a cenar con teco'... Nonno, Nonno... he had a blue suit."

Did he remember that dream? He was lost. All around him were mountains and tall buildings. Suddenly out of nowhere came Mozart singing, "A cenar con teco." The sound of music opened a way out of the labyrinth. He walked in the direction Mozart indicated, without knowing where he was going. He felt happy and confident.

Music, that was something nice, like the smell of espresso coffee or clean clothes.

They told him that his father had finally received permission to come to Rome for a few days.

He was a strange man in a uniform who spoke strange words that Nestor couldn't comprehend perfectly. When they were in Oran, Nestor used to speak all day long to the *ordonance* and that way of speaking was called Arabic. The priests had their own language too, but they spoke it only in church on Sundays and, after all, it was very easy because it sounded so much like Italian. Nonno had told him that this way of speaking was baptized Latin: the language of the emperors. Nestor knew that sooner or later he would have to learn the language of the French soldiers, but at least he could learn it from Nonno.

He felt like running away when his mother ordered him to kiss his father.

Nestor felt his ribs squeezed against the brass buttons of the uniform and his father's pungent beard irritated his delicate skin.

"*Mon chéri... mon chéri... mon chéri...*"

"Strange words," thought Nestor.

"Is he eating enough?" asked the French officer.

The French and the Italians share a deep interest in food. It was the Egyptian heritage and Mamma almost believed that food could bring corpses back to life. For those Latins, food was the most important thing after religion.

"Yes, but he spends the whole day in the library with his grandfather," answered his mother.

The men of his family had been scholars for a few generations and the women had learned to fight keenly the power of books. There was a war in his family: books against food. God, the Saints, and the Angels didn't need food, and the Greek meaning of Bible was book. Was the food better than the books? Nonna used to mumble. There were books in the library, in the bedrooms, in the kitchen, and Nonno used to take a book to the bathroom. Already Nestor had joined the male reading club of the family.

Nonno's beard was soft and white; so was his mother's breast — he still remembered that. Soft was something like chocolate. When nobody was looking, it was easy to put your fingers through the chocolate cake: it was so soft. Everything that was soft couldn't hurt. His father's beard was very hard. A first conflict with his father took place when he was three years old. Papa, as they called him, was back home for a few days. When you were sick, they gave you lemons. Lemonade was good for headaches, toothaches, colds, fat necrosis, deafness, cramps, cervitis, mongolism, nausea, tumors, obsessions, flatulence, gastritis, and many others, including yellow fever. In the summer, the only kind of ice cream allowed to enter the doors of the Delamin house was lemon ice cream. A lemonade was lemon aid. His father tried to make him drink the pale yellowish liquid. Nestor became very violent, and by evening was very ill. Bitter was something like lemons.

The books in Nonno's library had a nice smell. Old volumes were almost perfumed. There was nothing calmer than a printed page. Words were strange objects. *Amore* meant love and *Amaro* meant bitter. When Mother and Nonna would tell him *"Amore mio,"* he would automatically think of lemonade.

A father, what was that?

He breathed in the smell of coffee and thought that the answer to his question could be found in the library.

Breakfast was ready.

The milk was white, so was Nonno's beard and mother's breast, but they were so different. Everything was so mysterious, every idea had a father.

White was the father idea for milk, breast, old men's beards, and clean clothes.

"Go and tell Nonno that breakfast is ready," ordered Mamma. He moved slowly, trying to hide the fear that was invading his eyes, remembering that he had once seen a hand playing the piano in the dark hall.

"Quickly," shouted his mother.

He tried to hurry through the dark hall. His legs felt unsure. The hall was dangerous and full of devils and communists. He began to shake. His teeth were chattering. The devils and the communists in the hall were invisible —just like God. Again a cold shiver moved like a wave down his back. Thinking that they were rushing after him, he ran to Nonno's room, always with the impression that someone was touching his back.

"Nonno, Nonno! Breakfast is ready."

"What's the matter? You look sick."

"The communists and the devils in the hall were after me."

"Did you see them?"

"No, but..."

"Don't believe a word of what the women say. If you don't see them, they don't exist."

He didn't believe in them anymore because Nonno had said that they didn't exist, yet he was still scared of them. God was invisible; therefore, he didn't exist. Why did Nonno keep going to church every Sunday? What about the smell of coffee? They walked to the kitchen holding hands, and Nestor kept turning his head, just to make sure that nobody was following them. The smell of coffee was invisible yet it existed. Could Nonno be wrong?

"Don't tell stupid stories to this child."

"Instead of preaching to us you'd better come home early in the evening. You were drunk again last night."

"I am the head of this house and I come home whenever I please."

"She's right, you were drunk."

"Not as drunk as a French soldier."

"They won the war, didn't they?"

"Listen, women, your place is in the kitchen, so take care of the politics of your oven."

He looked at them with his big eyes and added in a much louder tone, "By Bacchus... I am head of this house!"

Finally seeing that he had quieted them down, he added, "Come on, this child must eat. What are you waiting for?"

Now it is total silence, thought Nestor, but as soon as he leaves, they will begin to criticize. Women!

They were both against him, and he kept going to the office day after day so they could eat, buy flowers and dresses, and have a maid. Nonno was very rich before the war, but he lost almost everything because he had been a friend of Mussolini. It was annoying to hear the same story all over again. When Mamma and Nonna began their complaints, Nonno had to swear to quiet them down. Nestor knew they would end up by making the sign of the cross and by remaining silent until Nonno left for work. Even though Nestor had been accustomed to such scenes, he couldn't help crying every time they occurred.

"Nonno, would you like to be my father?"

Nonno explained that he was his grandfather and therefore he couldn't be his Papa. His father was fighting the Algerians, but soon the war would be over, "Then you will have a father." Nestor didn't answer, but deep down he knew that he had to keep looking for a real father who surely wasn't going to be a soldier.

It was so easy to see Him in the sky.

A kind of white ghost with huge wings held by the sun. The father of every created thing, of the beetle and of the coffee bean, was smiling at Nestor. "Come and take me with you!" he whispered.

"Let me touch your long white beard, bring me to the great Sunday mass, the mass that you say for the stars and the moon, come and take me with you, invisible father, teach me to fly, things must be so beautiful from above."

He waited and finally began to weep because the white ghost of the sky didn't answer him.

From In Rome (Toronto, 1980)

CATERINA EDWARDS

ASSIMILATION

At the end of his first month in Canada, Nino is convinced that he has made a mistake. This is not the place for him. But he cannot go back defeated, a failure, a fool in the eyes of Daniela, his family and his friends. He wants to return with something in hand, something to show for his sojourn in this wild west, not just money but accomplishment. He needs to be able to say I did this, I made this.

"Give it time," says Cesare, who has rented him a room.

With a year of high school English, Nino thought he would be able to manage, to make his way. He discovers that though he can read signs - stop, walk, men, women, immigration, passport, police station - when people speak, he understands practically nothing. When a cab driver or a clerk or a prospective employer opens his mouth, Nino hears a flow of unintelligible sounds. He must rely on gestures, or Cesare, to communicate. And Cesare's own English is broken. Even Nino can hear that.

On his second day in Canada, another man, a tailor from Treviso, who does speak English clearly, if not correctly, takes him to an employment office for an insurance number. And in an hour, he has his very own number. He is certified legal; he can work in this country.

. He is impressed by the tailor, by Cesare and his wife Amelia. They do not know him, Cesare's father was a friend of his father, but the tie is tenuous, and still Cesare helps him, they all help him automatically, without question. "That's what we do," Amelia says.

Nino is also impressed with the ease with which he registered for work. This is a better place, he thinks. Of course being able to work and actually working are separate things.

His first job is with the Canadian National Railroad working on a stretch of track an hour out of the city. The first new words he learns to say in English are pick and shovel. And that is what he does hour after hour: drive the pick into the ground and then shovel. He lasts three days. His legs, his back, his arms, his hands and even his head hurt worse each day. "This will kill me," he says.

On his second job, he lays plywood subflooring. He is fired by the contractor, who points out that the nails he takes so long in hammering consistently miss the beams. "You didn't get it right once," the man says.

"This is the land of possibility?" he asks Cesare. Who answers "patience" and "give it time."

Nino joins a work gang traveling through Northern Alberta pouring foundations. They work fourteen-sixteen-hour days, but he hangs on until the company cites lost contracts and lays him, and many of the others, off. "Thank God," he tells Amelia. "You wouldn't believe the food in those small town cafes. Garbage: fried, greasy garbage."

He goes to work at a car wash. At the end of the week, he realizes that he is earning half as much as he was as a tour guide in Venezia.

He phones the tailor and together they take his diplomas, high school and university, into the employment office. A plump woman, dressed head-to-toe in florescent pink, smiles and smiles at him; then tells him, through the translator, he will have to be reeducated, reassessed and reexamined here. Different standards, she says, different criteria.

The immigration official in Milano, the embassy staff in Rome, they told him that Canada needed skilled and educated workers. They recruited him. The Canadian government paid for his airplane ticket. They had all misled him, all of them. And he had been stupid to believe them. He, of all people, should have known that you couldn't trust anyone representing any form of government. There are no jobs for him. He isn't needed; he isn't wanted.

At the Italian grocery store, he meets an engineer, who feels as frustrated as he does. The man has been in Edmonton for over a year and is working as a waiter in what passes for an Italian restaurant. He had visited a local lawyer of Italian origin who acts as a vice-consul. "I demanded that the Italian government pay for my trip home. I demanded that the government take responsibility," the engineer says. "Italy should be protecting its citizens, protecting them from charlantism and exploitation."

"I bet he laughed," Nino says.

"Mr Vice-Consul laughed," the engineer says. "I wanted to punch him."

"Italy doesn't give a shit. Glad to get rid of us."

"Italy doesn't give a shit. Canada neither."

At the end of his second month in Canada, Nino is convinced both that this is not the place for him and that there is no easy return. Then, as the days grow shorter and the air colder, giving an inkling of what is to come, he rediscovers hope. He hears about a rich and successful Italian architect whose company is building all over Alberta. He hears that Peruzzi, a Florentine, prefers to hire Italians. And he must need architects, technicians, surveyors, assistants, designers; Nino is eager and qualified to fill any of those jobs.

He puts on his best suit and tie; he takes out his diplomas. He cannot deal with phones and English-speaking secretaries. He goes to the company offices. He is persistant: he waits, he will not leave. At closing time, with his chin up and his back straight, he walks into Peruzzi's's enormous office. But the man does not receive Nino the way he expected.

When Nino recites his qualifications, Peruzzi assumes an expression of distaste, as if Nino is a panhandler with his hand extended. "I don't need an architect."

Nino, who checked out a couple of his high rises the day before only to be disappointed by their ugliness, would like to differ. "I am a certified geometra as well. It took me several years to decide what I wanted to do. I studied one thing, then the other. They are related, of course. See -- my diplomas."

"I don't give a flying fuck about these pieces of paper." Nino has heard this before. He will hear it again, many times. In Canada, whenever his education is mentioned, it is dismissed. Strong arms, a strong back and money. That's what matters, he is told over and over. "Anyway," Peruzzi shuffles the pages of Nino's curriculum vitae. "You never practised or interned as an architect. Not that I can blame you. Who can be an architect in Venezia?"

"Renovations?" Nino says. "And on the mainland. But you are right, Signore Peruzzi, there is not much work. Not for anything new."

"Restorations, restorations, restorations. Don't I know it. In Firenze, it was a nightmare. And Firenze is not yet Venezia. The rules and regulations that have to be followed, the government boards to be pleased. A nightmare. You couldn't put up a building over four stories. And it had to blend in with the old ones. My creativity was in chains."

Thinking of those two high rises he had seen, Nino again has to supress the urge to say something pointed. "Makes it tough to make a profit."

"Exactly," Peruzzi says. "But we are in Canada now, thank God. None of those preserve the past boards. Here they don't give a dried fig what you tear down. Or what the new building looks like. We are free." Peruzzi stands; he has short legs and a barrel chest.

"To make money." Nino can't stop himself.

Peruzzi draws out a thick wad of banknotes from an inside pocket. He tosses the wad on the desk between them. "This is the only kind of paper that talks to me," Peruzzi says.

Still, he gives Nino a job. "Let's see what you can do." He sends Nino to do odd jobs on the construction site of a warehouse. Nino is to assist: to fetch and carry, to clean up after, to follow orders. Joe boy.

Earning a measly $1.50 an hour, Nino realizes he is being tested, but for what: patience, loyalty? And if he passes, will there be a reward? A job that does not leave him with screaming muscles at the end of the day?

It is mid November and cold, too cold for anyone to work outside. But the work proceeds: a steel skelton welded, walls raised. When he complains, the other men laugh. "This is nothing," they say. "Wait till it gets really cold. Till your breath freezes in the air. Till your bare skin freezes in two or three minutes. It can be dangerous," they say boastfully.

On advice, Nino goes to a shop called Army & Navy and buys a heavy parka (par -ka he learns to say), deerskin gloves, and work boots. Still, when outside, his forehead throbs, his cheeks burn, his fingers and knees stiffen. He dawdles in the trailer, hovering over a heater, stretching out the breaks. To three friends from Reggio, adjusting hat brims and pulling on gloves before they brave the outside, Nino says: "Abandon all hope you who enter there." All three look mystified. "Out there is hell," Nino says. "And in here, purgatory. We're paying for our sins."

"It is only going to get worse," one of the three says. "You'll see," says another.

The temperature drops and drops; the snow falls. The site manager suspends the work. Nino is moved to a small factory where the parts of pre-fabricated houses are made.

Giacomo, who studied to be a lawyer in Rome, stands beside him on the various assembly lines. Together, they are rotated from beams to window frames, from counter tops to floors. He tells Nino that Peruzzi hires Italians, because he can pay them less.

"He waved this wad of money at me, as if it were a sign of his superiority, like a crown or a bishop's hat." Nino says.

"He did that to me too. His identification badge. And he actually said, this is why I am the boss."

Giacomo reports that the two architects that are working for Peruzzi as architects are from rich Florentine families.

"Wonder how much experience they have," Nino says.

"Money talks," Giacomo says. "Money talks.

Once a week, Peruzzi strolls through the plant, inspecting. Each time, he pauses when he comes to Nino. He plants a hand on Nino's shoulder.

"How are you doing, *bischero*," using the Tuscan word for dickhead.

Nino does not smile. "You can call me Nino." He uses the *tu* form with Peruzzi as Peruzzi has with him. The boss laughs, strolls on.

"You've got balls," Giacomo says.

"It irritates me. The condescension, the vulgarity."

"He's a Tuscan. They have the foulest mouths in Italy. Doesn't mean anything to them."

"He doesn't say it to you."

The next week, Giacomo claims that a building Peruzzi built in Italy, or maybe Argentina, fell down. That there was a scandal.

"I believe it," Nino says. Drill, drill, drill. "I believe it. The man is a bad designer."

"I heard it from Gerussi, the biologist. You know, his brother is the famous heart surgeon? He's also from Florence."

The following day Peruzzi and his trailing court make their appearance. Peruzzi's hand drops on Nino's shoulder. "Hey, fuckface, what are you fucking up today?"

Letting go of the drill, Nino turns. He looks straight into Peruzzi's eyes. "Look at your own face. You'll see that you're the dickhead." And he walks out - elated.

After the Christmas break, he finds a job as an assistant to a tiler. At last, he has found work that he can do competently. He is careful and precise, cutting the tiles, laying them. He is good at patterns, at colours and finishes. He makes his suggestions to the tiler, who passes them along to the store and home owners as his own. Nino starts an English class in the evenings. Six months in Canada and he is beginning to understand what is necessary.

Nino meets a girl at a bus stop. Haltingly, he asks which bus will take him to Woodwards downtown. He knows the answer, but seeing the girl standing there bundled up, shoulders hunched, a red scarf drawn across her mouth, only her dark eyes visible, he is touched. He wants to speak, to coax her out of her cocoon. She pulls down the scarf to answer. She smiles; "I'm going there myself," she says.

Of course, Nino thinks. I should have been doing this from the beginning. What better way to learn English? Nino is no Casanova, not like some of his old friends. Giorgio who had a different woman each week. Or Beppi S. who boasted of prefering two at once. He has neither the energy nor the interest to conquer for the pleasure of conquering. But he had his adventures. Especially with the pretty, eager girls, Swedish,

French, German, Yugoslav, who flood into Venezia each summer. So many of them are looking for an experience, a flirtation; they expect a latin lover to go with the palaces and the gondolas. And now and then, Nino had obliged; he had done his duty in service of the reputation of Italian men.

Of course, Nino thinks, as he talks to Colleen with his eyes and hands and broken sentences. "What better way to learn English?" he tells Giacomo. "To get to know Canada?"

"Be careful," Giacomo says. "You don't know the customs here. You're plunging in blind."

Nino shrugs . "It's all easy here. No problem." And Colleen is easy-going and placid, a big-breasted, thick-ankled Alberta girl. Her hair hangs down her back, and she prefers flowered, cotton dresses that reach down to her feet. "She lets me do anything," Nino tells Giacomo, laying a finger on the side of his nose. "Anywhere. I don't have to ask."

Once more, he thinks, Canada is about freedom, space, and possibility. Once more.

He is learning more English, standard and slang, by the day. Colleen introduces him to her group of friends. They have known each other since high school, they take turns saying. (Which, Nino thinks, is no excuse for being so dull.) Every Friday, they go the bar, which he discovers is not a bar, or even a place, but a series of beer parlours: The Riv, The Commercial, The Klondiker and the Cecil, a series of enormous, shabby rooms with rows and rows of small round tables, topped with terrycloth and glasses and glasses of beer. The friends pull a few tables together. They throw their dollar bills onto a pile. The waitress automatically brings twenty to thirty glasses at a time and wordlessly fishes the right change out of the pile.

A couple of the girls ignore him but the others flirt, hanging over him as they teach him new words or give him advice on Canadian life. "Your accent is so sexy," one says. "Don't you love it here," says another.

The men of the group don't like him. They mutter to each other; they exchange looks. "What sound does spaghetti make when it hits the wall?" one says. "Wop, wop, wop," say the others. Most of the members of the group (not Colleen) drain glass after glass of the beer until they slur their words and laugh or cry, fight or embrace.

Nino wonders whether all Canadian youths are like them. Unlike his friends in Italy, they never discuss politics or philosophy, Marxism or Capitalism, books or films, no ideas. They talk of hockey and football, of the cars they want, of the houses they will build, of their idiot bosses or customers, of how drunk they were or will be. I was hammered, wasted, stoned, they say. But when they stand up to dance at the beer parlours or at parties, the music is familiar to Nino, as is their freeform dancing. Some things are the same everywhere.

Nino has grown tired of Colleen. He is starting to find her as dull as her group. He must stifle the urge to say nasty things to her placid face, to slap her on the buttocks, to bite into her fleshy arm, anything for a reaction, for a flash of light in her eyes. "She just lies there," he tells Giacomo. "And that loses its appeal fast. Opens her mouth and her legs."

"Come out with me," Giacomo says. "I've discovered an Italian club at the university and met this group of students."

It is at this club that Nino meets Fulvia. And everything changes: Nino changes.

The first time, he sees her across the room, and his eye, his attention, is caught. She stands alone, self-confident and self-sufficient. He does not have to ask if she, like most of the girls at the party, is the daughter of Italians but raised in Canada or if she has arrived recently from Italy. Her posture, her creamy silk blouse, her high heeled shoes, her throaty voice, all proclaim her Italianita. The second time he sees her, he wrangles an introduction. Fulvia is polite but barely seems to register his presence. Her Italian seems almost too cultured, too perfect, the result, he will discover later, of hours of practice to obliterate her Sicilian accent.

The next time, he immediately maneuvers his way to her side. He leans over and speaks into her ear: *quando bella splendea/ negli ochi tuoi ridenti e fuggitivi.* Then adds unnecessarily "The splendid beauty of your laughing, fugitive eyes."

"Not Leopardi, please," she says. "You'll make me feel as if I'm back in high school."

"I'm serious," he says. "You are splendid."

She makes a face. "*Uffa.* Cut it out."

"Why? I am telling the truth. I am in your power."

"Look, try someone else. I'm immune." She looks away, as if the conversation were finished. He stares at her profile, trying to decide which approach to take.

It is a chill night. To his Venetian standards, they are in the depths of the woods. A bonfire and a few lanterns provide the only light. He stays beside her, watching as she chats and laughs with the others. He doesn't join in. Then, his opening comes over a marshmallow. Neither he nor

Fulvia has ever seen one before and when a cute, round girl hands out sticks and marshmallows, they are joined in their inexperience. "Some tribal ritual," he says as they point their sticks at the bonfire. She giggles. Her first is burnt. "Incompetent," he says. His drops off his stick. They both laugh. And when, finally, they do bite into these famous Canadian marshmallows, they roll their eyes at each other.

"Help," Fulvia says.

Courting Fulvia, Nino puts aside his habitual irony (with women), his detachment. He has had enough detachment. From the moment that he arrived in Canada, he has felt disconnected. As if everything that he saw was an elaborate hallucination. Or perhaps it was he unmoored who was unreal: a ghost, a projection.

Now he is involved, even obsessed, and he revels in this new connectedness. Not that he isn't surprised by it. He finds himself repeating her name and sighing, or making the most extravagant declarations, and then he is surprised to realize that he is not playing a role or assuming a pose. He means the sighs, the words. And this goes on for days, weeks, months. The longer, the better he knows her, the more obsessed he becomes. He discovers nothing sloppy, shabby or lackadaisical about Fulvia.

He tells Giacomo, Cesare, Amelia, the tailor, and the tiler how much he admires Fulvia. "She's working at two jobs." "She has embraced this country."

"Be careful," Giacomo says.

"She's from down there," Cesare says.

"What would your mother think? Would she be pleased?" Amelia says.

"It is as if all the women before were silver," Nino says, "And she is beaten gold."

Surprising himself again by how much he believes it.

Reprinted by permission of the author, 2004.

LEN GASPARANI

LAURA

A freak snowstorm diverted the London-Venice flight to Monfalcone
– an industrial town nestled near the Gulf of Trieste. There was a bell
tone. A sign blinked on overhead: FASTEN SEAT BELTS. The intercom
crackled once, and the pilot informed the passengers (mostly tourists) a
winter storm was raging along Italy's Adriatic coast; airports in Treviso
and Venice were snowbound; and when they landed there would be buses
to transport the passengers to a train station where they could continue
on to Venice. After a brief silence, there was a chorus of grumbling. *"What
a bloody nuisance!" "So much for la dolce vita." "I knew something would
happen." "Well, it is December." "Is the airline paying the train fare?"* As the
plane began its descent, stewardesses checked that everyone's seat belt was
fastened.

When the passengers deplaned at the small airport in Monfalcone, a
cold night of falling snow greeted them. There were no buses in sight. Not
even an airline official was present. With their carry-ons and two large
suitcases, a handsome middle-aged couple from Canada threaded their
way through a noisy throng of people. The woman bade the man wait
with their luggage in the bus area outside the airport; then she dashed off
to seek directions and information. Others, looking disgruntled, confused,
impatient, milled about or scurried here and there. It was cold in the open
air despite the canopy the man huddled under. He lit a cigarette. Just then
a bus pulled in. A crush of people surged toward it. The man wondered
what was keeping his lady companion. He couldn't see her anywhere.
Someone shouted that the bus wasn't going to the train station. The man
glanced at his wristwatch. He had forgotten to set it one hour ahead. The
woman returned presently. She told him that no one seemed to know
what was going on.

"Utter chaos," she said.

The man cursed under his breath. "Welcome to Italy," he said
sarcastically. "Let me go and find out."

The woman frowned. "No, just wait here," she said, and hurried off
again.

Suddenly, in the crowd, a woman with a suitcase was standing beside
him. She was alone, and her face was beautiful. The man smiled at her.
She smiled back. He guessed she was in her early thirties. She was wearing

a camel-hair overcoat, kid gloves, and she was hatless. Her long dark-blonde hair tousled slightly in the cold wind. Now and then she gave a toss of her head, or swept her lustrous hair aside with a flick of her hand.

"*Mi scusi. Parla inglese?* Do you speak English?" the man asked her.

"*Si.*" She nodded. "Yes."

"Were you on the plane from London?"

"Yes.

"So was I," he said. "But where is the bus?"

She shrugged, then smiled. "I hope the bus is here soon."

He could smell her minty breath. He could tell from her accent and manner she wasn't English. She's lovely, he thought, feeling suddenly protective toward her.

"You're Italian, yes?" he said.

"*Si.* I live in Treviso."

"Ah!" He was happily surprised. He was about to tell her that Treviso was where his maternal grandparents (his *nonna* and *nonno*) were born, but a stout, moustached man interrupted them and asked, in English, if they knew anything about the bus schedule. The young woman shook her head, then said: "I am waiting for the bus." Resenting the intrusion, the man looked at the moustache and said brusquely: "Better check inside the terminal." The moustache turned away and brushed past a clutch of people.

"You speak English very well," the man said to her, trying to resume the easy tone of their conversation.

"Thank-you. I learn English in school," she said. "Do you live in London?"

"No. I'm from Toronto ... Canada. I'm Italian, too; but *non parlo l'italiano*." He shook his head, with a little show of embarrassment. "This is my first time in Italy. I'm going to Venice."

"Oh. I am sorry the weather is so bad," she said. "It is not always this cold; but you will like Italy."

"Talking to you, I already like it."

She smiled demurely, then looked away for a moment. After a pause, she said: "You have a nice voice."

"*Grazie.* You have a nice voice, too. What's your name?"

"Laura."

He repeated her name, and then he told her his first name. "You're very beautiful, Laura." He would have liked to put his arm around her. She looked cold standing there. The noise and the milling, jostling crowd made small talk almost impossible.

Does she think I'm alone? he wondered. The thought made him mindful of his companion, who might return any minute with news of the bus that was going to the train station. He glanced around. Time and place seemed unreal. He looked at Laura. He couldn't put the make on her, yet he sensed she was waiting for him to say something that would reveal his intention. Or did she think he was just being friendly while they both waited for their buses? His mind swarmed with thoughts, images, possibilities. He felt that she was attracted to him. How could he tell her the things he felt? He was probably old enough to be her father. Omnia vincit amor. Ah, youth! In the endlessness of a few minutes she made him aware of all his years, all the women he'd known and loved who were not her, and he wished he were thirty again, the loverman he used to be. He wanted to kiss her lovely pink lips. Laura, her name laureled his memory. Laura, the classic movie. Laura Secord chocolates: his mother's favorite. Petrarch's love sonnets to his beloved Laura. He once knew a Laura. She was black and beautiful, as in The Song of Solomon. Was his sudden euphoria akin to love at first sight? She was like a missing piece of his past. He wished he'd gone to Italy, the land of his forebears, a long time ago; visited Treviso where Laura, his female counterpart, lived. Laura. Aura of Laura. He truly loved his companion. They were unmarried, they didn't even live together; but she made him happier than his ex-wives had, happier than any woman he'd ever known. Who was Laura? A chance encounter at a small airport on a snowy December night. A once-upon-a-time Laura. Maybe she was married, engaged, or had a lover. What was her life? He could only guess, or try to imagine. It wasn't merely physical attraction but a certain aura she had, as though her presence beside him had been predestined. This was a woman he could love if he weren't already in love with the woman he was with. Yet he wanted to embrace her, to feel the warmth of her body against his. He knew his sudden, intuitive, irrational love for her would be unrequited. How could it be otherwise? The probability of seeing her again was remote. Loving her in the flesh rather than from afar meant he would have to change his life dramatically. So many obstacles, so little time. The risk was too great; besides, it would have been unconscionable on his part. To kiss her, to leave her with an impression of his passion, so she would remember him. To express the words of the spirit; to flatter her; to seduce her. Greenwich time was against him. Geography was against him. Ditto circumstance. I love her, he thought. Age tempers love with knowledge. What was it the poet had said? "There is the world dimensional for those untwisted by the love of things irreconcilable ..." The only love which lasts is the love that has accepted

*everything, every disappointment, every failure and every betrayal, which
has accepted even the sad fact that in the end there is no desire so deep as the
simple desire for companionship. Metaphysical concerns were inimical to love.
Sometimes he believed reality began outside verbal language. Nothing existed
in the intellect that had not previously existed in the senses. A cliché is a cliché
is a truism. Love was free from the restraints of morality. Love had a good
reputation because there was so much hate in the world. There was no evil so
great that love could not accommodate. Yes, he wanted to hold Laura in his
arms. Laura. Her name sounded like praise. In the space of a moment he saw
her sleeping, eating, bathing, dressing. Laura of Treviso. Had the plane landed
in Treviso he probably wouldn't be talking to her now. He wondered what the
satyric poet Gabriele d'Annunzio would have done in a similar situation. Age
was the worm gnawing incessantly on life. He thought of adulteries, betrayals
of loving trust, love for love's sake. Did love justify jeopardizing another's
happiness? Was human love a disease? There were as many definitions of love
as there were lovers. Love was an ideal that presupposed an object. What of the
lovesick love subject? Yes, he truly loved his companion. She was his conscience.
He knew that she loved him. They loved with a love that oscillated between
the sacred, the Platonic, the sensual. "If dead men dream of anything in their
graves, it is to creep underground into the next grave, lift a dead woman's
shroud and share her sleep." He couldn't remember for love or money where
he had read that, and he didn't know why it suddenly came to mind. Ah,
Laura! She was the woman he had always dreamed about. She embodied the
unattainable by virtue of her radiant transience. Her hazel eyes seemed to
charm whatever they gazed upon. Clothed from neck to foot, with snowflakes
sprinkling down on her, she stood there poised, waiting...*

Shouts of mingled joy and irritation rang out. Three buses arrived one
after another. As the buses slowed to a stop, the crowd massed around
them.

"*Meno male!* My bus is here," said Laura.

"Which bus is going to the train station?" the man asked her.

"That one, I think," Laura said, pointing to a dirty blue bus, and then
picking up her suitcase.

The man extended his hand to Laura. "Well, it's been a real pleasure."
He held her gloved hand in his. "I've enjoyed talking with you. Maybe
we'll meet again."

"*Si.* Maybe."

"Have a safe ride to Treviso."

"I hope you enjoy Italy. *Ciao.*" She gave him a quizzical smile, then turned and headed toward her bus.

People were quickly queuing up to the buses. The man looked around worriedly for his companion. He saw her emerging from the crowd and waving to him.

"The number five bus!" she called out. "The blue one."

They gathered up their luggage.

"I thought you got lost," he said, and suddenly realized he didn't know Laura's last name.

"It was a madhouse inside the terminal. Let's hurry." She glanced at him. "What's the matter?"

"Nothing. Why?"

"Don't look so grim," she said. "It's not the end of the world."

Accenti, Vol. 2, No.1, Jan-March 2004.

DARLENE MADOTT

VIVI'S FLORENTINE SCARF

Vivi put me up to buying the scarf at a marketplace in Florence. She was a much older woman that I, nearly twice my age, and my hesitation angered her. In view of the price (even on my student's budget, this was a bargain), Vivi could not fathom what was keeping me from possession. The scarf was bright, almost gaudily coloured, and large – more of a sarong than a scarf. "But what will I use it for?" "Use? Why anything – to wrap yourself when you step out of a bath, *for your man.*" There was no man in my life at the time. Single, I towelled down after a bath. This scarf would not blot a drop. I had learned from the other students that Vivi was married to an rich German engineer, had four adult sons. She travelled alone that summer, as did we all, purportedly studying

Quattrocentro art in Italy. The notion of the scarf, the bath, and the man was totally impractical. Still, the vision stayed with me because Vivi could see it, where I could see only her impatience with me, not what prompted it – my own youthful preparedness to waste.

Vivi, dying of cancer, although undiagnosed at the time, took the scarf from the market vendor and threw it about herself passionately. The Florentine sun caught the gold threads between colours and the scarf transformed her.

"If you don't, I will."

Professor Lucke's first lecture (the only one to be in a classroom; all the rest will be churches, monasteries, graveyard chapels, before the objects of our collective gaze): "Why Tuscany? Why murals? Italy is the cradle of Western civilization and Tuscany participates in this fruitful exercise. It is the nature of mural painting that promises to remain faithful to the original location of the image by the nature of the word 'mural' – wall. Wall painting needs a technique. Fresco – 'fresh' – a technique in which paint is applied to wet plaster. The pigment undergoes, because of wetness, a process of intense binding. The result is a painting of remarkable solidity, with the capacity to face the attacks of time. The mural, like love, is not transferable. It keeps us, holds us, wants our response. This art, it speaks to me. I cannot hear it. I just see the lips move. It is as if, through the ages, the sound gets lost. I try to find the bridge from here to there. I don't understand because the language has been lost, like faith itself."

Professor Lucke tries to find a way back, to find it for himself. For every time he speaks to us, it is as if he is in intimate dialogue with himself.

Why Tuscany? Why murals? Does this answer for any one of us, his followers, why we were here? Why am I in Italy that summer – the summer before I start my legal career? *I do not know what this thing is, my life. I do not know what purpose it has, what to make of it.* To stay sane, study birds, study rocks, study anything. So I travel about Italy, with those firm, slender limbs, studying the "Allegory of Obedience," Giotto, Andrea del Sarto, Fra Bartolommeo, the upper and lower churches of Assisi, with the same lost intensity as I have studied law.

"Painting catches a moment. Prose flows like time. At a certain moment, Christ says, 'There is a Judas among us. There is one who will betray me.' Is this the moment the artist will choose, or the one when

Christ first breaks bread, transforming it with meaning? What moment do you choose?"

It must have been obvious for Eva to say to me after class, "The thirties are the most awful time for a single woman."

She had watched me talk to Branko after class – Branko, who in Rome had told me about his anonymous encounters with men under bridges at night, one turned to horror at knife-point. "Life offers us nothing but a series of opportunities to feel ashamed." Branko would not put his arm around me at the Baths of Caracala when an open-air performance of Tosca turned cold. Shamelessly, I had asked him to hold me. On the bus back to Rome, I had told him how, at thirty-two, I still sometimes went home to my parents for a hug. He said, "You know, sometimes you make me feel very sad. I could give you a hug, but it wouldn't be honest."

As we walked down the stairs from class together, Branko told me about the man he had just met. They had gone out last night and had dinner together, for hours. Now the man was helping him find an apartment in Siena. Generous in his happiness, Branko lavished me with a consoling little hug. I wanted to smack him.

Eva must have diagnosed my malady, for on the way back to residence, she said what she said about a woman in her thirties.

"In her thirties, a woman goes through an almost unbearable physical suffering if she has no mate. It is the first time you realize you may never find one or may never have a child. By forty, you have usually reconciled yourself to that thought. You don't suffer over it as much."

Eva had retired from nursing that year. She and I shared a bathroom at a *conservatori feminili* in Siena. There was a man Eva had loved in her late thirties, and who had wanted to marry her, but Eva had not made that choice for herself. He was ten years her junior. Whatever the reason, Eva made a decision against the man.

"Did you ever regret it?"

"No. It was not the man I regretted. I met him years later, and knew I had not made a mistake. *It was the child.*" She said this matter-of-factly, as was her way, so that I almost missed it.

"You had a child?"

"No. *The child I never had.*"

Professor Lucke, who professed himself to be without belief yet daily stood a starved man before a banquet table where he could not eat, compares two paintings of the same subject – a Guido de Siena and Duccio Madonna with child. In the first, both mother and child are preciously dressed, faces composed of geometrical forms. The child is less of a child than the visualization of an idea, our Saviour, who is Saviour the moment he is born. In the Duccio, the child is a baby. Again the mother holds the child in her left arm, but the baby has grasped a little bit of her cloak. Such a human gesture! You see the childlike playfulness of the gesture of her right hand, the way the mother holds these little feet. She holds a child's feet in her hands, at the same moment as she holds the feet of the crucified Christ. "Look at us and behold; we are human, he is human. You can come to me because I am a mother. This is my little child. I know about you because *I have gone through that.*"

The night before this lecture, I have a dream I am in labour, the birth pains pulling me to earth like the force of gravity. It is not the pain of a menstrual period. It is rather as if someone has reached up inside of me, taken hold of my womb, and is tearing me out – a cutting, annihilating pain. I wake on the single bed in my cell-like room, knowing my pregnant sister back in Canada must be in labour. I wake, relieved that it is she and not I, for I am terrified of her pain. I do not want this cup for myself, nor do I want to pass through life alone. In the terror of this night, these seem two irreconcilable fears.

Coming back to residence with Eva, I find the telegram and know, without opening it, that my sister's child has come.

"Look and behold, we were human. He was human. You can come to me, because I am a mother and this is my little child. I know about you, because I have gone through that."

And I thought what he meant was the pain of childbirth, never for a moment conceiving far worse. No, because in this painting, at *this* moment, the mother holds the child's feet in her hands. *"Ah," said my son's eventual father, watching me play with the little feet of my only son. "You kiss those feet now. Don't you know those are the feet that will take him away from you?"*

She holds the child's feet in her hands, at the same moment as she holds the feet of the crucified Christ.

Vivi is difficult to describe. Even her age is indeterminate. She might be sixty-five or fifty. She has been a model, has sold real estate, even taught – this in addition to having mothered four sons. Her pregnancies were terrible, with an overactive thyroid not diagnosed until she was in her late forties. She is Estonian – a tall, skinny blond woman, who does her makeup well, who dresses elegantly in melon-coloured silk dresses she made on her own – always elegant and womanly, with an innate artistry.

We met returning to the *Conservatori Feminili Reuniti* late one afternoon. Recognizing each other from class, we went to Nannini's for tea. She seemed lonely, though in my ignorance I could not imagine how someone could be lonely in a life of such density. She said she had a decision to make about that night. Her taxi driver had asked her for a date. She was nervous about agreeing because her Italian was insufficient to lay the ground rules for the evening; on the other hand, she wanted to break out of the circle of females at our residence. I told her I wished for male company, too. I told her about Branko, and how it was frustrating to be frequently with a male who elicited female response, but had no male response. She said she really wished she could meet someone gay, that she loved gay men – they were so intuitive.

The next day in Florence, Vivi saw me with Branko and ran after us. She announced that she wanted to have a really good meal with people who looked as if they weren't afraid to spend some money. At lunch, we had wine, perhaps were all a little drunk. Vivi talked and talked. At one point, she pretended to a weakness she did not have, and placed her hand on Branko's arm, as if for support. Branko preened at her touch.

"I do not believe you. You are a very strong woman," I said.

"You know that? I do not like the idea of being known."

On the bus, that evening, we sat separately – Branko way in the back, Vivi behind me. At one point, I turned around to hear something Vivi was trying to tell me, and Branko caught my eye, behind Vivi's back, indicating with his hands the quacking gesture for talk, talk, talk. That he should thrive throughout lunch on her attention, only to mock her now, diminished him in my eyes, at the same time as he made me his accomplice. I decided to distance myself from them both.

The next day, Vivi wanted to return to the same restaurant. I said I did not like to repeat experiences, so Branko and Vivi dined that day alone. On the bus back to Siena, Branko surprised me by taking the seat at my side. He told me Vivi had a terrible earache; they had tried to phone some international alert, for which her husband had bought insurance, and failing any contact, he had suggested that Vivi sit down and relax and eat something first, and when she swallowed her soup, the thing blocking her inner ear seemed to burst and the pain dissolved, after which she felt fine. I thought Vivi's illness a ploy, and was amazed that Branko had bought it.

Professor Lucke: "Monterchi, a graveyard chapel, circa 1445. Piero della Francesca. Here we have a tent motif, opened to the side by angels in a ceremonial way, so that we see the *Madonna del Parto*. This is not a common topic in Christian iconography – the pregnant Mary. You see the swelling of her body, hidden beneath a blue gown. Her feet are clearly visible. She turns slightly away from us. Her left hand on her haunch. Her right hand lies over a slit in her gown, a very soft, cautious touch; at the same time a gesture, which seems to point. This is a woman in every sense of the word, expecting. Inside surface – padding – inside of a fur coat. Outside a mantle. Promise of birth. Christ on the cross, promise of resurrection. Location, above the altar in a chapel of a graveyard. The meaning of the Eucharist. She is the chalice that carries the Lord. Like the tent that shelters her, her gown shelters her body, her body shelters Him. Pomegranate. Eucharistic symbol. Round and opened like her gown." Professor Lucke is excited as he points, his fingers flying here and there, dancing in his running shoes, his eyes on fire with the symbols on the wall. His loose cotton shirt billows like the wings of an angel as the sweat blossoms under each arm, with its pungent male odour, prompting Eva to comment, "He wants a woman," not in the carnal sense, but in the sense of a man wanting a woman to administer to the details, such as laundering his shirts.

I usually spent my weekends in Siena with Eva, lounging beside the *Giardino* pool. With Eva, there were no expectations, not even the necessity of conversation. We would sit side by side on our lawn chairs, observing the bathers from other countries over our respective books, in a parallel pursuit. Eva studied the course books in preparation for our final exam, while I read Boccacio. Thus, in silent companionship, our eyes filled with the same images. There was this Swedish girl in a loose white bathing suit, draped off her small breasts with their dripping nipples, perched with a single bronzed foot coyly fishing the pool. Her young muscular mate swam up to her, lifted the foot from the water and, astonishingly, sucked her toe.

"Isn't she gorgeous?" was Eva's singular comment, admiring the human animal which she had nursed in all its extremities. Eva was of an age – beyond surprise, beyond longing, accepting of seemingly everything. That day, and although Eva and I usually practiced our student economies, we ate at the *Giardino* restaurant. Without changing out of my black bathing suit, I simply wrapped Vivi's scarf about my waist and waited in queenly composure for the barbequed lamb to be brought to our table, treating Eva to wine. When supper was ended, I could not leave the bones on my plate. Wrapping them carefully in a napkin, I deposited them into my beach bag. Eva said nothing. Later, we laughed like complicit schoolgirls over the contemptuous silence of our Sienese waiter, removing my boneless plate. In the privacy of my cell-like room back at the *Conservatori*, I gnawed again upon my bones, with a hunger beyond need.

While I usually spent my weekends with Eva, one weekend I went to meet Vivi in Bologna. Our purpose was shopping. Vivi was taking me in hand. If I were to become a lawyer, I must dress the part. In Bologna, I would find Armani suits and Bruno Magli shoes. Vivi knew just the right stores, and there was a hotel across from the train station where we would each take a room.

I arrived before Vivi. Though discussed weeks before, we had not confirmed with each other before the designated weekend, so I was uncertain if she would, in fact, keep to the arrangement. Was it for this reason or some other that I made all my purchases without her? In the shoe store where I selected my shoes and bag, I told the saleswoman I would be practicing law on my return to Canada. "In these," she told me, "the judges will not be able to resist your persuasions." For the black Armani suit, with buttons up the left side of the skirt, I would find a handmade white-and-black shirt. I made my choices in an orgy of spending, all in one morning. Surrounded by a sea of tissue paper on the floor of my hotel room, I surveyed the purchases for which Vivi's approval had not been sought, and a wave of nausea overcame me. Was it the extravagance of what I had just done, or fear of my own choices?

At dinner, I told Vivi that I had been about to leave Bologna after my purchases, uncertain of her arrival. She burst into tears. Tonight was her birthday. I could not possibly have known...to have been abandoned by an alcoholic mother, a father unable to care for her, being given into foster care. She had grown up thinking of the children who came and went as her brothers or sisters, never to see them again, never knowing when they would disappear. Her father had thought he could get her back, had apparently tried – a fact not known to Vivi until the year after his death, when she had traced her birth parents and learned for the first time that she had been wanted by at least one of her life givers, that her father had tried. He had thought the child custody order temporary, not appreciating how in legal terms temporary can become final. There was one birthday when a man arrived at the door. She was sent to her room, but not before she saw the shadow of his form, the doll in his hands. They were delicate hands, with long aesthetic fingers – the hands of a pianist or an artist. The doll had a porcelain head, later broken by one of Vivi's foster brothers. Now Vivi had a vast collection of dolls at her home back in Canada, the one built for her by her German husband. She had four sons of her own. No, I could not imagine the sense of abandonment had I not been there in Bologna.

"Duccio: We look into an interior, into something that could be part of a larger structure. Time here is convincing. People are joined together, having a meal – drinking, eating, talking, but lively. There is one in the centre. Again we have the motif of the one who leans against him. For sure, these people spoke Italian. We seem to hear them. Notice how much Duccio operates with hands, in contrast to Giotto, who seems even to hide hands. When shown at all, Giotto's hands are at rest. In Duccio, in proper perspective, the lines should converge on Christ. That would recess him. The way it is here, in the Duccio, the convergence point is outside the back wall. What principles did these people operate with? There is a construction, a syntax, an order that brings the disparate parts into a whole. These splinters of perspective—are they renderings of observation or constructions unidentified with external sight? We can't see this painting from Renaissance eyes. This is a way of seeing the world unknowable to modern eyes."

In Assisi, we dine together – Branko, Vivi, Professor Lucke, and I – a rare night together, never to be repeated. Eva is bedridden, having eaten some tainted food. She takes her incontinence as a sign of demise, apologizes when I surprise her, weeping alone in the dark when I return with some tea. I had thought Eva beyond grieving, not understanding that one can always grieve one's own life. Eva, then, had been *afraid*. Alone in the darkness of our cave-like room in Assisi, Eva had been afraid.

That day, in Assisi, we learned of the Franciscans. "In the Franciscan
spirit, there is the discovery of the individual, who has the capacity
to judge, who in a sense needs to be converted." Like Professor Lucke
himself, whose deepest need is to be converted – to believe. It is easy for
those who do, impossible for those who cannot. Faith cannot be willed.
Like love. Neither for him, nor for me. "God is perfect. Man is imperfect.
Whatever is imperfect cannot be God. But Christ was born man. Yet
he was a spiritual being, was not man. This must have been a deadly
challenge to the Church, this Christian paradox. It meant in his very core
God was man, born man, became man, lived like man, died like man."

Professor Lucke, Branko, Vivi, and I eat together in an outdoor garden
of arbours and vines. A guitarist from the nearby campground plays
Neapolitan love songs. At outdoor kitchens carved into caves, there are
large open hearths; we select our meals at the cave mouths. I have quail on
a spit, cooked peppers and rapini. We bring Professor Lucke his favourite
pasta, *con oglio e aiglio*. And, of course, there is the wine!

In the arboured garden, our separate realities seem to coalesce. We draw
near. Professor Lucke confesses to the problems of teaching in Italy, how
he can see some people are coping with so much other than the course – it
may be a bug in the bathroom or something else. People are overwrought
because everything is different. We begin talking about opera and intense
experience when Branko repeats the Tosca story I heard in Rome about
the transposition in the music signalling some epiphany in the plot.
Professor Lucke tells Branko he likes opera because the music distances
the emotion. He has this abstract thing to contemplate, interposed
between himself and raw emotion. Vivi says it is only deep experience that
makes life worth living. I sit distant and silent, wrapped in the scarf. My
silence is willful, for Branko has told me that afternoon I am too caught
in the vortex of myself that I do not see people around me – the way they
move away, as if from a fire, realizing that I know exactly what I want and,
my God, I'm going to get it, and they had better get out of my way until
I'm done. "You are hard to be with."

Vivi tries to capture Professor Lucke's attention the whole evening. Then,
unexpectedly, Professor Lucke leans across the table and says into my
silence: "This is a beautiful scarf." His thumb catches the fabric, like the
scene of the lamentation with St. Francis outstretched, *and Girolomo,
the one who could not believe, he catches the fabric and pulls it up and free*

of the wound and then pushes his fingers into it. We see him do that with terrific concentration. We see him from the back kneel down in businesslike fashion. "I want to know," in contrast to everyone else, whose response is raw emotion. Professor Lucke brings his face close to the scarf, I can smell the sweat rise from his unwashed body. Vivi smiles triumphantly, taking the compliment as her own, but says nothing to betray me. She and I alone know that I would not have bought it but for her. It is her taste he compliments, but *I* am the scarf. It is my beauty he means. I am beautiful – for the first time in my life.

Toward the end of the evening, the others start asking Professor Lucke about art. I say our conversation will become too much like work. Professor Lucke says, "My God, you *know* me." Then, "We have four weeks still to go." We have come too close, too fast. In fact, we will never again break bread together with Professor Lucke after that. *For not much longer will I be with you.*

    The next day, on a street in Assisi, he and I pass each other alone. Professor Lucke says he wanted to thank me for my company. He was sorry he hadn't the chance to talk with me, but he was distracted by the full conversation on his other side. "You," he says, "are very independent. One can see that immediately. Often independent people drive away what they need."

    Donatello's "The Conception": "'Yes, I will be the handmaid of the Lord,' and the very minute she gives her assent, she conceives. She hasn't here yet given her assent. Donatello focuses in on that moment, and gives it to us with a kind of dynamism. She doesn't say 'no'; she says 'yes', but the conception takes place only when she says 'yes'. In this mural, it has not happened yet. This is the moment *before choice*."

Never, for a moment, conceiving there could be far worse…
    When they put you in my arms and I looked into your face at those eyes, wide-open and searching for me, I, who had heard your first cry, who could not stop crying, had heard that tall ships, passing before the mouths of caves at the very moment sun entered as through a shutter, left a negative of the ship on the back of the cave; thus you were imprinted upon me, your face like a negative upon my mental plate.

"Momma, how will I bear it?" I went to your father's apartment to tuck you in during those first nights of our separation. In the bathroom,

I washed your little face, contorted with pain, watched you square your little shoulders, and go out to face your fear. *You will bear it because you must, because you have no choice. I did this to you.*

"*She stares at her baby Jesus and sees right into his future. She says 'yes' to conception, knowing of His impending sacrifice.*"

It takes me over twenty years to understand the gift of Vivi's scarf. By then a middle-aged woman with only one son to my flesh, I have an afternoon of love. I have emerged damaged but not broken from a failed marriage. To my surprise, there is a man in my life, enough years my junior to make me remember Eva. Remembering Eva, *I do not refuse*. We have all we can expect – a few hours on a Sunday afternoon between our respective obligations, the children's hockey games, their birthday parties. How shall I greet you? Wear nothing, he says, we haven't much time. But I cannot bring myself to open my door naked. It is not the fear of nakedness, but of my own imperfection – that he will see the unholy blemishes of this sacred temple, the Caesarean section, the imperfections of a life half used.

Vivi, I wrap myself in a vortex of colour. I stand behind my front door, a woman, in every sense of the word, expecting.

Ah, the delight of his eyes when I open the door, of his hands, searching the colourful folds for an opening. Vivi's scarf is the wrapping. I am the gift.

Vivi will return that summer after Florence to find a different color of hair in her own hairbrush, left in the lavish master bathroom of her perfect home, while she went to Florence to study art. Is it always thus that we discover ourselves betrayed? What choice did she have? The choice only of reaction. I was not there to witness. I will remember Vivi as one moment – the moment she threw the scarf in all its colors about herself under the Florentine sun. *If you don't, I will.*

Vivi, I wrap myself in the vortex of colour. I do this in memory of you.

From Joy, Joy, Why Do I Sing? (Toronto, 2004)

ANTONINO MAZZA

URBAN HARVEST

My great-grandfather, Matteo, on my mother's side of the family, became a successful oil merchant. A loner by inclination or circumstance, after losing all his children to the Spanish fever, maybe to forget, maybe to start over, he joined the end-of-the-century stampede to America.

After six years burrowing holes in the stony bowels of an infinite city, he returned to the village, smaller, darker. A ghost of his former self.

Matteo didn't whine. Hard work never killed anybody. Those harrowing fourteen-hour workdays spent in the sewers of the new world were not the cause of his ills. The hard work meant unprecedented good savings. The blame could only lay with the insipid American diet.

Against such inarticulate languishing, his forlorn wife divined a half-pint of olive oil, served over diced hot peppers and a clove of garlic. The ancestral potion restored his desiccated soul. Angela regained a husband, soon giving birth to two daughters: Caterina and Maria.

I should say at once that this happened in Calabria, a Mediterranean region ravaged through the ages by an endless succession of calamities that history forgot. At a still archaic time some nine decades ago. In that indelible year of 1908, a cataclysmic tremor, together with a sea-quake, erupted in the night leaving in its wake untold devastation and a human toll of 100,000 dead in the two rival cities of Reggio and Messina, in dozens of sea-side towns all along the dreamed Tyrrhenian coast, and in hundreds of villages in the surrounding mountains.

Startled by the unearthly cataract of dwellings that suddenly went crashing over a rocky crag of the lower Aspromonte, forever burying half the inhabitants of San Roberto, Matteo and Angela awoke and crawled out in the dark from the pile of rubble that had been their house, reassured by the piercing terror in their children's cries. Their family was safe.

Now, Matteo knew nothing about our narrow end-of-millennium maxim that the greatest opportunities derive from the worst catastrophes. But he knew his elixir. So when the shortage in man-power began to show in the rising price of oil, he resolved to invest his American savings and divert a creek. He used it to convert a crude millenarian "trappeto" into a water-powered oil press.

Farm labourers and tenant farmers began to trek their hand-picked olives to the new press, more efficient than all the mule or ox driven presses that had dotted the hills since time immemorial. Matteo was paid in oil, which with the hot spices remained preeminent in his diet. He sold the rest to barefoot itinerant vendors who came from Fiumara and other nearby villages, and later, when roads again permitted, on two-wheeled carts from Villa San Giovanni, Scilla and other more distant coastal towns.

Matteo didn't become instantly wealthy, but he was able to stave off America for more than half a century. In the next twenty years he built a new house in the less precarious village of Colelli that rose nearby, and purchased several parcels of land, variously endowed with grape vines, olive groves, and citrus plants.

Meanwhile, unhindered by their taciturn father, free from the inhibiting presence of Calabrian brothers, the girls grew up empowered by the ownership of property. Under their mother's deft tutelage they learned the arduous tasks of cultivating lands that did not yield easily: from tilling with the hand hoe to making compost from animal manure and hauling it to enrich the poor terraced soil; from irrigating against the leonine summer to planting and tending plants. The string and fava beans required climbing poles; tomatoes needed to be tied for support and their leaves pruned to expose the fruit to sunlight as the plants grew, especially when the tomatoes were to be preserved as sauce. Other vegetables had to be cared for as well, sweet peppers and eggplants, zucchini and cucumbers; an innumerable array of garden salads that took root best nearest the irrigation ditches where the soil remained damp; and herbs and spices, from rosemary to laurel, from oregano to the aromatic basil, from the arduous garlic to rainbows of hot peppers.

It is hard to imagine their lives, but it seems that all Caterina and Maria ever did was toil. If not to till and plant a field, or to timely get in the assorted fruits and process them, or the grapes at harvest time, then to feed the chickens and hogs, milk the goat, the cow, and the endless other chores that went with a day's work, given that soon they each had families of their own, and that now their children too had growing families. They cultivated their gardens so copiously that I remember as a child how even below the orange trees, right in the shade, there were always more surprises growing.

And neither could their daughters be much help any more. This was incessant work. With certain tasks, they simply had to do everything themselves, those women, custodians of their ancestral culture, who had never even been to the nearby city, except once, to buy golden earrings for their weddings.

Still, hard work never killed anybody.

What killed was ill health and the far away world, which meant bad nutrition.

Coltura-Cultura, says a proverb by now forgotten. So, not only did Caterina and Maria cultivate their gardens to fend their brood from America, but to be able to keep cultivating they felt compelled to protect their lands even from the vagaries of their husbands, orange merchants both. In Caterina's case, her husband almost managed by the end of his life in the mid-sixties to bring her to the brink of financial ruin.

Caterina's first daughter, Angelina, very young married my father, a thirty-seven year old stonemason, who learned his trade in the antiseismic rebuilding of Calabria and Sicily, and who had just returned from the war.

Those years must have been brutal for the region as well. I don't remember, of course. If I ask my father, he tells me this story: "At war's end I came back from the Veneto. I hid there more than a year with partisans and comrades I escaped with from a burning train in Padova. Made prisoners in Albania, we were being taken to a German Camp, and we knew what it meant."

My father has told me his adventures before; his stories are one unrelenting journey.

"When at long last I arrived in Villa San Giovanni, I didn't recognize it. The train station I'd helped rebuild before the war had been bombed by the Allies. Reggio and Messina were in ruins again, just like the time of the earthquake. *U bonu jornu si vitti ra matina!*"

As he talks in dialect of those grievous days, I'm hurled back to my own very first memories. There was a battery-powered radio. And tango music. On the terrace of our house everyone is dancing. I'm dancing my first steps with my father, my bare feet pressing on my father's shoes.

I move closer to absorb more of what he knows, I know his story will capsize what I remember of those festive times. He's saying "There was no work, no money in circulation, no one was building. When I joined your grandfather's business, marketing oranges was a risky occupation. There was the odd year, '48 for instance, when we still could have saved ourselves, when after a mid-winter hail-storm the largest markets, Rome, Florence, Bologna, Venice, were clamouring for citrus fruit.

"That year, in Bologna, a friend had offered to sell me a licensed depot he owned, where we could receive and store produce, with all the amenities to clean, buff, and repackage merchandise for other firms, rather than play roulette from year to year with our own perishable goods. I advised your grandfather. We had profits of three million lire that season already, they were asking only one million. We could have paid for the depot outright. '*Micuzzu*,' replied your grandfather, the moment you see a few pennies you can't wait to scatter them every which way. '*Appena viriti ncentesimu nan sapiti comu l'aiti a sparpagghiari.*'

"The next year the orange groves we bid on were hit by blight, and we lost much more than what we made all the previous year. We were forced to scale down. The women refused to go to the city. They would not put up their property as collateral. So the banks extorted usurer's fees on our loans. We practically lived hand to mouth. Scarcely able to deliver on the interest payments.

"Nearing fifty, with a growing family, I couldn't just sit and watch as we sunk ever deeper into debt. That was the choice."

At this point my father always breaks off for a moment, and I wait in anticipation to know which of two recurring pronouncements he will opt for to close his voyage on this time: "*Fu a megghiu cosa!*' It's the best thing I ever did!", he concludes.

Or, "*Fu nu sbagghiu!*' It was an error!"

Error or not, I don't recall the day my father left for America, though America was clearly Canada by then. But I remember when my mother came back from the port of Naples. The radio was sealed and put away, and was never heard again. And soon the letters started, monotonous, tormented.

"*Cara Moglie...*" "*Sacrifici!*" "*Cari Figli...*" "*Sacrifici!*" I still feel the prick of the flesh I felt then when I hear this word.

I couldn't really know what he meant then. He was in America, after all. But the women must have intuited more, because soon grandmother Caterina was hording a multitude of herbs and spices; and hot peppers; and tomatoes dried in the sun; and dried meats; and goat cheeses; and black olives; and red vinegar and the all vital olive oil, that in my child mind became associated with death and migration, since, when the revered great-grandmother, Angela, died, the tinsmith who sealed the inner zinc casket for her burial left a singed scent at the wake that wafted back on the terrace whenever he came to seal the tins of balsamic vinegar and olive oil for America.

Those fruits of the earth of Calabria, however, which grandmother

cultivated and mother bundled with care, and I helped lug on foot, up
and down the craggy hillsides to every scorching village whenever anyone
who knew my father was about to embark for Canada, did not often
make it past the Canadian customs. Port officials looked on those choice
stores as a suspicious barbarian feast.

I imagine some of the prosciutto preserved in those tins may well still
be at the bottom of Halifax harbour.

Italy kept no tally of the foodstuffs that the poor of Calabria, and
the other impoverished regions of Italy, exported via immigrant crates,
destined for the happy nourishment of cod and lobster.

Yet, the food from his barbarian region was the immigrant's lifeline.
How else could a man survive the subhuman conditions of work in the
new world? The perilous construction scaffolding? The anachronistic
firings on the spot? Workers who were refused membership in union
locals because they worked too hard, and had no recourse? And what
could console a man of tiny stature after surviving the collapse of a
subway tunnel, of a building wall, of a failed bridge?

No, the word "sacrifices" in those letters had to suffice. Who can know
the cravings of a body walking for miles in deep snow, in the outskirts of
an expanding Ontario suburb, in sub-zero temperature, to a wind-swept
job site, and only when the foreman asks if he brought his tool box, he
realizes that his limbs are frost-bitten, and that all his tools and lunch box,
"a boxa ru lonch`iu," had slipped from his hands, who knows where, on
his way to get there at the break of dawn.

No, you needed the hot spices, and the garlic, and a steaming plate of
pasta, with crusty bread baked in the family's stove oven, and the harder
cheese, and the home-brewed wine to keep body and soul together. A
man in such a dire state would have to rebuild a home.

That is why the women followed their men across the ocean. With
them came their mothers, sometimes in person, always in spirit. And their
gardening seeds were hidden in their underclothes where customs officials
didn't dare get at them.

No Canadian census of urban agriculture exists. The 1950s, 60s, and
70s of the vegetable garden in every immigrant backyard, whose yields
were several times as high as those achieved by rural farmers, have passed
forever. The garden may persist in our cities, but mostly as a fetish. It will
never supply again almost all the vegetables for an entire household as it
did.

The 80s of the enigmatic identity of the children of those emigrants too have passed. And their mothers' blissful cooking has prevailed upon the jejune Canadian diet.

The 90s surprised us. One by one we bury those tiny women of giant cultivation. Caterina died first, then suddenly mother, Angelina, here in the new world; and again Maria, in the forsaken village in the hills of Calabria she never left. Our metropolises are built. They are jewels in the crown of the new country. *Coltura-Cultura.*

From Urban Harvest = Raccolta urbana (Ottawa, 2004)

IV

EXCERPTS

FRANK G. PACI

BLACK MADONNA
Chapter 12

Before the funeral they had the widow Angeline help them write a
cablegram to their Aunt Pia in Novilara. Joey had suggested calling her,
but there had never been a phone number as far as they could remember.
They had included their number in case their aunt could make it to the
funeral in time. An offer to pay her air fare had also been mentioned.

But Pia didn't call until after the funeral. Marie gave Joey the phone
since he could speak better Italian. She went downstairs to listen on the
basement line. The voice was thin and distraught, crackling over the
Atlantic from another world. Marie was immediately struck by the familiar
ring to the accent and idiom. No one from the West End had ever come
from anywhere close to her mother's village in Marche.

Pia spoke quickly, trying to explain how she had received their news
late because she lived on a farm a little way from the village. The cablegram
had gone to Pesaro first, since the village didn't have a post office. She hadn't
known what to do until a city friend told her to phone to America. But she
hardly used the phone in the first place, she said by way of apology. She was
afraid to phone so long a distance. Was Assunta really dead?

"*Sì,*" Joey said.

Pia went off the phone for a moment. She was talking to someone in
the background. Marie could hear two women sobbing. When Pia came
back she could scarcely talk. Joey tried to explain how it happened. It was
very difficult for him to get the words out, but he managed to convey that it
was an accident. Pia took it to mean her sister had died in a train accident.
Joey left it at that. She kept sobbing, *povero Giuseppino, il tuo papa e La tua
Mamma, c'è nessuno adesso* — there's no one now — as if Joey were a child.
It was the hand of God. And Assunta had so much wanted to come back to
visit. She hadn't seen her in over 30 years. From that day in the train station
in Pesaro when she left with a suitcase and her trousseau trunk to go across
the ocean to America.

"*Vieni in Italia,*" Pia said imploringly. "Come and live here, Giuseppe,
for I know you like my own son. Assunta told me so many things about
you. All she wrote to me about was you and Maria. I will take care of you.
My roof is yours until you are married. Here, here, say hello to your sister,

Marisa."

The shy timid voice of a young girl came on the line. It was a clear, resonant voice that seemed to obliterate the ocean that separated them.

"*Ciao,* Giuseppe." Marisa said. "*Zia* Assunta was like a mother to me. She used to send me gifts and letters. I'm so sorry for you. Such a terrible accident. We all share your grief. You must come to Italia for my wedding in the summer, no."

For some reason Marie couldn't help sobbing at the sound of that voice. It was as if she could speak Italian.

"Is that you, Maria?" her cousin said. "*Ciao,* Maria. You must come to the wedding. Please. Maybe we can change our grief into happiness. I want to meet you and your little boy."

Marie made an attempt to say a few words, but her voice deserted her. She was overcome by an indescribable feeling of loss.

Pia wouldn't hang up until Marie and Joey convinced her that they'd seriously think about visiting them for the wedding. They'd have to keep in touch from now on.

The funeral was a quiet affair. This time there was no wailing at the bedside. Instead the Black Madonnas appeared in church together, sitting in the pew behind Marie and Joey. They were like a heavy black shroud mumbling their prayers in Italian in a continuous drone. Throughout the Mass Marie felt their eyes on her neck, burrowing into her.

She felt it was such a short step from the black dress to the black-draped casket in the aisle of the church.

Her eyes were fixed on the casket during the whole service. At the funeral home she stared just as intently at her mother's shrunken death mask. Marie saw her own end sketched in the wrinkled and closed eyes — in the grey hair and the toothless mouth. She saw that her mother was nothing now, and that nothing had been passed on to her in a place just under her heart where it was ticking with every beat, waiting to explode.

It was so certain she could almost taste her own end. The charred flesh. The smoke.

The certitude had caused such an overwhelming fear that everything around her seemed to slip away into insignificance. Her heartbeat picked up. She could hear it reverberating in her head like a kettle drum. She had to close her eyes in the dimly lit parlour because the light was too glaring.

When it passed she burst into tears. Only a dizzy emptiness remained inside her.

After giving a short homily over the casket Father Sarlo, in an unexpected move, spoke personally about Assunta. His eyes glistened and his words rang with feeling and conviction in the empty church. He seemed to have to summon all his strength to speak.

He told of how he had come to know Assunta much more in the final months of her life. Of how she had opened her heart to him. She had trusted him. They had grown old together in the neighbourhood. They had eaten the Lord's meal together for a long time.

"She was a simple woman," he said, directing his eyes toward the living. "She came to this country from a small village. She was a peasant like you and me. It was difficult for her to leave her village. She was bewildered and very afraid, But she came nevertheless. God had destined her to marry someone in the new country, she said. Her parents were ashamed of her. She was well past the marriageable age. But they needed her to work on the farm. There was no dowry for her except a trousseau trunk. She knew this offer of marriage was her last chance. If there was one thing she wanted in all the world, she said, it was to have children. To make her life worthwhile, she said. She would have crossed all the oceans in the world for that. Her life had been filled with poverty and hunger. Where during bad years they ate *polenta* for months at a time. Nothing they had was theirs. She only wanted to be loved, she said.

"But I knew Assunta Barone before she told me these things. My mother was like Assunta Barone — and the mothers of many of my friends in our village of Calabria. And you know Assunta Barone, you older women who came to this country like her. Who were set in your ways. Who had the old country in your blood and nothing could wash it away. For Assunta it was harder than most. She couldn't even learn the language here. She watched so much TV to learn, she said, that the pictures spoke without the words.

"During the last months she told me often that she had failed her children. I tried to convince her that she hadn't failed anyone. That it was a different country with different people. She said that once she left the old country the only things she knew in life were to be a wife and mother.

"I say that she, with less than enough, has given all she had. May she rest in peace."

Immediately afterward Marie had turned around to look at the old women. Their eyes were downcast as their lips moved in prayer. They seemed not to have heard a thing.

The old priest's words, along with Pia's phone call, had left Marie deeply unsettled. She had the whole day to herself after the phone call. Joey had gone to Annalise's studio to do some work in order to keep his mind occupied and would be back later in the evening. While thinking of her mother she had a sinking fear that something had happened to Michael, that somehow she would be punished through her son.

"He's all right," Richard told her when she called. "I've just made him dinner and I'm beating the pants off him in Scrabble. How are things there?"

She told him about the funeral and the call from Italy. It gave her such a feeling of relief to know that her home was intact, that she had somewhere to go where she was cared for and where she could care for someone. Her parents' house felt like an abandoned sinking ship. Its emptiness and silence were like screams of agony in her ears. It made her wonder if Joey had jumped off in time.

"It was so strange to discover these people knew so much about me. They even invited me over for a wedding this summer. Marisa, my cousin, is getting married."

"Why don't you go," Richard said. "You'll have the summer off. It'll be good for you after all these funerals."

"No, I couldn't."

"Sure, it could be just the thing."

She thought for a minute. "No, it's impossible, Richard. I couldn't do it."

"Why?"

"Italy is... it's just too far away, for one. And what about you and Michael?"

"You could take Michael, or leave him here with me if you wanted."

"What about you?"

In his pedantic tone he said, "Italy is something you have to come to terms with on your own, Marie. I'll just be in your way." And then with much spirit: "Besides, I'm definitely going to finish my book this summer."

"Let me speak to Michael," she said quickly.

But the suggestion wouldn't soon leave her. She had had enough of death. A wedding would perhaps set things in order again. It could possibly be the large Italian wedding she had never had herself. She could take Michael and let them see that Assunta's side of the tree hadn't completely withered. She could go back for her mother — make the return journey that Assunta had always wanted to make.

Marie wandered through the large empty house, momentarily excited by the possibility of going to visit her parents' homeland. To see first-hand where they had come from.

But the doomed house soon brought her back to the inescapable facts. The smashed TV set was a hideous reminder of the farces that had been played out in that room. In the stillness Marie could hear Assunta's voice asking them again and again what the actors were saying. Then the inevitable flare-up when she or Joey got fed up with the repeated interruptions. But why don't you learn the language? They'd raise their voices to her. Why don't you learn for yourself?

As she passed the front door she heard her mother yelling for her to come in for dinner, her voice ringing through the neighbourhood. Mar-yeeya. Maaar-reee-yaaaaa. The name grating on her ears so much that she made sure it was Marie to everyone else.

In her old room she remembered the days of solitary confinement during high school. The endless books. The nights when all she did was homework until bedtime. The primping and preening in front of the mirror. To make herself different. To prepare herself for when she'd finally leave this island of foreignness and reach her true home.

Going downstairs again, she saw that she couldn't leave out her parents' bedroom any longer.

She opened the door slowly, half expecting to see them laid out on the bed, bordered by flowers. It was dark and stuffy inside. She noticed the time had passed quickly. Opening the windows, she saw the deserted street. The widow Angeline's house was boarded up. The few old houses beyond the block still standing.

The room hadn't changed since her mother had cleared it after Adamo's funeral. Except for the change of dresser and headboard of the bed it was actually still the room of her childhood.

Almost in a daze Marie began looking for the key to the Hope Chest. It felt as if she were a child again, trying to find out how much her mother cared for her. Her value hidden in that old trunk.

After she searched long enough she took away the piles of *Grand Hotel* from the top of the trunk. Marie opened one of them to see what her mother had found so fascinating in the magazines.

From the photographs she could see they hadn't changed much since she had looked at them as a girl. They were still the same serial depictions of love stories, with the dialogue set in comic-book fashion above the heads of the characters. As she leafed through a few of them she noticed that all the stories had well-groomed and handsome young men hopelessly in love with beautiful and fashionable young ladies, going through a series of difficulties before finding their right partners. Sometimes the love plots were set in a hospital, sometimes in a villa, but most often in a modern dazzling city where everyone drove the new Alfa Romeo or the latest Fiat. They were like endless soap operas, with people being shot at or suffering from unrequited love. But no matter what the difficulty, the characters always cut the *bella figura* of high Italian drama.

She recalled Father Sarlo's words: the pictures spoke without the words.

Taking away the cotton coverlet, she looked at the exposed chest for a minute. It was older and less sturdy than she remembered it. Its brown paint had peeled in places, leaving the grains of wood exposed like protruberant ribs. As if it too hadn't received enough nourishment over the years. The wood had become desiccated, and it sagged on top where the magazines had rested.

There was no need to fear breaking the top open now, she thought, as she went to the cantina to get the crowbar.

She noticed Adamo's mason's tools lying neatly on the workbench. The wine bottles almost all empty. The wine press and barrels in the corner. Maybe Joey could send her some wine every autumn. The potent stuff seemed to unleash a dark, wild animal in her.

Back in the bedroom she sat on her haunches before the trunk and paused for a moment. This was it, she thought. After all those fruitless years of searching. Yet it seemed to mean very little now. She had lost interest long ago. She had learned to live without her mother's Hope Chest.

Casually she reached over to see how securely the lid was locked.

To her utter surprise it moved.

She stayed still for a minute, thinking. She could hear the extra timepiece underneath her heart ticking.

Checking the locking mechanism, however, she shook her head and let out a sigh.

"*Stupida!*" she said out loud to herself.

There was no telling when it was unlocked. The mechanism looked rusted and unused, but it could have been unlocked only a few years ago —well past the time she had stopped looking. It was just that she hadn't conceived of it ever being left unlocked. She couldn't remember the last time she had checked, but it had to be before she was ten years old when her mother first started to tell her about the chest.

The lid opened easily. A reeking odour of moth balls and unaired clothing stung her nostrils. A yellowed sheet covered the contents like a shroud. By feel Marie could tell it was extremely old. She recalled Assunta saying that some of the contents went back for generations.

There was an assortment of bed linens and clothes immediately underneath. Pillow cases with ornate embroidery. A few towels. Some very simple cotton dresses. Common sense underclothes of various patterns and fabrics. These seemed to have been mended recently. Underneath these was a simple black mourning dress of coarse black cotton with a kerchief and stockings. Marie noticed that as she dug deeper the contents appeared to be older, as if she were unearthing various layers of a person's life.

Without thought she draped the black dress over herself. It seemed to be the right size. Quickly she removed her jeans and shirt and tried it on. It smelled like an old book. Going in front of a mirror, she looked at her thin spectral frame. She wasn't surprised that it fit like a glove. The dark patches under her eyes and her resigned ascetic expression seemed to fit the dress exactly.

Close to the bottom of the trunk were a couple of shoeboxes. She removed one and found what amounted to a shrine inside. There was a leather-bound frame that opened up into three pictures with a little stand underneath, One picture was of a sweet-looking young girl with her arms crossed over her heart looking angelically toward the sky. There were lilies in one hand and an aureole over her head. A church was in the far background. At the bottom was the name S. Maria Goretti. On the opposite side was a photograph of an old white-haired peasant woman, solid and self-possessed, with a black polka dot kerchief, smiling serenely into the distance. The name underneath was Assunta Goretti. The middle photograph was of a casket underneath an altar in a church. The sides of the ornately made casket were of glass and the body of a young girl rested inside. She was wearing a full-length dress of glossy silk decorated with white lilies, and there was a crown on top of her long black hair. Her young virginal face was so composed that Marie thought she was only sleeping.

There was also an assortment of milk-white candles, a small font for holy water and various other religious items, such as two small statues of the Virgin, scapular medals and rosaries. The candles appeared to have been recently used.

Marie pictured her mother opening the case and lighting the candles underneath in the dark of her room.

But the image only made her more curious. She placed the picture-stand on the dresser and arranged the candles in front. Then she positioned the holy-water font and the two statues of the Virgin. She found some matches in the kitchen and lighted the candles. Shutting off the light she sat on the edge of the bed and looked into the mirror. Her face appeared just above the flames. The candles were reflected onto the bed behind her.

For a minute she thought of praying. She wondered who the people in the pictures were. Her mother had never mentioned them. She wondered what kind of people would keep the body of a girl under an altar. Whether it was the actual corpse. Or just a statue. The hair looked real.

She lost track of time as she sat transfixed in front of the shrine. Every so often she caught her own expression in the mirror. It was slightly perplexed. Slightly awed. It might have been one of the most complex mathematical problems she was facing.

Sometime later she felt her mother's presence in the room. She seemed to be lying on the bed behind her, the flowers bordering her body like icing on a cake. Marie stared harder into the mirror, trying to make out the expression on her mother's face. But she was too far away. She had to peer closer. The face came closer. It was hard like a statue. She saw the thin curve of the mouth. The sharp angular features. The deep-set eyes.

"Mamma, I'm sorry," she said out loud.

She waited patiently. Any answer, even no answer, would be all right. She felt her mind unloosen, clear itself of all cleverness and expectation. Slowly it extinguished itself and there was darkness.

The statued hardness of her mother's face softened. Colour was restored to the bony cheeks. The face twitched with life. The corners of her mouth slowly turned upward.

But the effort seemed to have exhausted Marie. She felt extremely faint. She remembered the only food she had eaten in days was yesterday's snack. The weight of her head was too much to hold up. Slowly she fell back onto the bed and closed her eyes.

Sometime later the overhead light abruptly awakened her. She didn't know where she was,

"Marie, what're you doing?"

Joey was standing at the door. His voice was thin and fearful. He looked startled, as he noticed the shrine and the opened Hope Chest.

"What's this?" he said.

"Shut the light," she said. It hurt her eyes.

He did as he was told.

"Let me be for a minute, Joey," she went on, as casually as she could. "I was only sleeping for a moment. Go on. I'll be out in a minute."

When she got her bearings she got up and blew out the candles. She put the shrine back in the shoebox and turned the light on. She was afraid to look at herself in the mirror.

Closing the trunk she saw she had forgotten the other shoebox. To her great delight it was full of old photographs of Assunta and her family in the old country.

Marie took the box and brought it to the kitchen to show Joey. Her brother appraised her quizzically.

"Where did you get that dress?" he said.

"In the Hope Chest."

"What was going on in there?"

"I just found some things in the trunk. A religious shrine."

"You scared me," he said.

"Sorry, I only got tired and fell asleep for a while."

"You know, with that dress on and lying on the bed, I thought..."

"Look what I found," she said abruptly, dumping the photographs on the table.

They went through them without further word, as if starved for information on their mother. They were like still-lifes of Assunta's past. There were photos of Assunta playing in vineyards and under fig trees. Of Assunta's father separately, with a large bushy moustache and in his best dark suit, in a Napoleonic pose. Of Assunta's mother, thin and wasted, alone in a cave-like mediaeval kitchen. Of Assunta as a child squatting on the dirt floor of what seemed like a shed. Of Assunta growing up. Her first communion. Her first pair of good shoes. Of her and Pia doing their chores. Of weddings to which the family had been invited. Of the black-bordered commemorations of dead relatives.

Through the pictures Marie got a good sense of the land her mother came from. It was hilly, with every piece of available land used for cultivation. A few pictures showed men ploughing fields that were strewn with rocks. The village itself rested on top of a hill. It seemed to have been some sort of fortress at one time. There was a picture of Assunta, at about nine or ten, in a pinafore, walking with Pia down a winding road, with part of a large crenellated wall and gate behind them.

As she was going through the photos of her grandparents and various relatives she saw the kind of people she came from. Hardy men with grizzly sun-bleached faces and high cheekbones. Stout and black-draped women hunched and hardened by toil. People of the earth. Peasants who worked all their lives trying to eke out an existence from the soil. It was hard to believe their blood flowed through her veins.

It seemed the only son in her mother's family had died young and there were only two girls to help out with the farm.

"Why do you think Ma never showed us these?" Joey asked her, captivated by the photographs.

"I don't know," she said pensively. "I remember as a girl I used to think she was trying to hide some fantastic secret from us. A scandal maybe. Like she was the illegitimate daughter of a grand duke sent to America to safeguard a reputation. So I could be proud of being her daughter."

Looking over more pictures Marie went on: "It seems, though, that what Father Sarlo said is true."

"You were always asking why she force-fed us," Joey said, handing her a picture. "Look at this."

It showed a scrawny sickly Assunta at fourteen or so, with Pia and their mother, seated at the kitchen table. They were all wearing shabby nondescript dresses, There was an iron pot in the middle of the table, with empty plates for four. The mother, with her back to the camera, was ladling out what appeared to be a thin soup. Assunta and the younger Pia had spoons in their hands and were facing the camera with long sad countenances. Marie couldn't tell *why* the father would record such a moment, unless it was a happy occasion. In the background, a little way from the fireplace where the iron pot was obviously hung, a door was open and Marie could clearly make out the side of an animal.

Marie could only shake her head.

"Do you want these?" she asked Joey. "I'd like to keep the rest."

"Maybe a few of Mamma. And grandfather and grandmother. What else is in the trunk?"

"It's just a simple trousseau trunk with bed linen and some other necessities."

"Are you going to keep it? It's yours, you know." He was looking intently at her.

"Did you know it was opened?"

He shook his head.

She thought for a moment, noticing for the first time a framed painting resting on the floor behind him.

"I was thinking of taking it to Italy to give to Marisa as a wedding gift," she said in a resigned tone. "I don't deserve it and she can probably make better use of it than I can."

"Then you're going?" he said, excited for her.

She nodded. "I think I'll be able to make it. What about you?"

"I can't, really. There's the house still. Someone should be here. I still have to find a new place. Someday I'll go over, though, and see for myself."

Marie reached over and put her hand on his shoulder.

"What're you going to do with all their stuff?"

"I don't know about the personal stuff. But the rest — the furniture, wine press, and things like that — I'll keep or sell."

He smiled. She smiled softly back at him.

"Is that Annalise's work?" she indicated the painting behind him.

It showed the side view of a hockey player with a close resemblance to Joey skating all alone over a large expanse of ice in the outdoors. The skater was midway between the glassy-smooth ice and the reddish sky, his eyes intent upon a point in the horizon, his face dark and fervent. The sun was setting in a cloudless sky and casting a long shadow on the ice.

Joey laughed, "Annalise thinks she's transferred all the passion I've had for hockey onto her. Notice the fierce expression on his face."

Joey's spontaneous laugh was so unexpected that she was compelled to look closer at him. And as she saw his hard wide jaw and thick potent eyebrows it occurred to her how much more real he was to her than ever before. That somehow the way he felt life was the measure of his reality.

"I'm very happy for you, Joey," she said.

He shook his head. "I can't believe what I did to the TV set."

"You can buy another one."

His expression changed abruptly. He looked sorrowfully into her eyes.

"I have to tell you this, Marie. I told Ma about selling the house. I couldn't help it."

He told her about what happened that day with Assunta and Annalise in the kitchen. He had lost his temper. She had treated him as a kid once too often.

"I tried my best," he put his head down on the table.

Marie looked tenderly at her brother.

"It's all right, Joey," she said, her voice full of forgiveness. "It's all right."

She put her hand on his head and stroked it fondly.

On the table she looked into the hungry eyes of her mother and smiled.

From Black Madonna (Ottawa, 1982)

MATILDE TORRES

LA DOTTORESSA DI CAPPADOCIA
Capitolo XXV - La Partenza

La sala dell'aeroporto di Fiumicino era gremita di passeggeri. Il momento tanto sospirato della partenza era lì, a due passi, che mi ammiccava, eppure avevo paura di raggiugerlo, di toccarlo.

Non ero nuova a questo genere di sensazioni. Sempre, in passato, mi accadeva di prefiggermi una mèta, di logorarmi per conquistarla e poi, quando mi sarebbe bastato tendere una mano per coglierla, rinviavo la realizzazione ad un tempo successivo. Quando, ad esempio, dovevo sostenere gli esami del corso di medicina, studiavo con alacrità tutto il programma, tralasciando, però, le ultime tre o quattro pagine. Mi sentivo, all'atto di completare la preparazione, posseduta da "un'idea prevalente" che s'imponeva alle altre e mi ordinava di smettere. Mi rendevo conto dell'illogicità di tali pensieri, tuttavia, nonostante i miei sforzi di volontà, non riuscivo ad estrometterli dalla mia coscienza.

Incuriosita, chiesi spiegazioni ad un mio amico psicologo con il quale, casualmente, mi trovai a dividere uno scompartimento sul rapido Roma-Avezzano.

«La spiegazione è semplice», mi disse. «Con la tua modalità comportamentale, tenti di tradurre in termini pratici una situazione psicologica piuttosto comune. Tu sei portata inconsciamente ad indentificare la fine di un lavoro o l'esito di un'impresa con il "finire" della vita. Dall'equivalenza dei due concetti "compimento" – "morte", scaturiscono le tonalità spiacevoli di cui sono soffusi i tuoi traguardi; è per sottrarti ad esse che rimandi ogni adempimento, in un inconfessato tentativo di sfuggire alla morte, la "conclusione" in assoluto, la somma di tutte le piccole morti che si accumulano vivendo.»

«Non sapevo di covare tanto sconforto...», mormorai con rammarico.

«Al contrario! Ami la vita a tal punto che vorresti differire la morte!»

«Amo la vita, amo la vita ...», mi ripetevo mentre cercavo la mano di Vincenzo.

Ottenni di più; Vincenzo mi strinse a sé e mi guardò negli occhi con espressione intensa, per infondermi coraggio.

Ad un tratto una voce metallica dall'altoparlante annunciò:

«I viaggiatori per Toronto, Alitalia, sono pregati di avviarsi al cancello d'imbarco».

Ci alzammo e ci dirigemmo lentamente verso l'uscita. Avevo le gambe legnose ed il cuore che saltava qualche battito.

La giornata era splendida, il cielo azzurro, la visibilità perfetta. Nel pullman-trasporto-passeggeri rimanemmo abbracciati, senza pronunciare una parola, per tutto il tragitto che ci divideva dalla pista d'imbarco. Salimmo la scaletta dell'aereo, la *hostess* ci accolse con il suo sorriso "a gettone" e ci indicò i nostri posti. Socchiusi gli occhi, mi appoggiai alla spalliera e sentii la *sua* mano stringere forte la mia. Ormai stavamo per decollare: verso il cielo azzurro, l'avvenire che ci sorrideva. Una vita nuova che soltanto noi due avremmo avuto ii diritto di gestire.

<<I signori viaggiatori sono pregati di allacciare le cinture>>, ci comunicò la *hostess*.

L'aereo cominciò a muoversi di un moto accelerato lungo la pista di rullaggio fino a raggiungere la velocità di decollo. Finalmente ci staccammo da terra!

Dall'alto mi apparve Roma in tutta la sua impareggiabile bellezza: la testimonianza di millenni di civiltà era sotto di me. Ii Tirreno che batteva il lido di Ostia e che avevo sempre giudicato sporco e burrascoso, ora che lo stavo perdendo mi sembrò meraviglioso; infatti, azzurreggiava ridente sotto il sole, solcato da flutti biancastri.

All'improvviso ebbi la sensazione che l'aereo si fosse fermato a mezz'aria, attratto verso la terra da una misteriosa forza magnetica. Dovevo divincolarmi per sciogliere i legami che mi tenevano ancora unita all mia patria. <<Roma..., ineguagliabile, splendida Roma..., ti prego..., lasciami andare con lui..., lo amo!>>

In quell'istante l'aereo riprese quota entrando nella "fase di salita", e dopo poco superammo una barriera di nuvole che eclissò la terra. Avvertii un dolore nel mezzo del petto: avevo accumulato un'altra piccola morte. "Alea jacta est" (il dado è tratto) mi dissi. Avevo reciso il cordone ombelicale die mi legava all'Italia, la "nazione madre della civiltà umana," Mi ero annullata per risorgere in un'altra dimensione, tra l'azzurro infinito del cielo, sopra uno spumone di nuvole e con nel cuore la speranza che al di là dell'oceano avrei trovato la libertà, la giustizia, la pace e la felicità che sognavo. Avevo dimenticato infatti, in quei momenti d'esaltazione, che, come disse il Goldoni:

<<Tutto il mondo è paese e l'umanità è la stessa dappertuttos.>>

From La Dottoressa di Cappadocia (Roma, 1982)

THE DOCTOR FROM CAPPADOCIA
Chapter XXV - Depature

The lounge of the airport of Fiumicino was full of passengers. The long-awaited moment of departure was beside me, winked at me, yet I was afraid of reaching it, touching it.

I was not unused to this kind of sensation. Always, in the past, I had set myself a goal, worn myself out getting there and, when it would have been enough to stretch out my hand to reach it, I would put off the realization for another time. For example, when I had to take examinations in the courses at the Faculty of Medicine, I would study all the material industriously, but leave out the last three or four pages. As I was completing my work, I was overcome by a powerful feeling which mastered me and made me leave it. I was aware of a lack of logic in such thoughts, but in spite of my best efforts, I could not manage to drive these quirks from my consciousness.

Curious about them, I asked for an explanation from a psychologist friend with whom I happened to share a train compartment on the Rome-Avezzano line.

"The explanation is simple enough," he told me. "With your behaviour, you are trying to translate into practical terms a rather common psychological situation. You are unconsciously led to identify the end of the task or the outcome of an undertaking with the 'finishing' of life. From the correspondence of the two concepts 'finish'-'death', arises the unpleasant association which you have attributed to final acts. To avoid this you put off every finality, in an unconscious attempt to escape death, the absolute 'conclusion', the sum of all the little deaths which accumulate as we live."

"I didn't know I was so sick," I muttered sadly.

"On the contrary! You love life to such a degree that you wish to postpone death!"

"I love life, I love life," I repeated to myself as I sought Vincenzo's hand.

More was given to me. Vincenzo hugged me and looked into my eyes with an intense expression, to inspire me with courage.

Suddenly the metallic voice of the loudspeaker announced, "Travelers leaving for Toronto with Alitalia are requested to go to the departure gate."

We rose and slowly walked to the exit. My legs were wooden and my heart was skipping beats.

The day was splendid, the sky a clear blue with perfect visibility. In the passenger-transport bus we remained in the embrace, without saying a word, for the whole distance to the runway. We went up the stairway to the airplane, the stewardess met us with her mechanical smile and showed us to our places. I closed my eyes, leaned back against the headrest and felt his hand tightly clasp mine. Now we were ready to take off: into the blue sky, into the future which smiled towards us. A new life which only we two had the right to lead.

"Passengers are requested to fasten their seatbelts," the stewardess told us.

The plane began to move, accelerating along the runway until it reached take-off speed. Finally, we left the earth!

From above, Rome appeared to me in all its incomparable beauty: the witness to thousands of years of civilization lay below me. The Tyrrhenian Sea washed the beach of Ostia which I had always considered dirty and noisy. Now as I was losing it, it seemed marvelous; it sparkled blue and laughing under the sun, furrowed with billowing whitecaps.

Suddenly I had the sensation that the airplane had stopped in mid-air, attracted to the earth by a mysterious magnetic force. I had to free myself and dissolve the bonds which still bound me to my native land. "Rome…unequalled, splendid Rome…, I beseech you…, let me go with him…, I love him!"

At that instant the airplane began to gain altitude as it went into its climbing phase, and shortly afterwards we passed through a barrier of clouds which obscured the earth. I noticed a pain in my chest: I had accumulated another little death. "Alea facta est," I said to myself, "the die is cast." I had cut the umbilical cord which bound me to Italy, the "mother country of human civilization." I had annihilated myself in order to rise again in another dimension, in the infinite blue sky, above a froth of clouds and with hope in my heart that beyond the ocean I would find liberty, justice, peace and the happiness I dreamed of.

In that moment of exaltation, I had forgotten that, as Goldoni said, "All the world is one country and everywhere mankind is the same."

Translated by Ann Cameron

CATERINA EDWARDS

A WHITER SHADE OF PALE

As George waited for Cynthia to arrive for her promised evening visit, he imagined the various ways he could tell her what the doctor said. Though the words he used varied, in each scene he was casual, ironic while Cynthia, for he imagined her responses too, was variously horrified, melancholy, and dismissive. Yet, when she did finally arrive, he found he could not begin. There were only fifteen minutes left before visiting hours were over, and she burned up the minutes complaining about the snowstorm, the sidewalk that needed shoveling, a neighbour's child who had bitten Sara, and George's parents who were off on a guided tour to China and, as usual, not around when you needed them. George could have interrupted; she did punctuate her monologue with "but how do you feel" or simply "sooo?" But the tightness in her mouth and around her eyes stopped him. He knew her concern and her frustration were there, underneath, but to demand a demonstration seemed a bit cruel, or, at least, risky.

She was worried enough, he guessed from the closed face, the wandering sentences. Worried enough: too worried. She was trying to show the appropriate amount of emotion, the expected response. Measured lives, theirs. They had to be balanced, always balanced. She had to be loving mother, and strong wife, even if the essential Cynthia was frightened or confused. Their marriage was an elaborate structure of demands, built up from the fragile base of their emotions. And most of the demands weren't even theirs. He was Daddy, the supporter and protector, Daddy, law writer and law follower, Daddy, citizen. Daddy –

Roles as they said in psychologese. Still, it was perhaps more to the point than the structure metaphor. You held a position too long, your attitudes hardened: petrification. But what choice did he have? He could keep moving and shifting the way Ted had: from a follower of Buddha to a follower of Rajneesh with Reich and Perls in between. Or Anne striding briskly through marriages and marathons onwards, ever onwards – faster, faster – and better. She insisted it was better, always better. As did Ted. His face gaunt from fasting, his new orange clothes already hanging on his frame. Her body so hard, if you touched her you'd bounce off; and her face, just try saying a slack or silly phrase to that face.

No, with potential and promise gone, the only choices were the inessential ones: that not this, this not that. Taken solemnly, often with much thought, discussion, and reading. A ritual invocation of the household gods. That car, this lock, that bed.

Terracotta, cooked earth: shaped by hand.

Terracotta, cooked earth in the different colours of the earth: sand, buff, pale gold, peach, mauve, apricot orange, reddish orange, vermilion: deep red, strong red, blood red.

By touch, he knew, by touch.

Evidence such as burial inscriptions and tomb paintings point to the fact that Etruscan women were considered equal to Etruscan men. Women played at gymnastics, ran businesses, took part in the public life, and, most scandalous to the Greeks and Romans, reclined and ate with the men at feasts. Their position, so unusual in the ancient world, led to calumny against the Etruscans. Authors as different as Theopompus, Plautus, Horace and Aristotle believed that this egalitarianism pointed to Etruscan degeneracy and immorality. The women were obviously "common to all men," Theopompus claimed. Yet it is the number of individual couples (loving couples) arm in arm, or holding out their hands to one another that is notable in Etruscan art.

And later it is the couple that he remembers, that he returns to, that he wonders over. "Terracotta, 525 BC, Cerveteri, the Sarcophagus of the Bride and Groom." *The couple*, he thinks of the statues in that way: distinct, underlined.

The actual couple, of course, was reduced to dust centuries ago. This couple represents that particular man and woman. More precisely, these statues give shape to the idea of the specific couple through the material of terracotta. From the material to the idea to the material. Despite such distancing, who can ignore the gentleness of his hand on her shoulder, the vitality in both their eyes, the common yet separate stance. This is no empty form. This is a marriage shaped, defined, and tender. Radiantly tender. Well might they smile.

Ahha! she says.

Ahha? he says.

Now I know why you're obsessed with those statues.

You do.

I do. Here you are presenting your interest as a fascination with the wisdom of the past. Dignifying it with theories.

What have I done?

Sit up. No, hold that expression. Look over there. See.

It's awfully dark.

I'll open the shutters a crack.

I'm grinning.

The archaic smile. Admit it.

I never knew.

And your eyes. Wrong colour but still. And the curve of your cheekbones.

I'm embarrassed.

You're not the first. A linguist from Tuscany has a book on how traces of Etruscan (an unknown language right) survive in Tuscan pronunciation. Then there's the Jewish historian who proved that the Etruscans were Semites and the Italians who insist they didn't come from the East at all but were indigenous. The Greeks....

O.K. Enough.

Oh, and D'Annunzio –

Fascist.

Exactly. He thought the Etruscan's message was that life is basically anxiety and fatality while –

Sophie, I understood after your first example.

Contradictory fables springing from the same evidence.

Different readings but I still think –

Yes?

Eighteen years old. His first time away from family and home in that first isolation, in that first lack of connection to the parade of sights, of tastes, of sensations, an intoxicating freedom. He had invented a new self in and out of that eternal sun. He presented himself as he wished to be and now was. In the cool dimness of the tombs. In the half light of Sophie's shuttered room. He'd had girls before (in the backseat, and once, difficult to imagine now, in the front seat of his Volkswagen bug, on the sofa in the rumpus room or even, when his parents were out in the country, on his narrow bed), but she was his first woman, those times together in Rome his first affair, not fooling around, not doing "it" but making love. Varied, inventive, and discreet love. She had insisted that they could not be open: she could be fired if it was known that she dallied with students.

"This is dallying?"
"Of course not."
"With students?"
"You know what I mean. It's what it would seem, from the outside"

And he had acquiesced at the time. They rarely sat next to each other at meals, they faded away from the group at separate times, she wouldn't even look at him at the dig. George hated that most of all. His eyes were drawn; he couldn't help it. She looked so right in khaki shorts and white T-shirt, so tanned and strong and long-legged.

"I could stare at you all day."
"Such gallantry."
"You'd be surprised."

She did move to another pensione, where no one from the group was staying, so he could come unobserved on the odd siesta break or late at night. He never said anything to Julian. He thought Julian guessed who he was with those nights he wasn't in his bed. Sophie did occasionally join the two of them and Jackie on an expedition or an evening of wine and talk. And the one time she came to his room Julian had answered her knock. She stood at the door looking embarrassed and upset, and Julian had glanced at George in a way that had seemed knowing and then excused himself. "Jackie's waiting." Instead, all along, Julian had thought Jackie was the woman. After Sophie ended the relationship, there was no outward sign it had ever existed. No one else knew. Sophie didn't want to remember. And George tried not to.

So why now?

Pursued by broken limbs, shapes from another time.

After so many years?

A hole in the nose, a hole in the knowing and not knowing.

* * *

Early the next morning, the professor was informed by the ward nurse that he was being moved to a private room. "The tests must have turned up something," he told George.
"Nothing serious, I hope"
"I suspect so." He was fussing with his top sheet, smoothing it out. "I'm at that age."
"You're not that old."
"Middle age, I meant: children almost grown, separated from wife, six or seven years till retirement. Everything slipping away."
George was embarrassed. He wanted to offer some wise words "Buck up, you still have – " blank but could think of nothing to fill that blank. "It doesn't have to be like that."
"Doesn't it?" The professor was suddenly amused. "You think you'll be any different in twenty years?"
Rolf was already gone, either discharged or moved, George wasn't sure which. He had made lots of noise going: loud goodbyes, long jargon-filled

explanations of his condition, but George hadn't paid attention. Rolf's replacement was young, still in his teens. He had a large blond mustache, and a certain swagger. He was dressed, of course, in a hospital gown, but it was easy to imagine him in tight jeans, a work shirt (cigarettes bulging) and a trucker's hat. Shit, he kept saying or hot dooggee. He was telling a story to the now subdued boy in the bed opposite. It involved two women, cunt number one and cunt number two, a case of the clap, a night of drinking, a fall from a balcony and his kidneys. "The doc says...." Every now and then, he would look over at George and nod, as if to acknowledge him as a fellow man of the world. You know, the nod said, these things happen.

It was time to make a move. George was cautious. Although he edged himself off the bed, when he stood, the floor lurched, the walls shifted. He waited until all was still, then adjusted his gown and pulled on the flimsy robe. He felt exposed; the robe and gown skimmed his knees and he was very aware of his bare buttocks. There must be no falling. At least he wasn't hooked up anymore. He'd hated trundling himself and the metal apparatus. Clomp. The hospital slippers flapped on his feet. Clomp. Clomp. He nodded to the silent, head-bandaged boy, then the wattle-necked old man by the door. When he moved his head, his scalp felt as if it were attached only on his forehead, as if there were an inch of air between his brain and his hair.

He wouldn't hold onto the wall. He'd concentrate. No glancing in at the private rooms. No pausing before the nursing stations. The corridor was full of sounds: the intercom paging doctors, the television sets blaring, but his footsteps and his breathing echoed ever louder. Careful. Slow but steady. Dept of Nuclear Medicine, Radiology, Urology, Rheumatology, so many parts to the human body that can go wrong, breakdown. Watch the wall. Through the doors. One floor down. Over and over, his hand to his cheek, no longer a search for sensation but a habit, almost a tic. A long glass passageway, two more corridors and finally the women's pavilion.

He paused for a moment's rest, threw a glance at the mural by the elevator and then looked again. It was a fresco of the Alberta landscape: prairie, foothills, and mountains. In the foreground, an Amazonian-sized pioneer woman was staring fearlessly into the future. She was wearing the traditional costume, but one shoulder and the breast were bare. She was woman holding her babe to her breast, woman clear-eyed and clear-browed, facing the future.

"Can I help you?" The woman at the information desk was eyeing his bare legs. Two flower-laden men got off the elevator. They also stared at his legs. The smell in this section was different, the undertones acidic rather than bitter, animal rather than chemical.

The halls here were busier. George had to dodge several clusters of visitors, besides numerous shapeless women (in fuzzy or shiny polyester housecoats) and the odd abandoned stretcher. He began checking room numbers although he knew he wasn't quite there. This was still miscarriage and hysterectomy territory.

Another station, nurses chatting about some movie, did they ever do anything but talk to each other? The usual crowd around the nursery window. George stopped; he couldn't help it. He'd spent so long staring through that window, joyfully at Michael and more ambiguously at the twins, that his response was habitual. An ugly bunch this one: all wrinkled faces and swollen heads. But then, though he and Cynthia had found Sara, Jane and Michael perfectly beautiful as newborns, perhaps a non-doting eye could have found fault. When they re-looked at pictures of those first weeks, the children did look odd, not half as cute as they were now. Their vision had been determined biologically; they were new parents. But what is not determined? Wherein do we think and choose? There is no choice of gender, class, culture or age? Especially age. The terrible twos, the balky fours, sulky adolescence, carefree twenties, responsible thirties, it just went on and on. And time? How to think outside of the moment.

Do events have a meaning because they have happened or do they happen in order to express a meaning?

2266. The door was half open. George knocked and, without waiting, entered. The first bed was mussed but empty. Jackie was sitting with her baby on the other. She was obviously startled to see him. She gazed blankly at him, her breast out. And only when he drew a chair up to bed and sat gratefully down did she, with a quick, fussy gesture, pull the top of her nightgown up and then smile.

"My goodness, George."

"Jackie, how's it going?" He was rather startled himself. He had been expecting the old familiar Jackie, not this slatternly woman with tangled hair, lumpy body, and tired, tired face.

"I heard you'd been beaten up, but I didn't think...."

"Julian's been up here too, has he? Talkative boy, that Julian. I didn't get beaten up. Doctors did most of the damage."

"Oh, do look at her. Isn't she gorgeous? I just can't believe that she's here.

That I have her, after all those years of...."

"Gorgeous....Got your eyes."

"Do you think so? She's got Mummy's eyes, poor little thing, Mummy's eyes." The sudden spurt of animation, the abrupt switch to an arch tone, these were familiar: remnants of the old Jackie. "She's so stubborn. I just can't believe it. She won't nurse properly. She won't. Either chews, Christ it hurts, or she gets this set stubborn expression. Now my nipples are cracked. You can't imagine...."

"You should talk to Cynthia."

"Right, anyone who can nurse twins." Jackie continued the baby, nursing, labour, and delivery talk, talk that embarrassed George but which he encouraged nevertheless. (He was a courteous man.) The baby twisted itself about in Jackie's hands. She offered an engorged, blue-veined breast; the baby began to squawk; she tried massaging its cheek and then moved it to the other breast. George went to get a bottle of sugared water from the nursery. Once the rubber nipple was wedged through the baby's lips, it began, contentedly, to suck.

"Rejected again."

"It takes time."

"What do you know?"

"Well. I do have..."

"I can't do this. I'm too old to start."

He patted the part of her body closest to him, her knee. "This is just a stage. Feeling like this. It passes." She shook her head, her eyes full of tears. "Just wait. In a day or two.... And you're not alone. There's Alan."

"Sure." She shook her head again. Her hands on the bottle and the baby were steady but her face contorted.

Not another teary, George thought, just my luck. "It'll be fine. You'll be fine, better than fine – terrific." Unconsciously, he had fallen into the soothing tone he used on the children.

She jerked her knee away from him, sat straight up, and thrust the baby with bottle at him. By the time he had adjusted the squirming bundle and blanket, so that it lay comfortably in his arms and he was gazing into its ageless infant eyes, Jackie had locked herself in the washroom. "You really should talk to Cynthia," George shouted at the door.

The baby let out a squawk. Awkwardly he rearranged it against his shoulder and began to pace the small room. "Brings back memories," he said to the wall. (The feel of a tiny body in his hand, the almost inhuman sound of a newborn's cry, he had forgotten much.) "You'll be surprised how fast it goes." Then he remembered Cynthia's words: "I mean, it seems eternal at the time, but then, boom, they're on to the next stage."

"Pardon me." A pretty young woman in a bright pink housecoat with matching cheeks and lips had entered while his back was to the hall door. She arranged herself on the other bed, fanning out the bottom of her housecoat, undoing the top button. "You a relative of Jackie's?" Her smile was amused, knowing. Her fingers were busily fluffing out bottle blond hair.

"Friend. Old friend."

"Another one, eh? Well, she needs y'all. Keeps turning on the waterworks. I keep telling her. Leave the kid in the nursery. Try some formula. We'll be stuck with them soon enough. But she's read too many damn books. Bullshit experts. I'm one of -"

The washroom door opening. Jackie had washed her face, tied her hair back with a ribbon, and drawn her characteristic dark lines around her eyes. " – six and my Mom always said –" Jackie held out her hands for the baby. "- the watched flower -" Her expression still solemn, she lay it down in its cradle.

"Shouldn't you be getting back. The nurses will send out a search party."

"I doubt it."

"Yeah, what are you in for? Though I got my suspicions." Pretty in Pink seemed as determined to keep him there as Jackie was to have him leave.

"It did start with a fight."

"He-man, eh?" Pink's smile managed to convey yet another level to her knowingness.

"It's time for baby's bath." Jackie insisted, although the baby had fallen asleep.

"I was completely innocent. Just sitting drinking my beer." George found himself sitting on the edge of Pink's bed.

Jackie was standing just behind him, speaking almost in his ear. "And April, weren't you going to that exercise class?"

"Gotta work on the old abs. Why don't you come? You could use -"

"I need my rest."

"Look Jackie. It won't take long, honest, but I have to talk to you about something else. Just a couple of minutes."

Jackie looked at him and then nodded. "I know."

But, after April left and he and Jackie took up their former positions, she sitting up in bed, he in the chair by the bed, he realized he didn't know how to begin. The part of his face that he could feel hurt and he was suddenly conscious of how tired he was.

It was Jackie who broke the silence. "I'm sorry. I just hate for you to see me like this."

"Come on. We're old friends. And you've just been through a rough time"

"'*Old Friends. Set on the,*' is it sofa or shelf? '*Set on the sofa like bookends.*' No, that's not it. I always liked the melancholy in that song."

"Julian did come up and talk to you yesterday."

She stopped humming. "He talked at me. I was even more out of things yesterday, as you can imagine."

"I've been remembering that summer in Rome. I mentioned it and he started going on and on." George stopped. Her head was turned, her eyes fixed on the cradle. "Right, talking at me." He has a weird version of things. He must have been saying the same things to you." George stopped again.

"So?" She spoke softly.

"Well, he's wrong."

"So, what are you waiting for me to say?"

"Well, this stuff about, about my being in love with you and you choosing him over me."

"Yes?"

"It wasn't like that."

"Yes, I see." Her head sank back onto her pillow and her eyes closed. "You certainly were not in love with me then or any time after. If anyone was pursuing anyone, it was me you. Finally I gave up, turned to Julian. You want me to tell him."

"No…. I just wanted -"

"What? What is the point now. I mean, who cares. Besides Julian, of course…it has been a long time."

"I wanted the past to be clear."

"Clear? If it's that." And she shrugged. "Anyway, if we're playing truth or consequences, why did you hang around so much?" She stopped, shook her head. "Anything else I can do for you?" This directness and impatience was new. George was tempted to label it postpartum prickliness. He would have thrown the phrase at the old Jackie, and she would have laughed. But he couldn't say it to the woman before him.

"No. It's just…. We are good friends. We got that out of those days. That summer." He stopped.

Then she had been as oblique as George. And he had found it restful, a pleasant change that lack of taking things head on. No expectations. "Look,

George, out with it. I can't read your mind."

Out of the sun, in the dimness of shuttered room. Sweating from the heat. From Sophie's touch. Each place her body meets his, pools appear. Her head is turned to one side on his pillow. A tear marks her profile. Rivulets, streams. They are not flowing with this river but riding it out. (Ease off, yes, a bit more to the left, hold back, hold.) And afterwards, she gets out of his bed. "we're swimming," and stretches out on Julian's. She faces George as she talks, the top part of her body propped up on an elbow. In the gloom her damp skin glows like marble. He wants to speak, to answer, but his mouth is puckered, his tongue numb with the taste of salt.

"I was involved with someone else." He stared down at the baby as he said it.

"I had an inkling. Girl at home, I'd say to myself. Though, hey, I know I'm very resistible."

"Sophie."

"Sophie…. Of course. But why are you telling me this? I can see you discussing it with Cynthia but -"

"It seemed right. You were our cover before and after."

"Fine. I understand. Your point has been made. I was used from beginning to end. You can go. The past is clear. Sordid but clear. Part of it anyway. You know George, I didn't need this now. Not at all."

"I'm sorry."

"I didn't need it. I don't need it. Why don't you go? You just keep sitting there, staring at me. Why doesn't a nurse come? or April? No one's ever around when you need them."

"Please, Jackie. You'll wake the baby. I didn't mean to…. We did, after all, become friends. You know I think the world of you…. Look, Sophie didn't want anyone to know. And then when her fiancé turned up, I understood why. I didn't want her to know how badly I felt." His words did seem to register. At least, as he spoke, the colour faded from her cheeks. She leaned back on her pillows and again closed her eyes.

"You wanted her." Her words came in a tone so casual that, what with her closed eyes and somnolent expression, they seemed to come not from her but through her. "I wanted you, or thought I wanted you, and Julian thought he wanted me. A-common-story." Her words floated out of her mouth and up, up to the ceiling.

"And if, underneath, you did want me a little bit and Julian didn't want me but you, that's also a common -"

Did she actually say those words or had they sounded only in his mind? "Pardon," he said.

"There's always another layer," she said.

He knew he should go. He had managed to say what he came to say. Still, the exchange seemed incomplete, and he felt confused, even deprived. He sat watching her face, waiting for a further phrase or a sign, waiting to sense that the long ambiguity between them was over. But Jackie did not speak or even open her eyes. He intended a dignified exit: a kiss on the forehead and a gentle phrase, but as he stood, the ceiling lifted then plunged.

So that in the years to come when he looked back on that time of the nosebleed (his phrase) often the first image he would remember was this: his sitting in Jackie's room his head down between his knees.

From A Whiter Shade of Pale (Edmonton, 1992)

NINO RICCI

LIVES OF THE SAINTS
Chapters XVIII, XIX, XX

XVIII

If the cock was in the fields, the men of Valle del Sole said, the hen would lay her eggs in someone else's nest. Yet that was what the men had always done, left their wives behind while they travelled out to farm their own fields or to earn a wage, away for days or months at a time, or now, if they worked in France or Switzerland, or across the sea, sometimes for years. Their fears had given birth to a wealth of proverbs : 'Guard your women like your chickens,' they said, 'or they'll make food for the neighbour's table' ; or 'A woman is like a goat : she'll eat anything she sees in front of her.' Yet it was the women of the village who had been harshest towards my mother, and who watched hawk-eyed from their stoops for the slow progress of her disease, as if they had taken it upon themselves to keep the disease from spreading ; and even at mass now, and afterwards as we filed back into the village, the men seemed merely awkward and put out by my mother's presence, passing by us stoop-shouldered, their eyes averted almost guiltily, as if they had been forced into a posture that did not sit well with them, while the women avoided my mother still with a cold-eyed rectitude, hurrying their children around us with their backs straight and their eyes forward.

But later, after we'd finished a sullen meal with Zia Lucia and Marta, my mother just clearing away the dishes, there was a knock at our door. Marta's eyes darted to the door with a look of wild-eyed curiosity, but for a moment no one moved to answer it, as if we could not make sense of the sound we'd heard there.

'Go on, Vittorio, open it,' Zia Lucia finally said.

A moment later Giuseppina and her husband and children were huddled in a close group inside the doorway, reeking of winter and looking stiff and formal in their Christmas clothing. Almost in unison they uttered a forced '*buon natale*,' Giuseppina moving awkwardly towards the centre of the room, offering a tray she'd held in the crook of an arm towards my mother as she pulled a white cloth from it.

'I brought you some pastries,' she said. 'You probably didn't have time to make any yourself.'

She'd brought a tray of *ostie*, paper-thin wafers like large communion hosts sandwiching a thick layer of honey and chopped almonds. Every family in the village had irons for making their *ostie* and their *cancelle*, crusty diamond-shaped waffles, at holiday times, their irons made up by the blacksmith in Rocca Secca and bearing the family name or initial on the plates, so it came out in relief on each pastry; but this Christmas our own irons had sat in their corner of the kitchen untouched.

'*Grazie*,' my mother said, but she didn't reach out to take the tray. 'Why don't you offer some to the children ?'

Giuseppina's husband still hovered near the doorway, cap in hand, his children grouped around him awkwardly, as if for a photograph.

'Come in and sit down,' my grandfather said gruffly. 'Cristina, get a glass for Alberto.'

'It's so nice what Father Nicola did with the church this year,' Giuseppina was saying. 'The wise men and the little animals and the baby. I went up after and even the diapers were made of silk. Silk diapers ! The whole thing must have cost a fortune.'

'You paid for it,' my mother said.

But now there was another knock at the door and Di Lucci burst into the room, his wife and one of his sons (he always left the other at home on Christmas, to tend the shop) hanging back behind him.

'Oh, *buon natale!*' he called out, plunking a bottle of brandy on the table. '*Bicchieri*, Cristina, glasses for everyone ! A christmas toast !' And he immediately helped himself to one of the ostie.

'Sit down, Ando, my grandfather said. 'Cristi, bring us some more glasses.'

And so our home, which for months had known only a lenten silence, was once again filled with a little life and conversation. Some consensus had been reached, it seemed, at dozens of houses across the village, my mother's presence at church, debated and discussed over Christmas dinner, finally taken perhaps as some kind of a sign, the sign of the repentance and guilt which the villagers had no doubt long been waiting for; and now they felt free to flock to the sinner like comforters to Job, for the matter had passed out of their hands and into the hands of God. If anyone had noticed the cold defiance with which my mother had walked down the aisle of the church and taken her place at her pew, they had chosen to ignore it; what my mother thought, after all, was her own business, but the people had to have a sign. It was as if my mother had simply written a character in the air, a cipher, and those who looked on it were happy enough to give it the meaning that suited them.

As the afternoon passed our house began to fill. Alfreddo Mastroantonio came by, former head of the *comitato* and, it was rumoured, a candidate to fill the position of mayor my grandfather had vacated; though he stopped in only to offer an overly hearty *buon natale*, straining to force a little gaiety into his usual stiff formality, and to drop off a bottle of *amaretto* for my grandfather. But several of the neighbours stopped in too, as well as my grandfather's nephews and nieces; and soon the tray of *ostie* was empty, everyone taking a ritual one as they entered the house, to be replaced by platesful of *cancelle* and other pastries, children flittering between grown-ups like ghosts to dart a quick arm towards the kitchen table and then retreat to a corner with their catch. A dozen conversations buzzed at once, swelling to a peak and then lulling suddenly to build again, borne along by some secret rhythm; babies in their mother's arms cried loud enough to be heard above the din, until a mother interrupted herself suddenly to cry 'Oh, *basta!*' and her baby retreated into a brief whimpering silence.

The room had gradually divided in two, the women standing near the side counter, where my mother was constantly pouring drinks and washing glasses, the men grouping around the kitchen table, straddled backwards over chairs. But a strange shift seemed to have happened since that morning; the women had dropped their straight-backed rectitude, as if they had suddenly remembered some sin or crime for which they themselves had gone unpunished, now openly solicitous towards my mother, offering to help pass out drinks and pastries, to wash glasses, even though my mother refused them each time with the same tired smile; but the men, when my mother came round to serve them, made way for her with a casual indifference, as if she were invisible, and wrapped up in their own conversations they did not bother so much as to glance up at her as they took a drink or pastry from her proffered tray. It was as if something in my mother's misfortune had made them suddenly feel invulnerable and strong, and they joked with each other in a way that seemed strangely candid and coarse, all their timidness gone. My grandfather, though, sat by saying little, downing glasses of brandy in quick gulps. He reached an arm out feebly once to draw Giuseppina's little girl Rosina to him as she reached out to the table for a pastry; but Rosina shied away from him, and he quickly withdrew. From a corner of the room Marta watched over us all like a fate, nibbling on a host, and when I followed her eyes they seemed always to light away from the centre of things – on my mother scrubbing glasses at the sideboard, her back to the room, her shoulders working with a restrained violence; on my grandfather turning suddenly to spit into the fire.

But as twilight descended, the light from the fire casting long flickering shadows across the room, the guests began to take their leave. Soon the last of them had gone, leaving the same air of desolation as the village square had after the festival, the kitchen quickly reverting to its familiar heavy silence. My grandfather sat staring silently into the fire while my mother lit the lamp that hung above the table and set out some bread and cheese. She poured out a glass of wine and my grandfather reached back to take it up, his hand trembling.

'They came here,' he said, still staring into the fire, 'to laugh at us.'

My mother sat down at the table and took up a slice of bread, tearing it in half with a quick pull.

'They're idiots,' she said finally. 'It was only for your sake that I didn't chase them out of here with a whip.'

But my grandfather wheeled round suddenly and slammed his glass onto the table.

'For my sake ! Was it for my sake you behaved like a common whore? Do you think you're better than those people ? They are my people, not you, not someone who could do what you've done. I've suffered every day of my life, *per l'amore di Cristo*, but I've never had to walk through this town and hang my head in shame. Now people come to my house like they go to the circus, to laugh at the clowns ! You've killed me Cristina, you killed your mother when you were born and now you've killed me, as surely as if you'd pulled a knife across my throat. In all my days I've never raised a hand against you but now I wish to God I'd locked you in the stable and raised you with the pigs, that you died and rotted in the womb, that you hadn't lived long enough to bring this disgrace on my name!'

My grandfather had taken up his cane and risen from his chair, his face flushed. My mother flinched, as if she expected him to raise up his cane against her; but without looking back at her he crossed the room to his bedroom and slammed the door shut behind him. But the silence was broken again now by muddled sounds from his room – a crash, a thud, a cry of pain. In an instant my mother was at the door; but when she had opened it a crack it wedged up against some obstacle.

'My leg,' my grandfather said, his voice tight with pain. He had fallen, his bedroom table toppled onto him and one leg stretching up at an awkward angle towards the door, blocking it. My mother knelt and reached a hand into the door to move the leg aside; but my grandfather let out another cry of pain.

'Don't move it.'

My mother rose and stood a moment undecided, her eyes wildly searching the room till they alighted finally on the axe by the wood pile.

'Stand back, Vittorio.'

She had the axe now. She clicked the bedroom door shut again and swung the axe hard against the door frame near the bottom hinge, the wood there splintering with a sharp crack.

'Go get Di Lucci,' she said. 'And tell him to bring the rack from the church. We'll need it to carry him.'

But I stood for a moment frozen, awed by the force of my mother's swings – she nearly had the bottom hinge free – until finally she turned to me and shouted, 'Hurry, *per l'amore di Cristo!*' and in a flash I was out the door and running once again up to Di Lucci's bar.

XIX

By the time I returned, Di Lucci and Father Nicola hurrying behind with the rack from the church, my mother had axed the door off its hinges. We had picked up a small crowd en route, and all along the street now the word was going round that *lu podestà* had been hurt; within minutes half the village had gathered, crowding into the kitchen and around the front doors, craning for a better view. Father Nick, in his black cassock and wide-brimmed cleric's hat, stood next to my mother and me at the doorway to my grandfather's room, rubbing his hands against the cold, while inside Di Lucci issued instructions to two of my mother's cousins, Virginio Catalone and his brother Pastore, who had elbowed their way through the crowd and were struggling now to wedge the rack into the tight space between the bed and my grandfather's prone form. Virginio and Pastore, identical twins, sullen and thick-set, had kept clear of our house since my mother's troubles had started; but they had not hesitated to push their way to the front of the crowd when the word had gone out that my grandfather was hurt.

'Try to slide it under him, like a spoon,' Di Lucci was saying. But finally the two men, ignoring Di Lucci, tilted the bed up against the wall with a single thrust and laid the rack flat on the floor. My grandfather let out a grunt as they lifted him onto it, his jaw clenched with the pain.

'Careful,' my mother said sharply. 'Can't you see you're hurting him ?'

'He's broken his leg,' Father Nick said.

'*Grazie, dottore.*'

We stood aside as Virginio and Pastore carried the rack through the crowded kitchen and into the street where a few thick flakes of snow had begun to fall. But now it was suddenly obvious that there would be no way of getting my grandfather into Di Lucci's cramped Fiat in his present state. Someone suggested that the front and back windshields be smashed away, and the rack slid through them.

'Don't be crazy' Di Lucci said, paling. 'And anyway how would I drive, tell me, squashed under that rack like a worm?'

'Vittorio,' Father Nick said, standing by with a look of forced calmness, 'go inside and get a blanket to cover your grandfather.'

When I had come out again with a blanket, my mother was coming down the street trailing Mastronardi's mule and cart, a lantern swinging from one hand.

'At this rate you'll be here all night,' she said, pulling up in front of the house. 'Load him into the cart, there's no other way. Has anyone thought to cover him?' Then, seeing me standing with the blanket still in my hands, she took it from me and bent to drape it over my grandfather, brushing away the snow that had already begun to collect on his clothes.

'*Ma*, Cristina,' Di Lucci said, 'it'll take you half the night to get him to Rocca Secca on that cart. In this weather.' It had begun to snow in earnest now.

'Do you have any other ideas?'

'At least I could drive to Rocca Secca and see if they'll send out the ambulance.'

'You know as well as I do that ambulance hasn't left the garage since the war. And on Christmas night ? They wouldn't come out here for Christ himself. But go on, if you want to, see what you can do. In the meantime I'll start out on my own. Someone bring some more blankets, *per l'amore di Cristo*'.

Di Lucci stood by hesitantly for a moment.

'*Dai*, Ando, smash out the windows,' someone suggested again. 'They'll freeze to death before they get to the hospital in that thing.'

'*Si*, smash the windows,' Di Lucci said, already moving to the door of his car. 'You and your foolish ideas.' And in a moment he had heaved himself into the driver's seat, gunned up the engine, and sped off into the snow.

My mother had already motioned Virginio and Pastore to lift my grandfather onto the cart. His eyes were closed now, but he was muttering softly to himself, as if in troubled sleep, his face beaded with droplets that may have been sweat or melted snow. With a single discreet finger Father Nick made a quick sign of the cross over him as the two men slid the rack onto the cart. Several women had come forward now with blankets; my mother covered my grandfather with a thick layer of them, then draped one around her own shoulders and moved up to the head of the cart.

'Go back to your suppers,' she said to her cousins. 'I can manage on my own from here. There'll be someone at the hospital to help me carry him in.'

'Don't be an idiot,' Virginio said, moving up to take the reins from her. 'Pastore and I will take him in.'

'No. This is my affair.'

'Let Virginio take him in,' Mastronardi said, eyeing his cart proprietorially. 'The woods are full of thieves. And in your condition—'

'I can take care of myself,' my mother said quickly.

And while Virginio and Pastore still hovered uncertainly near the cart my mother heaved herself onto the bench and gave the reins a quick jerk, the cart lurching suddenly forward as the mule raised up his head and thrust himself against the bridle.

'Wait, Cristina.'

It was Father Nick. My mother pulled back on the reins.

'What is it?'

'I'll come with you,' Father Nick said. 'Thieves won't harm a priest.'

'You?' My mother stared at him hard a moment. 'All right, then, let's go,' she said firmly. 'Put a blanket around yourself, that padding on your belly won' t be enough to keep you warm.'

There were a few muffled laughs, quickly suppressed. Father Nick blushed and hesitated a moment, but finally he took a blanket that was offered to him and draped it over his shoulders. He hiked up his skirts and walked briskly up to the cart, pulling himself onto the bench with surprising nimbleness.

'I'll take the reins,' he said, suddenly stern. 'You can get back in the cart and keep the snow off your father.'

'Suit yourself.'

Father Nick jerked the reins and the mule set off with a snort, the cart wheels creaking, flattening the snow beneath them with a soft crunch.

The snow was falling heavy and thick now, and shortly the cart had been swallowed into its white hush; but for a long while we could still make out the haloed haze of my mother's lantern. Finally this too faded into the snow and night, and the villagers still gathered in front of our house brushed the snow off their shoulders and moved quietly back towards their unfinished suppers, and home.

XX

My grandfather had fractured his hip and broken a leg, the same one a horse had shattered in the war. He was in the hospital almost a month, my mother and I riding into Rocca Secca in Cazzingulo's truck once or twice a week to visit him. A metal frame enclosed his bed like a cage, his broken leg, wrapped in thick plaster up to his thigh, suspended from an upper bar of it by a cable, as if he were a strange sculpture that had been set out to dry and harden. His skin had taken on the same pallor as the white plaster of his cast, and when we came to see him he'd mumble to us as if talking out of a dream, hardly aware of our presence, his face limp with fatigue. Once the doctor came in with a nurse to give him an injection, the same doctor who had tended to my mother's snake bite, his eye going down to my mother's belly now with a gleam, as if he shared some secret with her about the bulge there.

'You've been well, I hope?' he said, in his burnished Italian, taking a needle from a tray the nurse held out to him and sucking a clear liquid into it from a tiny bottle.

But my mother took him quickly aside.

'Is it necessary to keep feeding him all those drugs ? Look at him, he hardly recognises you. You'd never know I was his daughter.'

But the doctor moved aside my grandfather's blanket and jabbed the needle with a quick thrust into the soft flesh of his thigh.

'The bone in his leg shattered like glass,' he said when he had finished. 'We got out what we could, but there are still some splinters floating around there now, moving every time he breathes. Do you know what it feels like when one of those splinters brushes up against a nerve ?' He set his needle back into the nurse's tray. 'Like a knife.'

'He's had to deal with pain all his life,' my mother said. 'I'd rather see him in pain than like this.'

'Maybe that's a little selfish of you,' the doctor said.

Once when we visited, my grandfather called out to me by name, and my mother motioned me to stand beside him.

'Vittorio,' he whispered, taking my hand in his own and squeezing it feebly; but his hand was moist and clammy, and I pulled my own away as soon as I felt his fingers loosening.

While my grandfather was still in the hospital, letters began to arrive at our house from America. Only a few came at first, but soon they were coming almost daily, Silvio the postman handing them to my mother each day with the same sheepish shrug, each of them bearing the unmistakable scrawl of my father 's hand. The inevitable had happened – someone had poured some poison in my father's ear. Some word from a friend or a family member or from one of the messengers who departed regularly from Castilucci and Valle del Sole for America (and from Valle del Sole itself there had been already three departures since *la festa*) had finally pierced the veil that shrouded my father's mysterious life across the sea; and now he let forth a fury of letters, my mother reading each with the same wild-eyed impatience before crumpling them and flinging them into the fireplace. 'He's crazy,' she'd mutter, and for the rest of the day a silent rage would seem to simmer inside her, and I'd know not to cross her. I thought that she would sit down soon at the kitchen table and write some response to him, the way she used to, then send me off to Di Lucci's to buy stamps for it and to post it at the mailbox there; but the days passed and still she had no letter for me to post. Late at night, though, I sometimes heard the scratch of her pen from her room, and the next morning she would be up early and gone to Rocca Secca, on what missions I did not know.

When my grandfather returned home, ferried to the village in the back of the mail truck, his leg still in a cast and his hip wound round with wide bandages, the fog that had clouded his mind during his stay in the hospital seemed to have lifted.

'I'll rot in his bed!' he'd shout out from his room. 'I'll die and rot here, you might just as well have put me straight into the grave !'

The muscles in his face never relaxed now, screwed into a perpetual grimace, and his eyes were ringed round with the pink of an infection he'd gotten at the hospital, as if the skin there were raw from crying. My mother served him his meals on a wooden stand the carpenter had made up to fit over the bed, and every night she emptied out the sack at his bedside fed by a long plastic tube that came down from his groin. Then once every two days or so my grandfather would call out to my mother with an embarrassed, angry shout, and she would close the door of his room and come out several minutes later with a pile of linen in a basin.

'Like a baby,' my grandfather would rumble. 'Sixty-six years old and my daughter has to change my diapers.'

But after months of silence my grandfather's curses seemed almost comforting, as if a storm had broken less disastrously than it had threatened; and my mother, too, had refound her voice, an almost ceaseless banter going on now between her and my grandfather, the subject of which was the letters which continued to stream into our house from my father. Long arguments were carried on daily between kitchen and bedroom, tensions hovering around a critical point but never seeming to move beyond it, the arguments finally petering out to a resigned silence that was more the calm after a storm than the one before it.

'He doesn't know what he wants!' my mother would say. 'One day he says he's coming back to wring my neck, the next that I can go to the dogs, the next that he wants me over there on the next boat. Last week he sent me a letter to give to the embassy in Rome, to get a visa. As if I'm going to travel half way around the world in my condition. And then to put up with the same idiocy there that I put up with here!'

'*Sei scimunita, Cristi!* Idiocy? Who's the idiot? You're lucky if he doesn't crack your skull and throw you in the streets!'

'Then to hell with all of you! I'll go to Rome, Naples, anywhere--'

'*Ah, bello!* Like a gypsy. And what will you live on, the few thousand lire you've saved from what he sends you? Because you'll not see a cent of my money, I swear on my grave. And with two children to take care of, you can work in the streets. *Disgraziata!*'

'Ah, *si*, he's probably slept with every whore in America by now, but for me it's a disgrace. Women had their face up their asses for too long, they let their men run around like goats and then they're happy if they don't come home and beat them!'

'*Brava.* And you, *communista*, are going to change all that. With your communist boyfriend. A foreigner no less, who's just a coward and a beggar. Yes, you think I'm blind, but I know all about him. Where is he now, your communist boyfriend? Go, go, to Rome, to America, to the devil for all I care! Get out of my sight and let me die in peace. I'll sell the house to some rich Roman for a summer house or I'll burn it to the ground and feed the fire with my own bones, and all the bones of my fathers who worked to build it.'

The arguments and curses left me with troubling images. I had a vision of my dark-haired father looming suddenly large and angry in our doorway one day, bringing with him some unspeakable doom; of my mother and me left to wander the streets of Rome or Naples like beggars, or packed suddenly onto a ship and sent off to a dark future across the sea. But a few weeks after my grandfather had returned home a final letter arrived from my father which seemed somehow to carry more weight than the rest.

'He thinks we're still in the dark ages,' my mother said the day it arrived, 'when women used to dump their babies at the back door of the convent in the middle of the night and leave them there to die from the cold. Let him carry a baby for nine months and see if he feels that way.'

'You'll do as he tells you,' my grandfather said. 'The orphanage is full of babies just like yours, don't think yours will be special. I'll not have that bastard child living under my roof.'

An uneasy truce settled over our house now, and it seemed that despite my mother's objections the matter was settled: whatever my mother was carrying in her belly – 'that bastard child,' as my grandfather called it, which I thought might be a reference to the snake-headed baby Alfredo had warned of – could be got rid of at the orphanage in Rocca Secca, so that for the time being we would be troubled by neither arrivals nor departures. Gradually an air of normalcy began to assert itself again in our household. My mother still kept up a tight-lipped aloofness around the other villagers; but she went about th town freely now, and the villagers did not skirt her as they used to, only nodded in greeting and continued on their way. And with the last day of March set now by the town's election committee as the date for the election of a new mayor, a hand-painted sign announcing the decision posted prominently on the front wall of Di Lucci's bar, some of the older men in the village had begun to visit my grandfather in his room, talking strategy and politics long into the night.

But I had learned by now that Valle de Sole had more than a single face.

'Still holding her nose up like a queen,' I overheard Maria Maiale say at Di Lucci's. 'Quella Maria! Maybe it's a virgin birth.'

'Maybe it's the other Mary, Magdalena, you're thinking about,' Di Lucci said.

'We'll see what happens when her husband gets his hands on her. He'll crack her skull, you remember what he was like, like his father. Then she'll see how good she'd had it here.'

But there were other scandals too, more cryptic, which seemed about to surface. The election, it seemed, had stirred up much emotion in the village. My grandfather's party had chosen Alfreddo Mastroantonio, the former chairman of *il comitato della festa*, to replace my grandfather; but this time the election was not to be decided by acclamation, as it always had been during my grandfather's reign. The Communists, too, had fielded a candidate – Pio Dagnello, son of Angelo the Red, who every night now rose up on a crate in the square, his face flushed with emotion, and told the villagers how the government of Rome had ignored them since the war because no one among them had had the courage to raise an angry voice. At first the villagers paid him little attention, as if they took for granted that the government in Rome would ignore them, and it was useless to think it would ever be otherwise; but night by night the crowds around Pio began to grow. Alfreddo Mastroantonio, who did not make speeches in the square but held small private meetings in the back room of Di Lucci's bar, seemed alarmed: one day all the walls along via San Giuseppe were suddenly covered with large posters that had been printed up in Rocca Secca, an unheard-of expense, Alfreddo Mastoantonio's plump-cheeked face beaming its strained smile from every one of them. But still the villagers continued to flock every night around Pio, and every night Pio grew bolder in his denunciations, until there was no mistaking who he blamed for the village's ills.

'You see how he paid for it in the end? He was the first one to take them in when they came. Roads, he said! Lights! *Viva il Duce!* The communists will eat us alive! But where are the roads now? Where are the lights? He sold us to the devil for fifty *lire*, and because the people are like sheep it's taken them twenty years to open their eyes. You don't see Alfreddo Mastroantonio knocking on his door now. Alfreddo may be a horse's ass, but he's no idiot. He knows the old man sold us out.'

As election time grew nearer the visits to my grandfather became more and more sporadic, only a few old loyalists still coming by, mumbling consolations in response to my grandfather's increasingly bitter invectives.

'The village will go to the dogs, I tell you. Dagnello is a liar and a coward. Where was he during the war? I'll tell you where he was, gone out to some hole in the mountains the very day the letter came calling him up for service. If I'd half a mind then I would have turned him in. Now he makes it seem like he was a hero, when half his cousins died in the same war, just so he could come back to his house in one piece at the end of it. And Masroantonio is no better, the fool – you could buy him with the change in your pocket.'

Towards the end of February, another letter arrived for my mother; but this one bore a small neat script of bright blue, not at all my father's violent hand. My mother whisked the letter up to her room, closing the door behind her; and when I went up later I found her packing some clothes into a hamper.

'I'm going to Rome for a few days in the morning,' she said. 'I'll get Marta to come by to look after you and your grandfather.'

She drew open the drawer of hew writing table, rifling through some papers there and sliding a few into her hamper.

'I don't want Marta to come,' I said.

'Please, Vittorio, don't start. I have some very important business to look after.'

When my mother brought in my grandfather's supper that night, I caught snippets of subdued conversation between them.

'If you ask me he's as foolish as you are,' my grandfather said. 'You should have waited till after, the way you'd decided. He won't have that child in his house.'

'We'll settle that,' my mother said. But her words were curiously empty and dead, as if they were not her own. 'I spoke to Zia Lucia, everything is arranged. But I don't want you to say anything to anyone until I get back.'

'What difference will it makes? Now you think about keeping secrets. You should have thought of that months ago. I should have sent you away.'

'It would have been the same,' my mother said. 'Everyone would have known.'

'No. That's where you're stupid, Cristina. You carry your shame in the streets, you force people to point a finger at you. What you've done you've done, and may God forgive you for it; but that's not the way to be with people.'

'Please, don't start.'

Later, in bed, I heard the scratch of my mother's pen again. But when I went to her door she quickly slid the piece of paper she'd been writing on into her drawer.

'What is it?' she said, annoyed. 'You should be in bed.'

'Why do you have to go to Rome?'

She took in a breath in irritation; but after a moment her anger seemed to melt, and she drew me towards her and nestled me against her knees.

'Poor Vittorio. No one ever tells him anything.' She wrapped her arms around me, and I saw that she'd begun to cry. 'Do you promise to keep it a secret, if I tell you?'

'Yes.'

She pulled me closer, putting her cheek against mine.

'We're going to leave the village, Vittorio,' she whispered finally. 'In a few weeks, we're going to America.'

From Lives of the Saints (Toronto, 19th Printing, 2002)

V

POEMS

GEORGE AMABILE

ANCESTORS

It was already dark when I arrived.
In Genoa the streets
reeked with the same decay
Columbus must have breathed as a boy
 under denim sails
going to sea that first time.

Now that the imagined past
has led me through white light
on columns in the Forum, and around
the traffic circle of the Colisseum
I drift in cold shoes
under clotheslines and laundry
lit by windows, along
the crumbling wall of a Roman tenement
and come out blinking before The American Bar.

I sink like a wrecked tourist
into the red leather chair.
At the piano, fingers
flinkin the keys.
A girl with black hair
sits quietly, looking
as though she sees
notes clean as the handful of rain
sown by a windy branch
startling jewels and circles
from her table top.

Lamps flicker
in the stilled flow of walnut,
Eve might have had a mind like that.
I watch a layer of cigarette smoke
speed up into the mouth of an air conditioner
like the ghost of a river

lost in a city of dust.

Father, Mother
Grandparents
Great Great Great
something or other whose coat
of arms drew eagles on a red field
Etruscan sailor, herdsman perhaps
high in the coastal hills
or a dancer of some nameless tribe
stamping the earth for rain.

And before that
who knows what stone age riff-raff
fresh from the shaggy councils of the horde
rehearsing secretly in the sleep before birth
the same lit fuse of improbable changes
that blew my children into the air.

And behind this astounding *tour de force*
before the young sun's exuberant turmoils
the first hot flash, atoms
collected like stray thoughts
in a mind squeezing light out of nothing at all.

GENERATION GAP
to my father (1895-1961)

1.
I remember whining
about being dressed
like a fop-doll display.
You broke in from the back yard out of your work
as the mad builder
who cared for a chicken coop
at *me* you son-of-a-bitch.
I thought you'd bail me out of there
you beat me up instead.

2.
I wanted to blast your head all over the street
I didn't even know if you had a brain.
When we tried to talk
you'd back off
and lisp
for control
while I secreted macho like a weed.

But I'd seen the veins rise in your flushed temples
while American dicta flashed behind your eyes:
"Balls are made out of dough-power, boy."
"Doughboys eat gunpowder light."

In public you acted like a mild-mannered family man;
at home you played king of the roost.

3.
The one thing you taught me
was how to cut wood.
"Just the *weight* of the saw," you said.
"Learn to pace yourself."

I'd ride in those words for ten minutes
before the magic of technique
burst
with the vigour of a thistle pod
like the dream you had
of owning a chicken farm in rural America.

4.
You were a southpaw
in baseball, axe, hammers, brooms
& the two-man saw.
In human relations you led with your rights
as the son of an immigrant widow
who was a midwife
and the real father of us all.
She hit the roof

when you decided to marry
and make your little step-sister my mother-to-be.

Before that you were free
(except for the seasick troop ships of the first war
in which you cut meat
& developed a life-sized pain in the ass).
You'd gone on the road
with a brass Italian wedding band
strumming the twelve-string guitar.
Was it the wide open spaces
or the love-hunger
that brought you home to roost
in the double dream of chickens
& the State Highway Department?
It tore your mind to shreds
half of you starving for a patch of earth
the other set on becoming your big brother
who had dreamed of being a civil engineer
played mandolin
loved women
and died young of a poetic disease.

You kept your amazing balance
like a cat
inspecting girders in bad weather
for the first American Super Skyway
which is now obsolete
and cutting the throats of old hens in the yard.

I learned to play ball
with bullies
then hit them with bats.
They said I was nervous
but I was just practising
the *weight* of the saw.
Sometimes I lost control.

5.
You owned guitars
which I was never allowed to touch.
They stood in a corner under the stairs
covered with dustcloths
like a family of veiled totems.
An uncle told me you could make them talk.

I tried to get you talking too.
The closest I ever got
was the time I'd just come in from New Orleans
where I'd done great things
like working in a cardboard factory
reading Whitman to the stars by moonlight
while tight-roping a polished railroad track into town
partying for days on a forty-foot yacht
thumping a used guitar
singing black blues to hysterical whites
falling in love with B-girls
shitting my pants after forty hours on a barstool
starving in a downtown jail
and fighting a drunk ex-pug in a dusty boxcar.

My mother
who had stoned me with a cracked porcelain fire-holder
for vacating her control
and running around the house like Haley's comet
was up north in an orphanage helping the nuns.
She held you back the night I'd gone outside.
Now there was no one between us.
All I had to do was reach out
and put my arm around your shoulder
or punch you hard in the mouth.

I couldn't do either.
The outbuildings were a shambles by then.
The garage roof had begun to cave in.
The lawn was neat, though
in cool sunlight.

We stood there reeking of failure
making subdued remarks about the weather.

At the bus-stop
you gazed through Princeton's colonial storefronts
at the Agrarian Myth.
What did you say?
"Trust in the land"?
or "Land is the best investment"?
Your voice dried to a hoarse whisper
and sowed volcanic ash like straw in the wind.

6.
All I ever really heard between us
was the whack
of axes
& the ring of the two-man saw.

We cleared land instead of the air
& spread a garden with bat shit
from the brick-lined walls of a nineteenth-century farmhouse
called The Red Onion
that had gone to seed for the birds and a town drunk.

You killed the bats with a stick as if they were devils.
Was it a dream
you worked from or a mirage?
Once in the stalled traffic
I thought I'd caught you looking at death.
The distant afternoon light made your glazed eyes holy.
I felt seasick.

After that we spoke to each other
at the top of our lungs
off the top of our heads for years
until the night I asked you to step outdoors.
I wanted to punch the dry cement from between your ears.
I stood on the lawn under cold stars.
You never showed up.

7.
A wasp came out of the plasterdust tumbling in sunlight
& hit my cheekbone just under the eye.
The needle of pain it left
grew deeper.
You pulled me into your rough shirt
like a prized possession
became still
but tense
for seconds
then crushed it against an old beam with your thumb.
There were tears in my lashes
but not on my face.

Later I heard you curse
God
leaning on your workbench
in the back yard during my brother's wake.
He'd been your most recent hope for manhood.
In court after the accident
I knew you wanted to pay back
the black who had gunned him down with a rusty dump truck.
No luck.

I told an absurd truth
in feet
and inches.
The man went free.
He'd come lurching over the crabgrass.
I ran at him out of control.
He gathered me into a bear hug
and wept.
There was whisky in his breath.

8.
After that you quit
playing guitar
retired early

as a handyman jack-of-all-trades
& died watching a prize-fight in your sleep.

I threw flowers down at the coffin.
You died a month before our daughter was due.
I wanted to tap your closed mind.
I snubbed your grave instead.

9.
You had socked away
over thirty grand in three banks
hoarding one last dream:
to outfit a camper and drive
the roads, opening
chapters of free time
toward the end of your lives.
But always it was, "Not
yet, we need more
money, next summer, next spring..."

My share went
into family passage from New York to Genoa
on a rusty Yugoslavian freighter
a maid for Delia and Natasha
an ambassador's illicit sublet in the American section of Rome
etc. (which means The Luau & The American Bar)

10.
I left the apartment in a rage
& drank *strega* with a wagon-load of gypsies
in a night bar north of Rome.
I said nothing.
On the way back
I drove into the weaving light
of a motor bike
and nearly killed the heaviest male
adolescent in the city.
His head grazed the windshield
& dented the roof of the white Volkswagen

I rolled & totalled later in Connecticut
after a language exam.

I found him lying on the road
in the headlights & broken glass
blood oozing out of his hair
& soaking his white shirt.
He was snoring like my kid brother.

Was it all those years of walking away
& trying so hard not to fight?
I drove Delia and Natasha to the airport
then south toward Mt. Vesuvius.
At Praiano I tried to write but the past kept closing.
I ate *mortadella* sandwiches with wine slurp
in sunshine on the terraced hills like a sailor.

One afternoon I studied conchoidal stone chips
by spinning them into the cliff
until one turned into a buzzing flint-chip handsaw
that severed a lizard's tail.

I got drunk once
in the wind & streetlights.
The stones were old
the air clear
the moonlight very sharp over the bay.

I wanted to punch the pain out of your head.
I wanted to talk.
But there were green smells
& the withered folds at your throat were disastrous.
Your scratched voice blew off in the wind.

From The Presence of Fire (Toronto, 1982)

ALEXANDRE AMPRIMOZ

LA RÉALITÉ EST LE CANCER DE L'ÂME

Soleil il est temps maintenant de peindre
les momies de tes ennemis et de tous ceux qui se
plaisent à sculpter l'ombre
    la haine qui coule dans leurs veines est
le poison des dieux et des poêtes
    Soleil ce sont des hommes
    seuls les morts et les nuages sont des images
pures
    laisse les enfants croire que la neige a un
        coeur rouge
    entre avec moi dans cette forêt où leurs mots
sont stalactites de silence tandis que leurs histoires
s'en vont glacer le lit tendre du Nil
    père ailé de l'antique sagesse j'écris en
m'inclinant sous la barque dorée
    nous sommes les arbres timides qui frissonnent
sous la pluie du doute
    nous plantes désespérées pleurons quand les
serpents glissent sur nos feuilles comme des
mémoires
    mais les hommes eux sont prêts à couper les
joues de leurs enfants avec sabres ou rasoirs
    pour eux Soleil le mal est une forme de gloire
    j'en ai vu tant dans ce présent du toujours
inventer des noms de dieux pour pouvoir torturer
    j'en ai vu tant et beaucoup d'autres au-delà
de cette plaine plus humaine dans le mal que la bête
ne peut être sous les doigts de l'instinct
    il y a ceux qui montent les ânes sauvages de
leur noblesse onientale pendant que leurs femmes
urinent en se tenant debout sans même soulever
leurs robes boueuses
    il y a ceux qui se lavent trois foir par
jour et pourtant offrent les maladies de leurs

maîtresses a leurs femme
   il y a ceux qui rêvent de vices et de vertus
dont la destinée rejoint celles du ver de terre
   il y a ceux qui organisent des banquets pour
venir en aide aux famines de ce monde pendant que
leurs filles font la diète et vont a l'institut de beauté
   il y a ceux-là et d'autres encore dont il
vait mieux ne pas rêver

mes lèvres tremblent
comme celles de la vieille chanteuse
comme la chair qui déborde de sea bras
déjà la voix se brise contre un rocher
de notes et d'harmonies
mes lèvres savent que l'amour
est l'ancêtre doré de l'illusion
combien de coeurs moururent
d'une explosion timide
comme la corde
d'un instrument que l'on tourmente
Soleil vois ces âmes
qui furent harpe ou violon
et tombèrent dans l'espace
que la main avide du temps
creuse entre deux notes
malheureux Tristan
Roméo de torture
Don Juan brûlé

ne furent-ils égaux à tant d'autres

et voilà que mon corps
comme la pomme qui but trop
de lumière
commence à devenir
un univers de vers

et de nouveau tu pars Soleil
jaloux de grâces passagères

ce vent vient mourir
agenouillé aux pieds
de cette terre ridée
qui elle-même semble naître
de l'ombre
d'une déesse morte
ce vent vient mourir
il faudra vivre dans la tombe
de cette déesse
humble comme un ver de la terre.
silencieux comme un grand poète

et quand tu tournas le dos
il me lança dans un langue étrange
son dernir théorème
je n'est pas un autre en hiver

From Changements de tons (Sainte Boniface, 1981)

TO A COUNTRY WITHOUT NOSTALGIA

crushed squirrel
on the road
good material
for new prose
you think

where i come from
crushed legs
are part
of an old tradition
a gift exchanged
between men
who find it impolite
to share land

and impossible
to agree
on the definition
of universal mystery

DÉRACINÉ

this is not your landscape

you knocked
on a wrinkled door
to find time
with a cut wrist

and you sat under the wilted
lamp
    and you stared at the rug
    —eroded memory

look at the rain
how it slaps the window
leaving your heart
almost uprooted with fear
like a child's first tooth

this is not your landscape
no one talks to you
about venetian tunics
or tunisian venus
and it is alone that you dream
of holbein's hands
drawing erasmus' hands

From Fragments of Dreams (Toronto, 1982)

10/r

> c'est la fourmi   qui coucha avec le lion
> on aIla au baptême du fourmilion
> c'est fou   mais le pauvre enfant fur mangé
> par le curé   qui était   bien entendu
> un fourmilier

s/10

c'est le printemps
et sur le toit
de la vieille maison
on a oublié
le Père Noël en plastique

il restera là jusqu'aux prochaines élections
il compte déjà sur l'ardoise noire
les votes verts et blancs
des pigeons

From 10/11 (Sudbury, 1979)

ISABELLA COLALILLO KATZ

DZIKIR OF LOVE

1
first nights there was song. there was the baby scent of new breath. the
longing for sleep never overcame the delight of holding her tiny body in
my arms. her sweet smile. the panting sun moving towards her beauty. her
freshness. and me attuning to her needs.

long nights of song and sleepless abandon. her inconsolable tears. her grace when she lay sleeping; her smiles when she still talked to angels. I remember the way those baby fingers cried for mother-milk. the nights she refused to sleep and how my tired eyes traced the lines of her new face. the world became a sacredness when she suckled. she cried little then. she still knew the taste of heaven.

2

then. life's scars etching the tapestry of her skin. I cried to protect her from their bites; to hide her from the human face of sunlight. later, words that wound. the inevitable misunderstandings. the need between us for differentiation. her struggle to take back her god power. she doesn't think when she strikes out—her venom singes my soul. I scream to make her understand. defensive, disbelieving. how can love turn to such bitter dust? destroy the tango of years? pollute the purpose of our breathing lessons?

after giving her love, I stand empty-handed. a mother looking for love in the dustbin of time. a child crying from the sharpness of words. these are the questions I ask the goddess: why has my daughter become the arrow seeking her own destruction? why am I the enemy? did I think I could tame her heart with old remedies—trust, love, freedom?

she rants and rages. I have no words to destroy the venom. she splinters, unrelenting; fights me for the taste of life. why can't she remember the flavour of our nightsongs? how my milk grew her heartbeats? battle weary we cry. the listening moon urges the stars to twinkle. she's crying for new milk. her own taste of life. my wounded heart flutters. breaks open. tries to redeem her anger. fails. again.

3

did we ever dream it would come to this? did we ever guess that love is only part of the answer? in those days of delight and beauty, how could we have known that the need for love could terrorize us, as only real love can? I write letters to my daughter. she writes to me. we rush into tenuous answers. she is the princess who felt the pea of my love. I'm a mad Rumplestiltskin begging for my name. she needs breathing room. I give her sadness.

these are the alchemies of motherlove. these are its sad findings. this is

the poem I could not write this morning. the chant of incompatible
geometries. the space between us and how it teeters for the love of you,
my unredeemable daughter. sweet mother love.

*First published in Journal for the Association for Research on Mothering, Fall/
Winter 2002, Vol.4, No.2.*

WASHING DAY II

I cling to her blue cotton skirt
she chatters all the way to the river
on her head
a bobbing wicker basket filled with soiled laundry
the women are carefree
a half day washing by the river is a kind of holiday
the sun frolics on the mountaintops
stippled clouds play hide and seek
winking and glittering
the river water enjoys their game

my mother puts down her basket
shakes my hand free
finds her place on a wide washing stone
kneels and begins the wash
the sheets are first
then the smaller linen and other
· the women soap and scrub and rinse
laughing and cackling bawdy stories I don't understand

I see my favourite dress
the one we bought at the gypsy market
the green one with wine stains from last Sunday's dinner
my mother pushes it underwater
I run behind her wanting to see
to help

she screams
I wobble
splash hard the rippling water

when I'm safe in her trembling arms
a woman is laughing
another tugs at something with a long stick
my mother's chestnut eyes gazing
and then I see it
small and wet on the topaz waves
my favourite dress
gleeful
under the glance
of heedless clouds

First published in Journal for the Association for Research on Mothering, Fall/ Winter 2002, Vol.4, No.2.

A WOMAN'S IDENTITY

they wanted to marry me off,
I was barely fourteen;
a young man from the old village
came to visit three weekends in a row
all the way from Hamilton.
part of me was intrigued,
another scared to death.
the sunlit kitchen yawned
as he talked to my parents;

I felt funny,
a bit like a good horse at a fair.
my tender years my only defense
against any kind of quick agreement.
in my room, I studied French grammar

using the pluperfect subjunctive
to find a loophole in his plans.

I already understood the trap of marriage
the role it played in their traditions.
marriage was all they seemed to plan for,
to talk about. Sunday afternoons,
evenings of *paesani*
talking about who had married whom.
who had established what relationship
with what family over the past hundred years.
they remembered everyone's name,
dates of birth,
death and marriage.
family lineages carefully tracked for generations.
and even those who came to America,
the promised land of peasants,
were not lost to the tribal stories
repeated in these conversations.

that afternoon
and the Sundays that followed,
my parents claimed the purity of my lineage—
it was they assured the young man,
better than some.
honourable pedigrees on both sides.
no scandals of any consequence.
my father descended from Spanish blueblood,
my mother from French aristocracy.
landowners,
travelers,
all good stock and traceable.
I was saleable.
a good catch:
pretty
smart
educated;
a promising cook.
and though I could be headstrong,

too forthright—*too* English,
I could be counted on to do the right thing
especially in a family crisis.
for three weeks,
each Sunday, the boy came to visit.
he was twenty or so and though anxious to marry
he promised to wait if they agreed to the match.
and so they went over my pedigree,
counted my wifely attributes.
and each Sunday, the visitor asked about marriage.
she's keen on her studies, said my mother wistfully
with the voice of a proper woman.
she's keen to study all right, said my father
ignoring my mother,
but she'll soon be ready.
she'll make some paesano a good wife.

not me, I said to myself,
listening behind the closed door of my bedroom,
I'm leaving this transplanted village life—
leaving it far behind.
one day it will be a part of me
like this physics I don't understand—
I'll pass the test tomorrow and then it will be gone.
I'll become someone else,
someone even the familiar stars won't know.
more than marriage,
I want to discover myself.
learn everything,
go everywhere.
become the one I still don't know,
the one they don't suspect me of being.
the woman they can never
never sell into bondage.

First published in Journal for the Association for Research on Mothering,
Spring / Summer 2003, Vol.5, No.1

CELESTINO DE IULIIS

IN MY BACKYARD

I own a house now.
My father sowed his seeds
in his backyard,
and reaped the lettuce and tomatoes.
He had known who he was when
his hands formed the cheese
drawn from the milk of his flock.
Having come here, he was less sure
and worked in factories or construction sites.
He made his own wine and slaughtered still
the Easter Lamb for us
(and for himself too, there's no denying).
He loved what was his own with little show
and fewer words.
The language never yielded to him, strong as he was.
I wrote the numbers out on a sheet
so he could write his cheques,
pay his bills...
My youth was spent in shame of him.
My tiny face would blush, my eyes avert
on parents' night when he would timid come
to ask in broken syntax after me.
In my backyard
I have my grass and flowers
and buy my produce at Dominion.
My eyes avert in shame now
that I ever was that boy.

DIN DON

When church bells ring
four thousand miles away
there in those hills that do not bear
the fruit of former years,

when hardier hands caressed
small plots of land
— made smaller by the passing generations —
and reaped the nourishment for a six-month
sleep beneath the snow,
that is the way they sound
din don
at vespers and at morning mass,
and when the joyous festivals arrive
they swing in wild surrender
under the sun of August
singing their crazed song
din don din din don
din don din din don
while the growing hands of boys
engage in mortal combat
the writhing rope
beneath the dancing bronze.
You had not heard them pealing
in your tongue,
those bells that had announced
your coming hither,
for twenty-five long years.
But they had not forgotten you,
who in your time had made them sing
while waiting patiently to be a man
possessing his own flock.
Four thousand years away
one day in March
the bells remembered
as the slow sad constant note
rang don
      rang don
            rang don
and welcomed you back home
amongst your
hills.

From Love's Sinning Song (Toronto, 1981)

PIER GIORGIO DI CICCO

FLYING DEEPER INTO THE CENTURY

Flying deeper into the century
is exhilarating, the faces of loved ones eaten out
slowly, the panhandles of flesh warding off
the air, the smiling plots. We are lucky to be mature,
in our prime, seeing more treaties, watching
TV get computerized. Death has no dominion.
It lives off the land. The glow over the hill, from
the test sites, at night, the whole block of neighbours
dying of cancer over the next thirty years. We are
suing the government for a drop of blood; flying deeper
into the century, love,
the lies are old lies with more imagination;
the future is a canoe. The three bears are ravenous, not content
with porridge. Flying deeper into the century,
my hands are prayers, hooks, streamers.
I cannot love grass, cameos or lungs.
The end of the century is a bedspread up to the eyes.
I want to be there, making ends meet.
I will not love you, with such malice at large.
Flying deeper into the century is beautiful, like
coming up for the third time, life flashing before us.
The major publishing event is the last poem of
all time. I am a lonely bastard. My brothers and sisters have
had sexual relations, and I am left with their mongrel sons
writing memoirs about the dead in Cambodia.
Flying deeper, I do not remember what I cared for, out
of respect. Oh *Time,* oh *Newsweek,* oh *Ladies' Home Journal,*
oh the last frontier, I am deeply touched.
The sun, an ignoramus, comes up.
I have this conversation with it. Glumly, glumly, deeper
I fly into the century, every feather of each wing
absolution, if only I were less than human, not angry
like a beaten thing.

From Flying Deeper into the Century (Toronto, 1982)

THE HAPPY TIME

These are the most beautiful times
in my life; Mario and Alfred and the spirit
of life, the entourage always coming to
the door; the woman with her mouth flowering
into bouquets of honesty; yesterday's disasters
so distasteful to themselves they come
snivelling up to the doorstep wanting
a little bit of light; the poem spurring itself
on because hope draws the line by the teeth.
The virtues lining themselves up like street-lamps
down the avenue, at first sputtering, then making
the world sensible with daylight –
          I don't know what I want to ruminate
of the past, but the guts extend themselves
by the grace of something other.
          I have grown up to be a metaphysician –
an apple is a kiss, a friend is a smile,
and these things are not poetry –
I leave it to the post-modern to see a coded
transform for the song in their lungs.
          The visions return, after ten years
of watching faithlessness eat people out of one bed
into another. I do not wait for them to come awake.
I do not want company. I sledgehammer my
grief, without fear of repression, and it comes out
azaleas, marigolds, whatever you like –
the soul has its own tastes.
          Sentimentality is what the proud fear,
so they never get to the outrageously beautiful.
This is my only grief in a Protestant
country – they have no talent for metaphysics.
My friend Mario talks to Alfredo across the table
and describes him as a flower growing on his shoulder –
In a five mile radius they would laugh at this
In a five foot radius they would laugh at this
In a five inch radius they would laugh –
But Mario has become the hub of the world

and its circumference – two things at once –
and in Berkeley they are trying to get over
the Uncertainty Principle, how to be two things at
once, male and female, particle and anti-particle –
The Italians live with paradox as an act of faith
humbled to the ridiculous and courting the angels –
well, to be brutal about it, it isn't just the Italians
that could do this. The obedient to heart could do it.
Someday the scientists will localize pride in
the Protestant brain, and we will be having
a good laugh at this, and we won't say a thing –
we will have evolved into something other than a concept –
perhaps as a smile behind a tree, a poem, a song,
an old photo of the family in Molise – into the
unlikeliest thing, the way God makes something out
of nothing, under the quantum quiffs,
knowing that poetry is science wise enough to know
that you have to live with your metaphors.
      But, as it stands, this is the most beautiful
time in my life. When I am out of grace, I will
forget it, and you will see me long-faced, on Bloor,
discussing Kafka, and Germaine Greer and systems
holism. I would thank God, if he weren't so busy with
me, so I will thank Mario and the other angels –
There is one more apologia, every time I
forget to say *thank you*; and it occurs to me
grazie means thanks in Italian, while
the English say you're welcome, when they mean goodbye.

From Virgin Science (Toronto, 1986)

SOME SELF-REFLECTION

a bit of a codger.
an american codger.
not just playful, a little "furbo".

i learned from bro. anthony
to act a little crazy and they'd leave you
alone.

then there's the survivor
from my father's camps and
ambushing the rival gangs from
the dundalk woods.

growing up smelling danger, separating
it from the scent of hyacinths.

then there's the plain old sincere one
who can't hide from god;

who won't confuse charity with his own need,
who puts christ in front of him
when his own heart is salivating.

don't confuse the both of them.
the songster from tuscany,
the sleeper with one eye open,
the feminist nightmare,

the one who knows where this poem is going
but is open to the turn
in the neck of the woods.

a simple guy,
with a knowledge of human nature,

owing to nothing but death,
a plain birdsong,

and the resurrection of his mother,

the world.

From The Honeymoon Wilderness (Toronto, 2002)

COUNTRY PRIEST

now here's a kicker.
me in the dark
in a chapel on a hill, mid-winter, pines and
city lights fifty miles off.
150 years old the place is.
i light the mary candle and it flickers
among the city lights.   my mother is buried
fifteen yards away.
this is what I have wanted all my life.
i knew it would come to this.
a large statue of jesus with a broken hand
somewhere in the dark behind me. he has
beautiful eyes. he knows everything.
i know nothing.   looking at the skylights
and beyond
i would hate to come here to die
but I guess I will.

beauty is the name of as good a place as any.

SINGING IN MY SKIN

Singing in my skin.
Loving it. Always singing in
my skin. It's a hell of a good time.
Come in out of the weather.
We can see people from in here, like crabs
scuttling over a tent. Funny how we'd look,
only with arms, legs, that sort of

thing, human, godless.
And now it's warm in my skin, singing
like this, just you
and I, dumb,
touching.

SOMETHING OUT OF NOTHING

i still carry with me the first
fork i ever ate with. all else has been lost,
stolen, borrowed, maybe it's the kind of thing
i'll take in the coffin with me, my rosebud;
mouths are important symbolically and even
without symbols, it is where the poems and prayers
emerged, the exhalation of spirit, it is where kisses
drew the summer air, and where the curses came, the
exclamations that negotiated me in God, the thank
you at the xmas gift, the first plea for rejoinment
in the womb, the name of beauty, the lovely names
of friends who scattered shadows. this fork is stainless,
and rather mundane. if there is a feature on it i will
keep it to myself, it is that private, unlike everything
else i have spoken and said. and yet it is the final thing
i don't know what God means by; all else is gone, my father's
first transistor, first eyeglasses, 1964 muscle
magazines, so He must mean something by it, leaving
me this, as if a mouth must be something to Him,
a place from which to carol eternity, his gift of
song in life. i still use this fork, and if i lose it, i
will find one more last thing to make a fuss over, always one last
thing; it is last things that are important, what i would take
with me; i would, rather than a fork, your blue eyes taken
to my soul or the poem almost finished and filled with
everything, or the sublimity of an afternoon alone when
all friends form a confluence like a ring around your
heart; but the fork is also where i have been, cities
and witness in a stupid way to all the drama, was the fork
sleeping through all that? i look at it and it almost remembers for

me the things i though grander than eating; just a kitchen
table, mother, first breakfasts as if all social animals
crept out of the mire of weaning and placement of dishes
and adults in conversation while the child revels in his
own particular fork.
i would take so much, but we always travelled light
in our family, and this is the best thing I could have
been left, and where it ends up is maybe a box
carted into a secondhand store with invisible
stories that stalk the earth. it's good it is only a fork.
because it is the same with the gorgeous things
we are to each other, memories or books or
lifting a child to the air, it is something you do not
resent God for taking – a fork, it is where you started,
as simple as that, with the cartloads heard as
your heart goes away, heavy with crowns, tiaras,
love affairs and blood. you can't hear your life
crying, that's the beauty of the fork. it is the
beginning you could almost take up again, as if nothing had
happened, between your mouth and your hand, like the
first take, like the first frames, before God says action;
you are ready, and you miss nothing, yet.

From Living in Paradise (Toronto, 2001)

BRUNA DI GIUSEPPE-BERTONI

IL MACCHIONE - TERRA DI MIO NONNO

Il profumo di ginestra
Mi dà un' allegria
In questa terra scordata.
Ancora si distinguono i ruderi
dove la casa giaceva.
Il forno è ormai un monte
coperto da erbe.

Il noce, il pesco, il fico,
alberi robusti. Frutti perduti.
File di olivi, foglie color d'argento.
Quanto bel fresco offrono sotto
un sole rovente in questa terra
scordata.

MY GRANDFATHER'S LAND

On this forgotten land
the fragrance of the *ginestra*
brings joy.
Shattered ruins are the testimony
of the old farmhouse.
What was once the wooden oven,
grass has overgrown.
Robust trees of peaches, almonds and figs
stand as sentinels and guardians of the land...
Wasted are their fruits...
Silver coloured leaves of olive trees
provide the shade
under the scorching sun
on this abandoned land.

From Sentiéri d'Italia. (Toronto, 2003).
English translation by Alfredo Biafora.

PIER 21

I REMEMBER...
   My first steps off the boat.
   They are here, footprints of my past.
   Fresh ocean air caresses my wrinkled face.
   Halifax harbour embraces me again
I REMEMBER...
   Speechless,
   I envision the ghost of my youth.

Gratitude is felt within me.
Here my new life began.
I REMEMBER...
    The route to which I entered.
    The island, the snow.
    The rooms in which I waited.
    The food. Unspoken words.
I REMEMBER...
    The train.
    Framed nature's paintings
    zooming one after another.
    Glimpse of heaven.
I REMEMBER...
    Memories are not lost...
    Canada is home.
    Identities are regained.
    Youth is all I've lost.

From Valigia d'oro Project (Toronto, 2001)

MARY DI MICHELE

I   MIMOSA

Even more than a tired man, Vito is a sad man,
all Sunday afternoon finds him rocking
in the brighton rocker, in the backyard
of the house he's earned, under the sky he's created
of green fiberglass, jutting from the roof.
There is only one heaven, the heaven of the home.
There was only one paradise, the garden
that kept them little children even as adults,
until one angel, Lucia, his luckless offspring
fell, refusing to share in his light.

Sentimental music is being sucked up
from the stereo system in the basement
like a sweet gaseous pop
through a straw.
He listens to an Italian tenor sing Mimosa
and savours his banishment
with a ginger nostalgia,
ginger ale fizzing in a glass by his side.

Summer's finished.
The few roses left are such a dark red
you imagine the odour of menstrual blood.
There's a walk of broken tiles through the well trimmed
grass
leading to a vegetable patch, fenced and carefully tended,
a nursery for deep purple eggplant, whose mature passions
keep them close to the security of the ground,
garlic, the most eloquent of the plants,
with the grace of a lily, from white clusters of buds,
the flower, is sticking out a long green tongue.
Zucchini, tomatoes, peppers, tender peas, and Italian
parsley,
the season yields.

He tries to improve the English he learned in classes
for new Canadians by reading the daily papers.
Unlike his wife, he can talk to his children in the language
in which they dream, but he keeps that tongue
in his pocket like a poorly cut key to a summer residence.
He keeps his love for them like old clothes, in a trunk,
he no longer wears in public. He never wanted the girls to
grow up.
He wants Lucia to be three again and sleeping in his arms.

A small shack stands in the northwest corner of the garden,
his latest project, a hut for storing seeds and tools,
and now there's nothing left to build,
a lifetime of development, of homes under construction,

there's nothing left to be done,
the man's hands are idle and have found time to brood.

The years spent working in a stone quarry just outside
Toronto
taught him how to find the fault in rock
how to split it so that it could be used to build
a face of pink and white limestone for an old house
of red tar and plaster.
It didn't tell him much about the fault lines in his life:
the overtime and the extra Saturdays, the few hours left
frittered away asleep in front of the television,
accounted for a distance he didn't bargain for,
the estrangement like a border crossing
between himself and his children.
His good wife, he didn't have to think about,
she worked hard and cooked well.
He might have done other things,
but he married young, just after the war,
and hard times made him stop breathing for himself
and spend it all on his children.

He has no son but his daughters are rare and intelligent
and full of music.
He's not happy, he knows he's getting old
and Lucia abandoned him to live in an apartment on her
own.
He has little hope of finding his youth in grandchildren
soon enough. How can he be happy when he knows
that he'll die sooner than he cares to?
He still remembers his own father,
the left half of his body paralyzed
from a heart attack and how he died saying:
"I'll only have to close one eye when I die,
poor you, who'll have to close two."
After that Vito learned to sleep with his eyes open.

The voice of the Italian tenor is wailing
about mimosa and the moon which is american.

Vito listens and holds back tears.
He can remember the choice he had to make
as a poor one: to starve making fireworks
to celebrate the saints' days, in the family trade,
working as he had worked as a child,
bare foot until he was thirteen, with his father,
and always hungry,
or to make his way in a new world without mimosa,
where he didn't have to tip his hat to Don So-and-So
in order to eat or get a job,
where he hoped a man would be judged by his work
and paid for his labour.
The good life gave him a house and money
in the bank and a retirement plan,
but it didn't give him fruitful daughters,
his favourite makes herself scarce
and the other looks like her mother.

II   MARTA'S MONOLOGUE

All my life I've tried to please my father.
I live at home, teach school around the corner
at St. Mary's. I make a good salary
and help children to learn to read and write.
I have very little experience, that's true
but I know enough to risk nothing,
to live where it's safe,
to have a job that's secure,
to love those who love me, my parents,
and to offer the proper respect to our relatives
so that when my uncles gather with my father around the
table
I listen very carefully to all their bull shit
as they split *lupini* and throw the shells
into the bowl I don't fail to provide for them.

My elder sister, Lucia, is not like me,

she's not good. She's the first born,
the stubborn one, who wears Italia
like a cheap necklace around her throat,
with a charm that makes her heart green
with tarnish, Lucia, the poet
who talks about us in obscure verses
nobody reads for sure,
Lucia, who claims that someone in the family,
her twin, committed suicide, but it's not true,
she has no twin, I'm the second born
and a full year younger than she is.
Lucia is *putane* because she doesn't live at home
and because she won't say hello
or pretend to like uncle Joe
whom she calls a macho pig.
Secretly I know she has nothing to say
even though she pretends to write
and the family is ashamed of that gypsy
daughter, the bohemian, the cuckoo's
egg in our nest.
Sometimes we wish she were dead.
Sometimes we wish she were married.

At every family gathering
I pull out the accordion.
I play like a full orchestra
overtures by Verdi and Rossini,
the music he loves,
the music I've learned by heart
as an act of love.
Out of my musical box
spring the burnished grapes in wicker baskets
of Italia, the Appennini breathe with lungs
that are the bellows of my accordion,
La Maiella scratches his snowy cap
in the Abruzzi, he's the grand old man
of mountains, I've never seen him
but I've watched my father's head
grow white and bald.

The roads,
the mountain roads,
winding up
the steep flanks,
the round shoulders of the hills,
the geography **of** hearts,
winding up
like a complex thought about someone you love,
how you can never understand them,
how loving them is an act of faith,
a way of choosing to live
or to die,
by instinct,
something that you can't just back out of.
You can't really love unless you realize
that a mortal life isn't time enough to love anyone,
not time enough to know yourself,
so I love my father, who is from the beginning,
who stood to make water
and lay down to make love to my mother,
who knew me from the beginning
as a vague stirring in his loins,
as a burst of ecstasy
on a Sunday morning.

Lucia has other notions about love.
About love she says she's an expert.
I don't know when she adopted the sacred heart
of eros. Five years after she left the church,
she was still a miracle worker of sorts.
I never could understand how she had the visions
and I had the faith,
except that she was the prodigal daughter
and I was the one who resented the fact
that she was not punished, but rewarded,
for doing whatever she wanted to do.

Lucia says that love is a labyrinth:
you approach a familiar doorway,

the door is wide open or barred shut,
the door is too small or too big for you
to reach the handle,
the door is the first hurdle,
then you enter the tunnel,
frescoes and graffiti blister on the walls,
the light you walk by never fails
to reveal a shadow,
you are searching for the one you think you love
through passageways that lead nowhere
but back into the self.

What I really think about love is all mixed up
in my head with what I remember being taught as a child
in religion class at school, the lessons I parrot today
to another generation of squirming innocents.
The family is the first experience
and then what the priest has to say
is a kind of generalization,
the holy family being a prototype
for relationships sanctified by the church
and sanctioned by the state.
I remember how impatient this model of divine grace
working in the world made Lucia.
She was an artist and therefore a narcissist
and believed, when she believed anything at all
that a person's relationship with God
had more to do with the way you love yourself.
Yet we would pray in church,
light candles, and for her they flared,
for me they smoked. I couldn't understand it.
We were ten and eleven years old,
and she would talk about the old gods
as if they were related and equal,
mythology and religion,
a pagan temple and a catholic church,
and she would have her prayers answered,
(whatever she really wanted she seemed to get)
while my prayers, addressed properly to Jesus,

to God, the Father, in His name,
by which He was bound to answer,
were like conversations on a pay telephone,
He never rang back.

Every night I'm afraid I'll wake up
dead and find Lucia there before me,
that even my death will be a hand-me-down.
I know that I'm afraid of getting to the bottom
of the differences between us,
as if to really know her
would be to lose my soul,
and all the clothes she wore before me,
were gifts of shed skin
or cast off experience.
I made them my own and found the fit
gave me a form.
I didn't give a fig about fashion,
but second hand clothes from my sister
identified me as hers.

Lucia wanted to be smarter in her life than in her books
so she made me the butt of her poems.
She would experiment with herself that way,
by putting me in the pigeon box of her words
and watching to see what would happen,
that way she wasn't prepared to make any mistakes.
She demanded some clarity of purpose in her life,
she wanted to act with a vengeance,
not because she was mad at anything
but to clear up the confusion,
a dusty room would give her a headache,
a Marx brothers film on television would send her
running out of the room screaming.
In health class the film of a birth,
the untidy womb giving expression
to an anonymous morass of mucous and blood,
the human shape, a fish on a line,
made her sick and I heard her say:

"Never, never, never..."
in the darkened room,
and as the lights came on, I noticed she had
unbuttoned her shirt and was staring down
at her breasts. I think she feels
the same way about the family,
I think that by denying us
she thinks she can deny that she has legs,
that she's a woman, like any other woman,
servant to a dark blood she doesn't understand.

I'm not ambitious,
I find my art in the accordion
that entertains uncle Joe,
that makes my father hum
and my mother proud at weddings,
I always play and I don't mind,
in fact, I enjoy it,
but more when Lucia's not there
with her sulking face and rude
staccato laughter,
with that you're wasting yourself look,
half pity, more contempt.

But when a woman's life is so worthless,
I think she's got a perfect right
to do nothing,
to paint her nails,
to bake a cake,
and to wait for a man
to buy her shoes
so that she can go walking with him
on a Sunday afternoon
eating ice cream.
Not that I'm waiting for one,
but I like to be with friends
and to exchange tips on the latest
lipstick. I wear it thick and red,
the same shade I remember mother wearing.

Lucia and I would play when she wasn't looking
and paint big mouths with her rouge no. 5,
our lips quivering like blue gas flames
with excitement, as we prepared to be women.
A woman's always naked without her lipstick,
I remember mother saying.
One day I entered her bedroom alone
not prepared for the amazing transformation
I achieved by carefully drawing a cupid's
bow mouth with quick smooth strokes.
It stopped me for a moment as I looked up
from the lips I was defining
to see my skin, startling white,
my eyes, more intensely blue,
my hair, serenaded by the light
from the balcony,
and I saw that I was beautiful,
and I thought I must be rich,
and I thought there was nothing else
I needed to do. Then Lucia barged in,
grabbed the lipstick and painted her nose
bright red, ripped open her blouse,
her breasts like molted birds,
and shouted that a woman always seems naked
without her lipstick on,
and her ironic laughter brought mother in
and a tanning for both of us.

Friday night when I'm going nowhere
and I'm alone, I play with my kohl
eye pencils and become Cleopatra.
Friday night and I know what it means to enter
a room with the sparkling white heart
of a refrigerator.
I paint my eyes like a cat's so that I can look at myself
in nine different ways,
Friday night and I watch the late show to learn

the Hollywood way to the nirvana of a stunning face
and celluloid figure
which tells me more about being female
than the poetry of Emily Dickinson
or the epistles of Saint Paul.

But I learn most about being a woman
from watching my mother, Alma.
I learn from her how a woman is made for love
and for cleaning house.
She's very fat with eating pasta and the insults
of my father who takes for granted her loyalty
and would love a divorce and a younger woman.
He'll never leave her though
because the family's a landscape
he doesn't want changed.

For me she's the ring of smoke the wind wears
on the left hand, on the fourth finger,
open and generous, if somewhat gratuitous,
like a house built for birds,
a house with an entrance, but no door,
a house with windows, but no pane,
a house, where the wind never begs at the front steps
for nothing.

I have to admit I'm happiest when Lucia's visiting
and we all work together as in the old days
preparing preserves of vegetable from the garden for
winter eating,
peeling the burnt skin back from roasted peppers,
pulling off the black ash that sticks
to the fingers in brittle chips,
pulling off the pepper tops,
watching the oil squirt then run
along our fingers, an orange sticky drool,
watching what I'm doing and doing it well.

I confess there was a time when I wanted to be like Lucia,
when I thought her incredibly wise,
when I thought it courage that made her leave home
and generosity that made her experiment with love.
I remember how she used to say
with what seemed such a special kind of knowledge:
"I love you, no matter who you are,
that's not logical, but the axiom
on which logic depends."
I guess it's something like the love we learned about in
church
or from mother, it's so big and so perfect
it's like a circle drawn on the black board,
the imaginary lines of the imagined perfection
and then erased with an unthinking brush
by a monitor after dass.
But Lucia couldn't leave home without coming back too,
whenever she claimed to be flat broke or in despair,
she couldn't stop being the center of attention.

Disappointment is the unthinking brush
bloated with chalk dust and the promise of a better life.
I only want my fair share.
I want what's mine and what Lucia kicks over.
I want father to stop mooning about her
and listen to my rendition of Mimosa.

III   LUCIA'S MONOLOGUE

So much of my life has been wasted feeling guilty
about disappointing my father and mother.
It makes me doubt myself.
It's impossible to live my life that way.
I know they've made their sacrifices,
they tell me so often enough,

how they gave up their lives,
and now they need to live their lives through me.
If I give it to them, it won't make them young again,
it'll only make me fail along with them,
fail to discover a different, if mutant, possibility,
succeed only in perpetuating a species of despair.

Most of the time I can't even talk to my father.
I talk to mother and she tells him what she thinks
he can stand to hear.
She's always been the mediator of our quarrels.
He's always been the man and the judge.
And what I've come to understand about justice
in this world isn't pretty,
how often it's just an excuse to be mean or angry
or to hoard property,
a justice that washes away
the hands of the judge.

Nobody disputes the rights of pigeons to fly
on the blue crest of the air across the territory
of a garden, nobody can dispute that repetition
is the structure of despair and our common lives
and that the disease takes a turn for the worse
when we stop talking to each other.

I've stopped looking for my father in other men.
I've stopped living with the blond child that he loved
too well.
Now I'm looking for the man with the hands of a musician,
with hands that can make wood sing,
with the bare, splintered hands of a carpenter.
I want no auto mechanics with hands blind with grease
and the joints of a machine.
I want no engineers in my life,
no architects of cages.
I want to be with the welders of bridges
and the rivers whose needs inspired them.

I learned to be a woman in the arms of a man,
I didn't learn it from ads for lipstick
or watching myself in the mirror.
I learned more about love from watching my mother
wait on my father hand and foot
than from scorching novels on the best sellers lists.
I didn't think I could be Anna Karenina or Camille,
I didn't think I could be Madame Bovary or Joan of Arc,
I didn't think that there was a myth I could wear
like a cloak of invisibility
to disguise my lack of self knowledge.

The sky is wearing his snow boots already.
I have to settle things with my father before the year is
dead.
It's about time we tried talking
person to person.

More than a tired man, my father is a such a lonely,
disappointed man.
He has learned through many years of keeping his mouth
shut
to say nothing,
but he still keeps thinking about
everything.

"If I had the language like you," he says to me,
"I would write poems too about what I think.
You younger generation aren't interested in history.
If you want people to listen to you
you got to tell them something new,
you got to know something about history to do that.
I'm a worker and I didn't go to school,
but I would have liked to be an educated man,
to think great thoughts, to write them,
and to have someone listen.
You younger generation don't care about anything in the
past,
about your parents,

the sacrifices they made for you,
you say: 'What did you do that for,
we didn't ask you!'
right,
is that right?
These are good poems you have here Lucia,
but what you think about Italy!
'a country of dark men full of violence and laughter,
a country that drives its women to dumb despair.'
That's not nice what you say,
you think it's very different here?
You got to tell the truth when you write,
like the bible. I'm your father, Lucia,
remember, I know you."

The truth is not nice,
the truth is that his life is almost over
and we don't have a common language any more.
He has lost a tooth in the middle of his upper plate,
the gap makes him seem boyish and very vulnerable.
It also makes me ashamed.
It's only when he's tired like this that he can
slip off his reserve, the roman stoicism,
the lips buttoned up against pain
and words of love.

I have his face, his eyes, his hands,
his anxious desire to know everything,
to think, to write everything,
his anxious desire to be heard,
and we love each other and say nothing,
we love each other in that country
we couldn't live in.

From Mimosa and Other Poems (Oakville, 1981)

LEN GASPARINI

TO MY FATHER

Having argued with you, confided in you,
And sometimes listened to you
For most of my thirty-six years
On this accidental planet,
I think it's now time we had a man-to-man talk.

I confess I've been selfish and willful--
Perhaps hereditarily so.
I won't make excuses. You told me long ago
If I took my troubles to the market,
I'd come back with my own.

Well, father, avid birdwatcher that you are--
The blasted oak in which you placed a bird house
Still puts forth leaves. Did it sprout
From an acorn a blue jay forgot?
Is life a half-remembered dream?

The only difference is, your dreams
Are more practical than mine.
You point out the poison mushrooms, then rave about
Their elfin beauty. You add, I subtract.
I am your prodigal freedom enslaved by memory.

I remember when you were burdened with worry
And an aching back, you boarded a train
For Buffalo, New York, and journeyed all night
Just to visit me in jail.
A fellow jailbird said: "That's what I call a father!"

In my deepest shame I felt proud to be your son.
I remember when you spared the rod.
You made me read
The Complete Lectures of Robert G. Ingersoll.
That book spoiled my belief in God.

Although our world views sometimes clash,
We try to respect each other's space.
The craft I've taken so long to learn
Reveals its lines upon your face.
Wisdom reads the heart; age has that advantage.

From Breaking and Entering (Oakville, 1980)
Revised for this publication, 2004.

ANTONINO MAZZA

VIAGGIO

God pushed a boat into the mouth of the sun
and our planet began to swim.

In and out of the light, the milky waves:

the sea grew tongues, the evening gathered dusk,
the light that lapped our wooden walls,
the waves that chased us, that chased the yellow slopes,
the way the sea made love to the pebbly beach,
the earth, a butterfly
                    afloat.

The night our violet earth was lost beyond a disk of stars,
our half moon was a copper cup, and my heart,
inside a chest of bones, a broken child;
my ship rippling in a dish of honey: and I never thought
there'd be so much honey!

In and out of the waves, the polar chills;

it is a dream of copper sunsets, of cherished hopes,
the memory of our journey, between the daily loaves of dread,

between the whines;
                    still, it is ourselves we meet
when we meet love, when we meet our dreams: and life
becomes a dish we relish so much we don't want to finish,
if in her eyes the earth bursts back into the waves,
and our hearts break into the sunlight.

And we grow lips for a child, friend, lost
between two planets when we enter a tangle of tongues
as into a beehive to sting the sweetness and be stung.

And the chills, in and out of the waves,

the way a ship is thrust inside our rippling flesh,
the way a copper planet begins to drift towards us,
towards our lost hopes,
the way God can't hide behind a forest of leaves that cheer,
in and out of the light, that feast for us,
wandering souls.
                    And the chills!

But who would want to suppress a fleeting shudder
if it were a matter of arriving
arriving home
home   so soon   after so long?

From Italia America, Vol. 4, nos. 1 & 2 (1979)

OSSOBUCO

The earth arrives in a village with chestnut eyes
and I can't help myself if fire pours out of my mouth.

There was a purple road once.
It now returns; whine in my head,
the way the sky spins for the evening sun.

And the volcano again breaks the horizon. But my
grandfather... the clay pipe in the orange groves
belching mouthfuls of laughter?

When I arrived, what I'd remembered most died.
But the scent of it flows, invisible through ancient
windows. Inside me, it lingers for love with longing
fingers, the way a muscle smiles, for life.

And I can't help it. The poem
filled with heart enough to cup all bodies
of water, to flood all memories
pours out of me, like a bone with a hole in it.

And I can't help it. Like a dirt road bolting
uphill, my life arrives with me, in an orange forest,
and unfurls in a blaze of colours.

From Anthos Vol. 1 (1978)

RELEASE THE SUN
to the children

Poetry is about learning about sailing a boat
            in the rain
            in the rain and one acre of light
blue water changed to silver: the scales of the river
the colour of mirrors in turmoil.
                              There were women!
and flowers and mirrors and our women are nothing;
and I am in love in the rain. And my thoughts
go back home each time I'm alone.

In the rain we run indoors to the fire:
to the women who followed our men all over the world,

to the strawberries my mother was sharing with us.
                      There were men!
and dreams and colours and our men are nothing;
and I am a poet holding a mirror, in the rain, at night,
and there is our comet: harbour of light.

The way I remember it, there were holes in our sandals,
but a glass planet under our raw flesh, burning,
like the heart of the son of a man
         inside the body of a woman.
                         There were children!
and life and prayers we share and our children
are nothing; and I am alone in a boat, with the hard music
of tear drops, and our planet: a shattering body of silver.

And there is the world the way we want it:
         the word
         "dawn" echoes through our hearts, a surprise
of fire arrives, rising with the colours of flowers, slowly
flooding the air like an angelic cosmic prayer.

Life is about learning about flying a planet
         at night
         at night and I am a man learning about my heart
about this turbulent light. And its night. And a mirror
flies home, in the rain, to release the sun.

From Anthos, Vol. 2, nos. 1 & 2 (1980)

JOSEPH MAVIGLIA

FATHER'S DAY

under the water a boy blue
and swollen

hears a painter's maddened heart
and leaves his salted sticky
wings behind   for

someone else his innocence
now drowns   his rage
raises him to the face of god
bruised as he is   worn
nude and not given to much swimming

daedalus doesn't see this fire
     instead he mourns on mediterranean
shores how to explain
the accident to a dead boy's mother

god listens to the boy   begins
to measure new wings through his angels
and motions the boy forward   not
knowing the language of this god   the
boy steps back
falling off the cloud that holds him

whispers fill his ears in blue and
green   in flemmish tears
the fieldmen and fishermen now look
above
and resent an english poet's guilting eyes

the boy turns modern as he falls
meeting lucifer
and lands in new york city   he
wakes and shakes the dream out of his head

he calls for father but he is mute
   he looks down at his feet
and curls his toes   he tries
to call again and rain comes down
heavy and he runs   his

mother stares at empty bowls
goes out into the yard   looks
at the sea
and sees her husband with a noose   she
runs   she calls   and is too late
falling to her knees   daedalus

now swings in mid-day sun
    the english poet sees a wooden cross
considers abraham and issac for a turn
but chooses the painter's quiet brush

rain fills the streets of new york city

MICHAEL

michael
            steps on satan's head
sword drawn back
satan
laying brown beneath him

this is my saint patrick's
where the irish
devil
cries out his third-world looks
and position

            and my
gold and blessed   in blue
archangel
poses in eternity

  this is when
i do believe
most of what stained-glasss has rendered
more than ever

passing prayer to my dead mother

and the names on walls
both mic and mac
have spoken   still
in this ivory-green basilica
saint anthony
holding child high
but closer to himself than god
seems more her man

　he
and the mics and macs   they've
conquered devils for me in the past
they've sent me
home   making hosts of candy
have taught me rebel songs
and love for sammuel beckett
　　　　　　　liverpool and kennedys
even the undoing of mountbatten

here   in this church of childhood
michael's wings
hold back the light
and all the demons
sadder more than evil
　　　　　call on me to kneel

MONOLOGUE 1

Bobby Rabanzo here! I'm hangin' out. Gonna bust some lines.
Gonna make you weep! You know what they say about dagos now,
uh? Nothin'. They don't say nothin'. I fuckin' dare them!
Fuck it! I'll say it! It goes like this....You see, long ago this guy
stepped off a shore and became a fish. He didn't know why he

became a fish and saw no other fish around him. He thought he was himself. Young. Bright. Full of hope. Full of sun. Earth guidin' his step. As a fish…needless to say he…he lost his footin'… he…he lost his footin' and he didn't know because he thought he was a young man not a fish. So, he lost his footin'. There he was in the sea. Still thinkin' he was a young man and saw no other fish or young men around. He didn't think he was losing it or anything like that. He was just a fish he didn't know he was. When he finally touched land he stood up and walked to the nearest town. It was a farm. He smiled up at the sun. But it was a cold sun. And strange, the moon seemed somewhere behind it. It was callin' as if the moon could call from behind the sun *but it was bright daylight. From the corner of his eye he saw a man approachin'. He had a book in his hand and was yellin' back at other men. There were no trees around them. The man kept approachin'. He askd the fishman his name, The fishman answered and the man with the book didn't understand at first then realized he'd heard this way of speakin' before. When his grandpa used to hold him on his knee. He had forgot the sound. Though other guys, he was told, spoke this way. He opened up his book and held a pencil for the fishman to write with. The fishman stopped but took the pencil and looked in the book…….A fish. A man can never be a fish. How can a man be a fish? How? Fifty fuckin' years of swingin' picks and workin' shovels, buildin' homes, roads, the whole fuckin' city, country, and just because someone said "You're a fish!" Swim! Swim you bastard fish! Swim! C'mon fish! Baby's gotta eat. Folks are gonna die! Swim and you find out what's on the other side. There's no freakin' mailman in the water! Go! C'mon! Swimm! Swim! Swim!*

From freakin' Palomino Blue (Oakville, 2002)

CORRADO PAINA

OPEN COLLEGE

the bars of College street are opening
open Brooklyn
you of granita
and of espressos
tables on the sidewalks and children of immigratory waves

the Chinese State knocks noisily
"we will stop them on the waterline!"
from pool halls upstairs
appear young portuguese

night falls with a group of vietnamese
knifing each other
("sons of war" they say)
at night a gang of vigilantes
clean-shaven italoportojapokrainian
maybe chase a car thief

the yell in ENGLISH
poly, multi thugs

open College

they could close off the area
like in Rome
and put tables
in the streets!
the summer is different on College
and the distant sirens
belong
to the city
on College bells are ringing.
on College firetrucks are a civic event
on College they know you
on College there is a vagrant

that everyone knows
and that goes back and forth
along College
the pantograph of a streetcar
tears through the viscera of the sky
hunks of watermelon
bits of pistachio ice cream
scraps of tomato
and threads of parmesan and pecorino
rain
upon the tables of College

ITALIAN SATURDAY

the area awakens to the sound
of AlfaRomeo and Cherokees
"It's Saturday"
a spring Saturday
we must air out the garages
"wake up Nina and put on your best dress!"
Tony will buy cannoli
while nonno hoes the bekiarda
to plant flowers and not tomatoes
like they taught him
(in adult education)

here in the Petawawa of the rich
of the less rich and of the neveragain poor
the sun shines italian

it's nice to see the cotrarelli
playing be-se-ból
in the streets
and the old men sitting on the steps near
the neoclassic garage

it's warm and the linen clothes are lying
on the bed still fragrant

double-breasted suits and flowered shirts from
florida

the mothers and the nonnas are preparing cannelloni
the wine stirs in the cellars
waiting for relatives friends
how nice it is to walk along the empty streets of
Woodbridge

knowing each other
after years in the neighborhood
there are no cafes
there are no shops
the pools still dirty
the trees so young

there is shade only
near the neoclassic garages
there are no barbers
pharmacists
and the priest...

...it is an italian sun
that beats down on Woodbridge
flowered Woodbridge
one day they will put benches
for the old men
confined in their maximum security bekiardas

From Hoarse Legends (Toronto, 2000)

ROMANO PERTICARINI

EMIGRANTE

Trascinati d'antichi pesi
nel baratro dell'ingiustizia,
stiamo sulle bocche
delle piste pronti allo scatto,
sulle bocche dei "ramarri"
pronti all'agonia.

Figli d'antica madre
che nelle doglie più sofferte
ha voluto partorire
migliori uomini, e ladri:
e noi con i primi esuli,
stanchi d'un pane nero,
stanchi di correre, di cercare,
e nelle piatte città d'acciaio
ci lasciammo vincere, esiliare.

Nelle chiese dell'infanzia
ancora il Cristo muove
la pietà dell'uomo
che sta su pietre assolate,
su cave brecciose, di granito,
sul teatro del dolore,
sulle screpolate vene
della dura terra.
E nelle sere stantie
ingoiar insalate acerbe,
e vino per annegare mattini
d'erbe cotte, di pani duri.

Ha scolpito profondo l'aratro
sulle giovani gote
arabescate di sudore,
invecchiate anzitempo
e chi nella speranza vinse

le distanze, l'incerta meta:
lentamente muore di ricordi.
- Una farfalla all'ultimo volo -
Riposavano le fresche acque
sul palmo della mano
come in devota preghiera,
e l'acqua svaniva, cosi i giorni.

Sono anch'io uno di voi
ho contato mucchi di sabbia,
molliche di pane, gironi amari.
Il mio volo d'ape
dall'alba al tramonto, e quando
le monete d'oro delle piante
ad una ad una caddero:
si sollevarono le ancore e
soffiò il vento le mie vele.

Un asilo nuovo -- fiore di terra --
ma il tarlo della fatica
da sempre nelle mani.
Le mia ricchezza giace
in quelle antiche cave,
nei digiunati mattini,
nelle sere ubriache di stanchezza.

EMIGRANT

Dragged down by ancient verdicts
in the abyss of injustice,
we find ourselves standing at the gates
of the dirt-tracks ready to take off,
and in the grip of "green lizards"
ready for the agony.

Sons of an ancient mother

who by the crudest labour pains
has wanted to give birth
to better men, and thieves:
and to us among the first exiled,
tired of the darker bread,
tired of running, of seeking,
and in the dull cities of steel
we let ourselves be defeated, be exiled.

In the churches of our infancy
Christ still moves
to piety the man
who finds himself standing among scorching stones,
in pits of gravel, and of granite,
in the theatre of our sorrow,
in the chapped veins
of the toughened soil.
Who in the stale evenings
gulps down the tart salads,
and wine to drown mornings
of dried bread, and mushy greens.

The plough has sculpted deep
into the young cheeks
arabesqued by the sweat,
grown old before their time,
and he who with hope won
distances, the uncertain goal,
slowly is dying of his memories.
— A butterfly on its last flight —
The fresh waters had collected
in the palm of the hand
as in devout prayer,
and the water was vanishing, as the days.

I too am one of you
I have counted mounds of sand,
bread crumbs, bitter days.
My bee-line flight

from dawn to dusk, and when
the golden coins of the plants
one by one had fallen:
the anchors were being lifted and
a wind blew in my sails.

A new exile — earthly paradise —
yet the gnawing woodworm of labour
from time immemorial in my hands.
My wealth is buried
in those ancient pits,
in those mornings that were hungry,
and in evenings that went drunk with fatigue.

BELLA VANCOUVER

Sulle rive del Pacifico:
lungo le sponde del Fraser,
adagiata sul fianco dei monti
l'immensa città si distende,
come un'amante pulita, che sa
d'essere bella, bella Vancouver.

Un gregge in cielo cammina,
son lane bianche, grigie e pigre,
e sull'invisible rete s'adunano
lasciando spicchi d'azzurro,
dove si specchiano le mie pupille.

Sei tu pennello bizzarro
che dipingi il cielo turchino,
di bianco, di rosso corallo,
di luce, di stelle d'argento.
Mia tavolozza, mio cielo.

L'insuperabile scalpello di Dio
ha scolpito montagne rocciose:

file d'immobili cammelli, adorni
di laghi profondi, di valli.
Mio cuore, prigioniero felice
di questo paradiso che mi veste.

Basta tacere, chiudere gli occhi,
per naufragare sul tuo giardino
mia bellissima Vancouver.

BEAUTIFUL VANCOUVER

On the ocean shores of the Pacific:
along the banks of the Fraser,
reclining on the slopes of the mountains
the vast city lies
like an impeccable lover, aware
of her beauty, beautiful Vancouver.

A flock glides along the sky,
they are woolly clouds, gray and lazy,
that gather against the invisible net
leaving pieces of blue,
where are mirrored my pupils.

It is you whimsical brush
that paints the deep blue,
with white, with coral red,
with light, with silvery stars.
My master's palette, my sky.

The unsurpassable chisel of God
has sculptured rocky mountains: frozen
rows of camel's humps, adorned
with deep lakes, with deep valleys.
My heart, happy prisoner
of this paradise that clothes me.

Sufficient to fall silent, to close one's eyes,
to shipwreck in your garden
my most beautiful Vancouver.

RICCHEZZA DI UN SOGNO

Quella brocca
portata d'inverno,
nella tiepida primavera,
nel grigio autunno,
d'estate, ogni giorno,
sulla testa bianca,
questa notte ho sognato
e la mia sete ha spento.

Quella vecchia madia
dove accorto custodivo
le mie poche molliche
era aperta e generosa,
i fornelli accesi,
la tavola imbandita,
questa notte ho sognato
e la mia fame ha placato.

Ieri:
che ogni passo ricordo,
nei giorni di sole,
di neve o di primavera,
l'immacolata ventola
delle piume d'oca,
mai che avesse azzardato
vento sui carboni,
nuova la stagnata,
vecchia la mia fame,
appena cheta la sete.

Quell'acqua di fonte
oggi impetuosa

scorre nel petto,
e mi avventura per il mondo.
Ma dispero di trovare
negli angoli più remoti,
una madia aperta,
un fornello acceso,
un'acqua di sorgente,
un giorno da Uomo!

Solo sognando,
stringo l'immensa ricchezza
d'un pane e un pò d'acqua:
come un antico carcerato.

From Quelli della Fionda/The Sling-shot Kids (Vancouver, 1981)

THE PRECIOUSNESS OF A DREAM

That jug
I carried through winter,
and in warm spring,
through the grey autumn,
and in summer, each day,
on my white head,
I dreamt of it tonight
and my thirst has gone.

That old cupboard
where I kept well preserved
my few crumbs
was open and generous,
the burning stove,
the table laid out,
I dreamt it all tonight
and my hunger was appeased.

Yesterday:

of which I remember each step,
in the days of sun,
of snow or in spring;
the immaculate fire-fan
made of goose feathers,
that never dared steer
wind to the coals —
and new is my cooking-pot,
old is my hunger,
hardly sated my thirst.

That old spring-water
flows, today
impetuously, in my chest,
and carries me around the world.
Still I despair of finding
in the remotest corners,
an open cupboard,
a burning stove,
water from a spring,
a day of a Man!

Only in a dream,
I clutch the precious wealth
of a piece of bread and a little water:
like an old convict.

Translated by Antonino Mazza

MATT SANTATERESA

A FREEZE-DRIED NOTION OF BEAUTY
as heard and seen from a Barber's Chair

Icarus' old man has a shiny tanned face
And tells Icarus he loves to build things
While he cuts Icarus' hair on the balcony

Of their apartment. A summer sunlight shimmers
Off the Mediterranean. From nothing he says
Building what people love me to build the way

Bear's tongues drip with honey, bees madly buzzing
Around their heads. That love and desire so intense.
Icarus loves to hear this. He knows how bears

Steal into the night to hives hearing
Sweet inscrutable music in their ears. He loves it
When his father laughs and his eyes twinkle like

Bright waves. And his father says life is like a machine
That he builds that the world trusts completely
Until it breaks down, and then he says, death is like a repairman.

You call and explain what you think is wrong, only
To hear him say that there is nothing he can do, crucial parts
Have worn out, irreplacable parts, nothing can be fixed.

And yes, he knows everything was working perfectly yesterday
But that was yesterday. Now, Icarus smells the repairman
The haircut is nearly done and the fragrance of baby powder fills

His nostrils to the brain as his father tamps some talc around his
Neck to cool scissor burn. It is done. His father hugs him
And tells him to fly a middle air between water and sun, and

Shakes the bib empty of Icarus' hair, then he laughs and spins
Icarus in his swivel chair, it moves 360 degrees and he sees

All is beauty around him, that he could not before

All the wilderness that meshes in a sweep and slowing down.
He sees the farmer struggle to straighten his plow, a fisherman
Reset a line with bait, a boat with a sail like

A drying garment in a wind, and Icarus has an image of God
A form standing there gazing at the horizon, tanned, white bib in his hand
Barrel-chested, sun glancing off the blades.

From Icarus Redux (Toronto, 2003)

RHYTHM AND ARCHEOLOGY

Clang
Clang
Nate is shaping a horseshoe
It turns everything else to silence
Said Bishop and Graves too
Je vous aime beaucoup
Turning round wondering what to do
My love for you is tres tres fort
Rhythm that starts from an atavistic core
Rivers that edify in slipstream sleep
Sounds that ageless emerge and steep
Continue past lineage and longstanding staples
Of every possible notion and constancy of opals
What archaeologies make of shards resounds
Like river's repeated tolls, a spirit sounds
In anvil and oar, Aeolian harp, elliptic
Longingly, lovingly mortal

From *Icarus Redux* (Toronto, 2003)

OVID BY THE BLACK SEA

In remarkable lives many gaze at the sensual
the abusive and still fall under spells of wonder
at the audacity of genius' contribution to
our reflective world, our mirrored world
yet poets riddle old works for clues
to nail down their inspiration and have
some plausible insight to how this
worked so well

He walks the trails of Tsarskoye Selo
remarkable garden walks with thoughts and
haunting barbs no doubt, still his footprints
draft great poems under dark olive leaves

Priests in canticles subsume his greatness
though outcast, his body anoints transgressions,
what an exile! To roam lush aromas, speaking
easily to himself of deities' grace and wars
as waves transact the sea, a critical mass
of words, moonlit, delicate hairs
of the forearm, nape

From Icarus Redux (Toronto, 2003)

CARMINE STARNINO

WHAT MY MOTHER'S HANDS SMELL LIKE

Right now it's obviously garlic. She's chopping
a little of it for tonight's *pasta con alice,* my father's
favourite dish. The sauce calls for three cloves
and three fillets of anchovies, mashed with a fork,
all brought together to fry in some oil for about
two minutes. But after dinner – after she's scoured
the mucked pan and scrubbed the smeared plates,
after she's flushed the glasses free of wine-stains
and wiped the grease speckling the top of the oven –
take her hands, ruddy with the scalded burnish
of hot water, bring them to your face, breathe deeply,
and somewhere, worked into her red knuckles,
is the cool stowed in a pile of sheets just off the line,
is the scent of one's soul in a dry dwelling-place.

CREDO
After the feast of Sant' Anna

Ooohing over these floats – a ship, a hot-air balloon,
a windmill – is silly. To think of them as poetry
even sillier. But what else can we call the guilelessness
of a steelworker who takes his credo of nostalgia
and toys it down to an electric train, lit up and hooting
around a hilly Italian town? Or that ship? Surely
it's an object we can pair with some immigrant's
deep bid for bardic self-expression, the way it speaks
for the one great ark that delivered so many here.
But maybe that's too easy a metaphor. Maybe the ship
is closer to the fear of death, the fear with which
a poem caskets away everything it wants to rescue.

A FATHER'S LOVE

At four, maybe five, I'd hand-and-foot my way
into his lap, and, sleepily perched there, let my mind
tip back from that high ledge until I felt myself
plunge through the air. I say this and you think
it was a test of my trust in him, my imagination
having me plummet as he held me, knowing his love
would never let me hit the ground. Yet he'd slam
the front door, late from work, and stomp past
as I ran to greet him. He'd toss his jacket on a chair,
take a plate from the cupboard and pick among
the leftovers. He'd sit in the den, switch whatever
I was watching, and eat, slumped, in front of the TV.
That's when I'd hoist myself into his lap, scaling
his granite unconcern; and, drowsing, dropped away,
slipstreaming in his arms, hoping he'd catch me.

From Credo (Montreal, 2000)

Why a New Anthology of Italian Canadian Voices?

> A people may have its language taken away from it, suppressed, and
> another language compelled upon the schools; but unless you teach that
> people to *feel* in a new language, you have not eradicated the old one,
> and it will reappear in poetry, which is the vehicle of feeling.
>
> T.S. Eliot, *On Poetry and Poets*

In Canada the concern over cultural identity has generated a lasting debate and dialogue. The concern is set forth, among others, by those who view it as a dynamic, complex and not reductively unified identity, and those who advocate a unitary identity. John Porter's early study *The Vertical Mosaic* (1965), examines the Canadian people as they "are often referred to as a mosaic composed of different ethnic groups".[1] Margaret Atwood's 1970 observation, "We are all immigrants to this place, even if we were born here"[2] invites Canadians to realize, in the words of Marion Richmond in *Other Solitudes*, that "This awareness is a fundamental part of the Canadian sensibility."

The ongoing debates about colonialism, nationalism, and multiculturalism, [1] the discourse concerning cultural identity on Canadian soil conveyed through dualities — old world/new lands, foreign/ indigenous, past/present, immigrant/host, global/local — have roots in the language of early social communities, oral and written, of Canada's earliest missionary and settlers, such as, for example, the Roman Jesuit Francesco Giuseppe Bressani (1612-1672), the Africadians of the eighteenth century, the writings of pioneering women like Susanna Moodie (*Roughing It in the Bush; or, Life in Canada* 1853), and in the early twentieth century, the writings of Frederick Philip Grove. Bressani 's booklet, *Breve Relatione d'Alcune Missioni de P.P. della Compagnia di Giesù nella Nuova Francia* was completed in 1653. This work looks "at Canada and its Native people from an Italian perspective and with terms of reference that are Italian rather than French." [3] The earliest presences on Canadian soil, from the First Nation populations, to the colonizing Europeans, to the Africadians — "the Black populations of the Maritimes and especially of Nova Scotia" whose origins go back to 1783 and 1815 [2] — set the stage very early on for the dualities, the dynamics and paradoxes of identity that are fundamental components of what it means to be Canadian, as George Woodcock notes. [3]

In the decades immediately following World War II, European nations looked to Canada with a degree of admiration mixed with sympathy for the social concerns generated by the massive population influx from Europe in the 1950s and 1960s. In time Canadians are coming to view the diversity of their culture as a dynamic and living legacy of the global mosaic that Canada has always been and continues to be. Over the past two decades "globalization" or world-wide shifts in population have escalated. One of the results is that the debate about "cultural identity" has appeared in numerous nations which for centuries had considered their population and culture homogeneous, or monocratic. At the same time, prominent literary and cultural theoreticians such as Edward Said, Stephen Greenblatt, and the Canadian Linda Bortolotti Hutcheon among others, have pointed to the need to reconsider the model of "national" literature or literary history that has implicitly connoted singularity of language and ethnicity.

In Canada, to assist with research or publication of information in areas of culture and production considered unique or rare, funding bodies such as the Canada Council have for decades encouraged and supported active agencies of study with the goal to cultivate a heterogeneous culture as it arose from a heterogeneous population. In the late 1960s, for instance, the Humanities and Social Sciences Division of the Canada Council provided a grant for research on the short stories that novelist Frederick Philip Grove wrote during the 1920s to the 1940s. The research underscores how Grove's works depicts images of Canadian newcomers as well as host Canadians, at a historical and cultural time of a great influx of immigrants, people who struggle to realize their dreams and to maintain their identities during a time of major debates on policies concerning immigration. [4] Grove, a naturalised Canadian, was born Felix Paul Greve in 1879, in Radomno, Prussia, a border town that was later part of Poland. He was a published translator of French literary titles (Flaubert), before becoming a writer in Canada. Regardless of the continuing critical issues concerned with the literary value of Grove's fiction, the themes and attitudes he explores, the regard in which he is held as one of Canada's "literary forefathers" constitute Grove's legacy and "voice" as an eminent Canadian writer of European heritage and artistic formation. The cultural intersections and concerns evidenced in his works, which explore identity, memory, and the problems of acculturation in general, introduce the several characteristics that have become central features of the expanding, increasingly diversified, and inclusive geography of Canadian literature. Grove's presence on the landscape of Canadian literature with that of men and women writers before him [5], bears witness to the fact that notions of cultural homogeneity or "purity" and "cohesive national" modelling [6] become fictive or mythic in the light of the plural voices and multiple identities of early and contemporary Canadian literature and culture: Africadian, Scottish, Welsh, Irish, English, Cornish, European, Asian. [7]

The beginning of a new millennium and a new century presents a singular moment for Canada the nation, its culture and literature. In the words with which the eminent American poet Walt Whitman described democratic America in the 1855 Preface to his *Leaves of Grass*, "Here is not merely a nation but a teeming nation of nations."[4] The recognition of cultural differences that occurred in the 1990s in Canada and abroad continues to shed light on how distinct identities can come together and dialogue with one another. Today differences need to be re-visioned, not in relation to the concepts of "centre" and "margins" but in ways that can produce new and fruitful alignments. Among the developed countries, Canada best illustrates the diasporic pluralism that is the demographic and cultural reality of the globalized world of the 21st century. It may be worth noting the view put forth by Homi Bhabha, who regards expressions and problems of cultural identity in any community as "the construction of the Janus-faced discourse of the nation," a discourse which like the Greek god of doorways, looks back to the past and forward to the future. In the process of constructing a minority literary identity, the meanings that result "may be partial because they are *in medias res*; and history may be half-made because it is in the process of being made; and the image of cultural authority may be ambivalent because it is caught, uncertainly, in the act of 'composing' its powerful image." [5]

When identity thus configured passes through language and time, through questions of racial categories, of gender differences relating to who we are as men and women and where we come from, it becomes clear that the act of writing as a specific manifestation of self-inscription becomes also a mode of making history, of historiography. Mario Valdés refers to Miguel de Unamuno's idea of history as of a community's constant effort to create and organize itself, and historians are the recorders of this collective identity: "Consciousness is made by speaking. Those who do not speak do not have consciousness of their action. Those who do not express themselves can move but they cannot make. ... History is above all the mediation that the historian provides between the unwritten flow of life and the scant record that has been received thereby striving to facilitate the expansion from facts into the record of living. ... The spoken language of the community is the origin and ultimate recipient of literature. Therefore literary history ...would be a history of the identity of a people." [6] The epitaph by T.S. Eliot at the beginning of this essay and Unamuno's view of history seem to situate self-expression and self-construction at the core of a community's self-historicization.

We suggest that literary anthologies play a role in articulating the language of a community and mediating "between the unwritten flow of life" — what T.S. Eliot calls feeling "in a new language" — and what becomes in time the "record of the living." Anthologies facilitate in both writer and reader a sense of belonging and recognition. Anthologies can also work to enlarge our sense of what it is we belong to and recognize ourselves as being part of because anthologies enable instances of self-expression and self-creation to be brought together to create a polyphony of multiple voices with multiple layers of meaning, language, and style. Because anthologies are often structured according to a historical time sequence, as *Italian Canadian Voices* which moves from past to present, the polyphony of multiple meaning, language, and style can be exhibited in structure as well as content. Our purpose here is to focus on the creative and constructive aspects of an anthology such as *Italian Canadian Voices*, how it speaks about the past to the present and the future, and how it can serve as a meaningful tool to help us know and assess our stances in regards to the constantly changing countenance of Canadian culture, social behaviour, and Canadian politics.

Anthologies function as "cultural maps," we submit, for writers as well as readers: the recorded and validated "voice" [8] of the writer functions as a mirror for the reader in search of human experiences with which to identify, be consoled, encouraged so as to be enabled to grow and move beyond the moment. In the complex construct of cultures that Canada has increasingly become, anthologies play an extremely important role. It is often to an anthology that one turns, at least as a guide, when one knows little about an area of creative and cultural human activity. Anthologies are an invaluable tool to assist with a multicultural education, as they enable readers to grow cultural connective tissues to concerns regarding class, gender, styles and literary genres.

The many and diverse pieces included in *Italian Canadian Voices* bridge a span of two generations from WWII to today. They demonstrate that patterns of creative energy among Italian Canadians are not static and unchanging but rather dynamic and evolving. They create a tapestry of narratives of aspirations, memories, language, and styles which depict a larger story — one of community and human potential. Most Italian immigrants said nothing that we could hear about their individual stories, save what they recorded privately in diaries and in letters that they sent back home, and which at times neighbourhoods would gather to read and dream about [9]. Those of the first generation and their children who write in this anthology are particularly qualified to probe, analyse, evaluate and articulate the intersections of human as well as gender experiences between past/present and future, old/young and new, there/here and elsewhere. Anthologies in general have a particular meaning relating to the "voice" or identity of the selections included, since an anthology brings together a community of writers and a presupposed community of readers — the latter being the social group which through reading, analysis, and identification, provides the "meaning" for the texts included in this anthology. Anthologies also provide what Mario Valdés calls the "continuing potentiality of being read." His insightful article studies the dynamic relationship of writer to text, reader to text, and analyses the role of time in the interpretative process. His observations on the nature of a literary text apply whether the text is found independently or in an anthology when he states, "A text of course does not achieve meaning within its own formal boundaries, but only when it passes the threshold of potentiality into the experience of a reader. The most fundamental presupposition of a literary text is that it is a mode of communication." [7]

Italian Canadian literary history shows an intriguing development from the beginning of an immigrant literature situated in Canada in view of a powerful Italian presence (as shown by the first inclusions in this anthology under "First Voices"), to the maturing of an Italian Canadian literature both firmly rooted in Canadian reality and concerned with the influence, the role, and the values of a specific ethnos within that reality ("*Sacrifici!* I still feel the prick of the flesh I felt then when I hear this word " states Mazza in his "Urban Harvest"). The strong and unbroken literary tradition persisting in Italy for centuries is one of the indelible values that Italian immigrants have brought across the Atlantic. It is a tradition which has richly contributed to the style, the language, the courage and dignity of self-inscription displayed by writers in this anthology which fittingly opens with an author who has alluded to his love of language. In the piece that Mario Duliani prefixes to *The City without Women*, his fictionalized chronicle, he tells the reader, "... having regularly taught courses in French and Italian language, and the history of French literature and philosophy to a large number of internees, allowed me to maintain close and intimate relations with almost all my chance companions." This love of erudition contributes to the measured, spare but powerful language and memorable images that revive the drama and the pathos of the experiences of internment suffered by this community of men in Canadian concentration camps held isolated from home, family, and community at large.

The brief and incisive opening sentence in "Nocturne" sets the calm, confessional tone for the rest of Duliani's *The City without Women*, with the temper of experiences of confinement that unfold: "Majestic and fearful night has descended on the forest where I feel as though I have been buried." Focusing on the paradox of wonder inspired by the Canadian landscape, and fear imposed by the mystery and the injustice of imprisonment, the narrating "I" articulates in highly controlled prose the crippling denial of freedom that is equated with being "buried," "The joy of colours ... vanished into the dark abyss!" Several contrasting factors here introduced — the joy of daylight versus fear of dark, the love of nature versus rigours of camp life, the desire for movement versus confinement and stillness — become main leitmotifs for this work that is grim and sublime, suffused with pathos as the narrator, longing to inhabit as a free man the country that has welcomed him, is instead forced to submit to the indignities of the law that governed it at this time of crisis. Written in a style that eschews both sentimentalism and self-pity, this work chronicles the spiritual faith and hope that the fictive "I" (like many Italian Canadian immigrants) brought with him to the new world — a faith that holds despair in abeyance giving way to courage in the face of very real adversity. The chapter closes with a fateful exclamation: "Courage! Life must be accepted always as it comes...."

This confessional chronicle based on episodes from personal history concludes with the narrating persona's reentry into a world outside the camp in the time of postwar Canada: "The passage from Life to Death would not have been so long. But here it is my return from Death to Life." [8] [10] As a survivor of imprisonment and confinement, the fictive "I" takes up the burden of grim memories and the challenge of lost years to convey to the reader a remarkable sense of confidence in a mysterious and life-giving justice that governs human destinies. This early work by an Italian Canadian dealing with the repercussions in Canada of the European conflict illustrates also some main philosophical ideas circulating in these times as for example the distinctions between those who belonged ("we"), and those who did not ("you" or "the other") [11]. In light of the narrator's final words of reconciliation with "Life," it might be interesting to explore to what extent Mario Duliani, the man and the writer, may have been influenced by Manzoni's notions of Christian Providence. Duliani, like Manzoni, demonstrates not so much that good comes out of evil, but that evil is a moment of chaos within a cosmic timelessness that is rooted in and springs from an essential Goodness.

.   This year marks the 60th anniversary of the publication of this fictionalized chronicle of internment life in Canada during the Second World War. Strong thematic affinities link *The City without Women* with the great Canadian novel *Obasan* by Joy Kogawa, and the Italian Canadian chronicle may also be studied in relation to the large corpus of Holocaust memoirs and testimonials. Antonino Mazza has stated in the Introduction to his translation of Duliani's chronicle that it is "the sole extant first-hand account of the grievous years of internment Italian-Canadians endured as a consequence of deliberate policies of the Canadian government unleashed on its ethnic population in the name of national security." [9] [12]

The confidence and hope displayed in "Nocturne" are exhibited in different ways in "To Bruno," the second piece, a dramatic monologue dedicated to the deceased, beloved and widely esteemed friend, whom the speaker addresses as a listener. This eulogy pertains to the type of lyric that mourns departures and good-byes, *il commiato*, bringing to mind the graveyard poetry of Ugo Foscolo as well as Leopardi's celebrated lyrics which dwell so relentlessly upon memory and remembrance of people and things past. Like the narrator in Mario Duliani's work, the poetic "I" of "A Bruno" must come to terms with an inexorable loss — the dear friend and the familiar world of community and culture. Like Duliani's fictionalized chronicle, the poem ends with the certain confidence of the eventual retrieval of community. These two early works of Italian Canadian literature could be regarded as metaphors for the experience of emigration and displacement. The sustaining pillars of these experiences are unshakeable human and cultural values that shape the inner human world, as well as the manner in which immigrants address and resolve the life crises they encounter. Reliance on faith signals a harbour in the face of adversity, yet it also points to the limits of material and political possibility that characterized the immigrant condition in the war- and immediate post-war decades.

The excerpt by Giuseppe Ricci, "July 1930," which concludes this "First Voices" section consisting of creative writings first written in Italian, displays the fabric of an immigrant people in whom self-reliance, ingenuity, and faith were vital for self-refashioning. At the conclusion of the excerpt, the narrating "I" injects irony in the words of the presiding judge who tells him, "If you can make macaroni, you are a good citizen." The issue here is not simply that the new Italian Canadian immigrant is reliable because he "can make macaroni," but rather that, as the judge well understands, since this immigrant has the ability to become self-sustaining and independent in a matter of months, he certainly has the mettle to be a model citizen. This same mettle based on a centuries-old vision of the ennobling virtue of work, provides for the narrating "I" the certainty to believe that he would receive his "citizenship papers in a short time," which he did, and which he cherished "to this day." Like the first pieces, many other passages included in *Italian Canadian Voices* invite readers and students to heed some special points that the authors embedded in their texts. These points about Italian Canadians help to demystify the stylized "Little Italy" images at times unfairly superimposed on Italian immigrant communities around the world, communities where the cultivation of Italian values and the conservation of the Italian language and regional dialects tended to convey the often inaccurate impression of stagnation and exclusivity.

The selections in the first section of *Italian Canadian Voices* employ language stripped of rhetoric to depict the individual's plight within the newly adopted society in the environment and the culture he inhabits. In each selection the speaking "I" refuses to submit passively, and resists adversity, convinced that a better human condition and a better life are possible and can be achieved. Following Aristotle, the Canadian political philosopher Charles Taylor has drawn attention to what he calls the "affirmation of ordinary life" and to how he views this affirmation as a preliminary step for the person's participation in the "good life" as a free and productive citizen. [10] In each of these three pieces the narrating person is shown as overcoming adversity with a view and hope of engaging in a better life. It may be fair to state that these pieces are suffused with a vision of Italian literary tradition based in part on the classical and humanistic model which assigned to art the highest mission: to instruct and to please.

The fact that these early writers employed most often Italian or

French denotes their preference (or need) to deal with realities of the new culture in terms of an already familiar mode of articulation, as opposed to the "borrowed" and more alien English language. For much of the nineteenth- and the first half of the twentieth century, French functioned as an unofficial second language in Italy, thanks to enduring close cultural and political links between the two countries, so that educated men like Bressani and Duliani would have been comfortable writing in French, which was also the language of their immediate milieu at the time of writing.

As is true for the compositions in the first section, "First Voices," the voices in "Roman Candles" resonate with the notes of a universal human predicament that is exposed when the flow of human wholeness is interrupted or shattered. Fittingly, this section is given the title of the original publication from which the selections derive. "Roman Candles," as noun and as metaphor, while connoting a type of celebratory firework display, also stands to represent here, as in the original anthology, the poetic compositions that resist and reject a bleak forward vision, but point rather to origin, to light as life, as knowledge and hope for the future. These selections continue and further develop the attention given to literary style as noted in "First Voices." Several of these writers have become teachers or members of the professoriate at Canadian universities. Acculturation, memory, and identity remain central concerns strikingly outlined in a language charged with visual imagery, musicality, literary techniques, whose seductive power becomes the effective conveyor of meaning. The compositions in this section, first published three decades ago in *Roman Candles*, have become classics of Italian Canadian lyrical literature.

The sequence of the eleven pieces here reprinted acts as a metaphor for Italy's cultural history (from Roman Empire to postwar emigration), and for the poetic "I's" own odyssey. The first piece, "Roman Return," works out in its twenty-two verses an impressive contrast between on the one hand, the lustre of ancestral Rome with its still standing landmarks

("Castel Sant'Angelo", "il Colosseo"), and on the other, the modern weary metropolis "where water sobs and suffers / where seeds are stranded and rare" and ancient "walls are sleeping, holy in their pagan nightmare." The anaphora that recurs throughout the composition, the structural parallelism between the first and last, the second and fifth, the third and fourth stanzas lend deliberate control to a composition which in a short space yokes together great contrasts of historical time, of settings, and of the speaking "I's" individual perceptions. Such intense poetic experience is conveyed by each of the poems that follow, whose thematic centres address key moments of human experience in the context of cultural displacement. But this first selection, "Roman Return," by its overt and insistent evocation of the great Roman past juxtaposed against the disillusionment of modernity, brings to mind the canonical tradition of the Italian lyric from Petrarch to Leopardi — as well as the compelling, twentieth-century musical compositions of Ottorino Respighi. In addition, the motif of *ubi sunt* ("where are ..."), the elegiac longing for the past, runs subliminally through the poem ("The bricks are chattering with strident sounds of long ago"). Through many of the compositions of this section the poetic "I" as wanderer, as stranger in a land that was once his own, works as metaphor for an internal anxiety about the location of selfhood, a longing for stability and certainty. This poem points forward to "Ancestors," the introductory lyric to section V that recaptures an "imagined past" evoking courageous Italic forefathers from the point of creation, the "Etruscan sailor," the "Roman tenement" leading up to Columbus "as a boy under the denim sails." The finest examples of Italian Canadian literature, while born of the experience of displacement, transcend the limits of individual experience to become works of art that encompass a broadly lived emotional geography: "Life was a long distance telephone call/ across the Atlantic" ("The Immigrant"), "the man works for nothing, because his english/ is less than fine" ("The Man Called Beppino"), "Looking into my sister's eye/ I see Italia behind my shoulders" ("Tree of August"), and "Canadese, you must never forget/ what you are... never!/ because when you do, they'll remind you" ("Canadese").

Like art galleries which exhibit communities of creative energies and methodologies, so an anthology like *Italian Canadian Voices* may be regarded as a veritable gallery of literary art. Readers reviewing its pages may examine and appreciate the diverse "voices" of a community, its literary and its social energies and styles as they have grown and evolved over six decades. The anthology mirrors slices of experience from this community. Umberto Eco reminds us that "Above all, literature keeps language alive as our collective heritage," and "By helping to create language, literature creates a sense of identity and community." [11] The "Short Stories" segment provides a variety of slices of time-interrupted, stolen moments of life in Italy, where the narrating persona encounters very real people and unforseen circumstances. They speak of chance encounters that play key roles in the narrators' realization of the difference between the lived, everyday realities of their lives as opposed to the "ideal" they momentarily glimpse, tantalizing yet evanescent. Most of the five stories unfold in the context of a significant feature of Italian culture.

"Urban Harvest" highlights the significance of a life in contact with the earth of Calabria, a preindustrial agrarian society, whose immigrants transposed their passion for cultivating land to building the Canadian metropolis. Taking the reader back to early end-of-the-century migrations from Calabria to Canada and the frequent returns to Italy, the story builds upon the saying "*Coltura-Cultura.*" The association of the two words intends to demonstrate the fact that for the poor yet resourceful inhabitants of the Italian South, "coltura," the art of cultivating land, was only one vowel distant from their spiritual and intellectual "cultura" back home. With culture in their minds and hearts, they set about cultivating Canadian culture while setting foundations and erecting buildings of its modern metropolis. The story seems to connote with subliminally elegiac tones, that what is interrupted in the immigrants of the Italian South is not the rich humanistic culture within, but rather the cultural fluidity in contact with the land of origin. Disjunctions and values of agrarianism become implicit in the new world in the purposeful work of creating the metropolis, "If a rural dweller, surrounded and humbled by natural beauty, feels no need to create more, in a city one is challenged to construct Culture, the second universe, where human imagination and aesthetic sensibility matter much more."[12] The meaning and conservation of "culture" continue to occupy an important place in Italian Canadian writings. [13]

Concern with culture is also the subject of "Vivi's Florentine Scarf," a story depicting an inspirational encounter between two women within the artistic context of Tuscany's Renaissance heritage. This story's several references to Tuscan painters and their works provide a link with the foregoing story, "Laura," whose ties with Tuscany are literary. Here, an Italian Canadian male visitor strikes a chance conversation at an airport with the beautiful Laura. The deliberate use of the name of Petrarch's "ideal" woman sets the ironic, playful temper of this story that gently satirizes the "Latin lover" stereotype. Yet what remains very real in the reader and in the narrating "I" of these stories is the bitter taste of life's joyful, fortuitous but very fleeting moments. In fact, beginning with "Preludes" and Nestor's desire to have his father near him, this third section of *Italian Canadian Voices* dedicated to the short story, offers — within the cornice of an Italian landscape — a rare, stylistically compact glimpse into the chemistry of desire, and the disconcerting moments when desire is frustrated or banished from the human heart by unworkable circumstance.

It may be of interest to underscore the fact that the literature here anthologized has already appeared in publication. *Italian Canadian Voices*, as an anthology, goes beyond the notions of François Ricard as quoted by François Paré: "Large cultures, more established (but not necessarily older), tend to give rise to reflection (produced inventories), whilst *smaller* literatures, in their fragility, create an illusion of existence by accumulating surveys and anthologies (productive inventories). ... Anthologies are often the only mode of 'public' existence of *small*, especially minority, literatures." [13] The first edition of *Italian Canadian Voices* of 1984 reached an audience largely unfamiliar with the variety and abundance of Italian Canadian literature then already extant. Several contributors to this revised edition, however, are already well published authors included in Can Lit anthologies and curricula. Frank Paci, Nino Ricci, Pier Giorgio DiCicco, Mary di Michele, and Caterina Edwards are among the most celebrated examples.

The novels and novella excerpted in section IV situate the woman at the centre of the social and cultural world of family and community. Second-generation children are shown as being of, as well as estranged from, the culture of their parents. The juxtaposition of the old and the new world yields a continuous and sustained tension that informs each of the four works excerpted. The resulting irony and conflict prepare for the moment of disorder and chaos experienced by the children when the world of the adults comes to an end. Joey and Marie in *Black Madonna*, as well as Vittorio in *Lives of the Saints*, for instance, are forced by the passing of their parents to come to terms with their own ambivalence toward their ethnicity, a coming to terms that involves their re-examination of values and attitudes toward the industrial and technological society that they now confront, unprotected by parental mediation. Both Paci and Ricci, high priests of the Italian Canadian novel, place generation differences, issues of acculturation, and problems faced by women squarely on centre stage of their artistic agenda. The social and spiritual predicaments of their fictional characters acquire a wider significance within the Canadian cultural context, crossing over boundaries of ethnicity. Their novels that often appear on postsecondary CanLit curricula share with other Canadian novels the issues of identity and cultural realism. Referring to views expressed by D.H. Lawrence, Paci maintains that the task of the novelist is to "present Reality. Note, not 'reality.' ... The Real is the truth, and the truth is the whole." [14] In relation to themes and language for the Canadian novel, Paci writes, "We must speak in the Canadian idiom. We must make the zones of influence ... speak Canadian"[15] and "So what matters more than the fact that a novelist is a Canadian or an immigrant is that he has created a good book that adds something to life. ... That maybe twenty or fifty years down the road some person in a small town will pick it up in the local library and experience a moment of revelation. Because the part of the soul that was ripped out to write the book will still be warm, will still be breathing." [16]

Julia Kristeva has stated that an immigrant is somebody who lost his mother — something that could be said also of the second-generation children of immigrants. While discovering a world where utilitarianism and materialism have greater currency than shared human values, while experiencing a type of acculturation that is contradictory and discordant, first- and second-generation Italian Canadians have often returned to Italy, where they consciously sought to reappropriate and/or question aspects of their Italian heritage. The trope of the Etruscan "archeological dig" in *A Whiter Shade of Pale* by Caterina Edwards, for example, functions as a telling metaphor for the rediscovery and reappropriation of past settings, realities and values. In their quest for identity, the characters Edwards presents often straddle two worlds: the Italy of a lost childhood and the Canada of their adult experiences, as Mary di Michele poetically illustrates in "Enigmatico": "... with one bare foot in the village .../ the other busy with cramped English speaking toes in Toronto,/ she strides the Atlantic legs spread/ like a Colossus."

The excerpts given in this section are derived from prose works that convey much more than the "voice" of the speaking "I", who "reconstructs and deconstructs the story of the Italian and Italian Canadian order ... enabling the textures of society to hover between oncoming modernity and lingering medievalism." [17] Published between 1981 and 1991, the novels and novella in question exhibit, within the Italian Canadian ambience, a consciousness of dislocation that at this same historical time had its parallel in the larger framework of Western value systems. Since the 1970s the worker has been made keenly aware of his alienation from his product, from the activity of work, his fellow workers, and from his individual humanity. The predicament of many characters in the Italian Canadian novel may be viewed in terms of the paradox of how to become a modern person but at the same time be able to return to the sources of one's unconscious and collective culture. This predicament is inscribed also in the problem of how to become "a Canadian," while preserving a root culture. As a consequence, the widely encompassing and varied Canadian novel often deals with people who are still "becoming," still retrieving experiences and forming identities from the fragments of a conscious or unconscious trauma of uprooting and migration.

The Italian Canadian writers excerpted in *Italian Canadian Voices* are attuned to dualities springing from tensions between the mainstream centre and pluralistic periphery: loss and gain, alienation and attachment. While exploring cultural dualities, they are also able to write from a vantage point of duality, or indeed plurality. It is hardly surprising, then, that a character's search for authenticity and transcendent values, in these times of late modernity, is fraught with incredulity, unbelief, and cynicism. The tragic end of the central female figure and the crisis of the root-culture in the novels by Paci and Ricci are perhaps emblematic of the skepticism, the "permanent crisis" atmosphere of our times and of these authors' subsequent novels — a modern form of tension tied to the questioning, the unmasking of tradition and assumptions. The attitudes of rebellion, the symptoms of malaise and maladjustment in second-generation characters of these and other Italian Canadian novelists such as Maria Ardizzi, remain to be studied in greater detail in the context of Canada's socio-economic development and the concurrent Western ideological climate. The notion of the self as a multiplicity of subjects is gaining currency in the West. Set against the political and cultural backdrop of the European Union, ethnicity and pluri-cultural identity can be viewed as providing access to a greater understanding of human experience and possibility. Charles Taylor concludes *The Malaise of Modernity* with a significant observation on our era, "As Pascal said about human beings, modernity is characterized by grandeur as well as by *misère*. Only a view that embraces both can give us the undistorted insight into our era that we need to rise to its greatest challenge."[18] [14]

As an anthology, *Italian Canadian Voices* brings together already published works displaying salient issues that recur in Italian Canadian literature over the past six decades. The concluding section illustrates the styles, themes, and concerns that have currency among Italian Canadian as well as other Canadian writers. Several poems are of recent publication. This last section evidences the stylistic and thematic variety, the individuality of voice, the fluidity and spiritual vigour that are the signature qualities of the present generation of Italian Canadian writers. Some arrived in Canada as children, as adolescents or adults; others arrived very recently, while some are Canadian citizens by birth. For the majority of these writers the language of choice is English, while French and English are preferred by a rich constellation of Italian Canadians living and writing in Quebec. [15] Unlike the novel where the presence of Italian or italianate diction tends to hinder the flow of the discourse (Canton), the poetry in English here presented benefits from the sparse Italian words (*paesani, ossobuco, putane, zucchini, canadese, pecorino*) which, pertaining for the most part to an international vocabulary, punctuate the verses with a note of familiarity that enhances meaning.

The thematic diversity of the several lyrical compositions of this final section cuts across ethnic and national boundaries, echoing the more general concerns of contemporary Canadian literature: identity, relationships, family, urbanization. Poems satirizing the negative effects of urban industrialization and consumerism convey and critique social realism through a grating vocabulary (vigilante, firetrucks, multi thugs, repairman, swivel chair). In addition, the rapid succession of images and active verbs, as for instance, in Maviglia's song-poem "father's day," point to hardships in the modern metropolis under the sway of violence, despair, and loss. Maviglia's composition concludes with a memorable pathetic fallacy where nature empathizes with human suffering in today's sprawling city: "rain fills the streets of new york city." Paina's studies of Italian Canadian suburban and urban life focus on the cultural impoverishment that is born of the traumatic shifts from transcendent to material values. The poetic "I" often exhibits a reproaching irony verging on the carnivalesque. His poem "Italian Saturday," for instance, implicitly laments the fraying of spiritual energies by ironically juxtaposing material status symbols (AlfaRomeo and Cherokees, cannoli, linen clothes, double-breasted suits), against Italian-English words (*italiese*) that denote a shared and unreflected everyday commonness (*bekiarda, be-se-ból*). The life of the successful Italian Canadian in Woodbridge, which on the surface appears as a little slice of heaven ("it's warm and the linen clothes are lying/ on the bed still fragrant ... from florida/ ... the wine stirs in the cellars"), is unmasked to reveal a suburban Canadian internment camp, reminiscent of the War years: "here in the Petawawa of the rich/ of the less rich and the neveragain poor/ ... it is an italian sun/ that beats down on Woodbridge/ flowered Woodbridge/ one day they will put benches/ for the old men/ confined in their maximum security bekiardas." The poem "Open College," outlines with tongue-in-cheek, the visible social transformations which have occurred over the decades in Toronto's College street; what was once the beating heart of "Little Italy" is today the site of gang wars, "a group of vietnamese/ knifing each other/ ... a gang of vigilantes/ clean-shaven italojapokrainian/ maybe chase a car thief." This former core of the Italian cultural community, underscored by the repetition of "College," has acquired the semblance of a "prison, or reformatory," connoted by the additional dictionary meanings of "college." The concluding image of "scraps" of food that "rain/ upon the tables of College" further intensifies the sentiment of this Canadian metropolis as a hell of corruption and suffering, since the image of food and rain immediately recalls Dante's *Inferno* (Canto VI), where liquid and solid food waste rain upon the souls of gluttons. Through a biting depiction of symptoms of urban decay in this largest of Canadian cities, the poem laments the weaknesses of communal ties, the paucity of spiritual values, the excesses of corporate capitalism embedded in the overcrowding and the cultural degradation that characterize the metropolis of today's industrialized global community.

The works presented in *Italian Canadian Voices* illustrate to what extent the person and the human condition are the focal subjects of much Italian Canadian writing over the past six decades. In his theoretical essay "Mediterranea: Notes toward a Poetic Manifesto," Pier Giorgio Di Cicco has stated: "The ontology behind Italo-Canadian poetry is non-dualistic. The name is the thing named. ... heart is immanent in mind and mind is immanent in heart in the creative epigenesis. ... Italo-Canadian poesis is hermeneutically dynamic and not party to post-modern trends of deconstructivism .... [it] seeks, rather, to preserve the 'self'."[19] Di Cicco's own corpus leading up to *Living in Paradise* (2001) and extending into his most recent collection, *Dead Men of the Fifties* (2004), is centred upon a hermeneutics of the human condition expressed, in the words of Dennis Lee, through "snatches of harsh, even brutal music, and a bruised jocularity that conveys the plight of a civilisation running on empty." [20] As well, the contemplative and self-reflective compositions in *The Honeymoon Wilderness* (2002), recreate "the texture of acceptance, of serenity"[21] of one who has laboured to understand and come to terms with the human condition.

The artistic world of Di Cicco, and of several Italian Canadian writers, is pre-eminently one that seeks to unlock, to interrogate and attempt responses to the ever changing dynamics of what it means to be human, not excluding, for instance, the subject of maternity, an overarching concern explored in varying degrees by Isabella Colalillo Katz and Gianna Patriarca. Maternity was given prominence in Canadian poetry by

Dorothy Livesay in the early 1940s. Yet as a subject of critical analysis it has garnered close analytical interest only recently. [16] Colalillo Katz's monologue, "Dzikir of Love," offers a mother's perspective in key moments of a mother-daughter relationship. After childbirth and the early months of ecstatic symbiosis ("the world became a sacredness when she suckled"), there follows initiation into life's pain ("why has my daughter become the arrow seeking her own destruction?"), leading to eventual disintegration of mother-daughter relations ("she needs breathing room. I give her sadness. / these are the alchemies of motherlove. ... my unredeemable daughter. sweet mother love"). The dramatic and extended monologues by Mary di Michele, on the other hand, present two daughters' perspectives on their difficult relations with parents — more explicitly with the father. The speaking "I" in di Michele's compositions challenges and resists very real gender issues including the schizophrenic tension between female desire and a daughter's "duty." The open-ended plots of each monologue bring little comfort or closure to either the children who leave to make their way, or to their parents who celebrate their life, but grieve their leaving.

The French feminist theoretician, Hélène Cixous, has written that the journey of a mother [and we would add, that of a father], begins in plenitude and is inscribed by loss. Its understanding of love is not acquisition, or holding on, but letting go. [22] In these poems the central issues pertain to generational estrangement, to the constitution of separate identities that only in part resonate with the immigrant experience. They are part of a much broader, global human debate about belonging and identity-construction of special relevance to Canada, whose national anthem: "O Canada/ Our home and native land!" underscores precisely the notions of home and belonging. These monologues addressing difficult feminine predicaments can be viewed as attempting alternative responses to the boundedness of home and nation. Some of these issues are also found in other contemporary Canadian women writers, such as Dionne Brand, whose fictions, according to Marlene Goldman, "express a longing for and, ultimately, a rejection of origin, belonging, and possession associated with being part of a family and, by extension, a community." [23]

While speaking about Italian Canadian literature, the writer Marisa De Franceschi states, "Regardless of where the seeds come from, the end result is the same: we seek universal truths relevant to any gender any race and culture." [24] The treatment of the figure of the father in several poems in this fifth section serves to illustrate this statement. It also provides a sense of circularity with the ancestral "voices" in the first section of *Italian Canadian Voices*. The introductory poem "Ancestors," for instance, celebrates the past through rich visual imagery from the point of creation ("astounding *tour de force*"), to "stone age riff-raff" and nameless tribes "stamping the earth for rain," moving forward to the courageous exploits of Italic forefathers "whose coat of arms drew eagles," the "Etruscan sailor," and the Roman "Colisseum." Columbus is remembered "... as a boy ... going to sea that first time," a foreshadowing of the explorer of the American continent, future home of the children of the Romans. The speaking "I," portraying himself as "a wrecked tourist ... lost in a city of dust" is at odds with the emptiness of the modern city, but seems to gain more concrete self-definition by rediscovering his ancestral cultural environment ("Great Great Great/ something or other"). The critic Stuart Hall has said that an active engagement is required of us in order to recover our cultural past because that past "is not waiting for us back there to recoup our identities against. It is always retold, rediscovered, reinvented. It has to be narrativized. We go to our own pasts through history, through memory, through desire, not as a literal fact." [25]

Parental figures that so often appear in the lyrics of this last section are emblems of a historicized and cultural past that is both desired and resisted, revered and distanced. The poem, "A Father's Love," which concludes this section as well as *Italian Canadian Voices*, recounts in its last lines, a childhood experience of bonding: "He'd sit in the den, switch whatever/ I was watching, and eat, slumped, in front of the TV./ That's when I'd hoist myself into his lap, scaling/ his granite unconcern; and, drowsing, dropped away,/ slipstreaming in his arms, hoping he'd catch me." These verses outline in their essence, the process of human and cultural development, while each generation learns and builds upon the experiences of the preceding one.

Some of the poems speak of individual epiphanies, peak moments of consciousness and gratitude for the achievements and strength of forebears ("... knowing his love would never let me hit the ground"). The grating language of struggle ("Fifty·fucking years of swingin' picks and workin' shovels,/ buildin' homes, roads, the whole fuckin' city, country" from "Monologue 1"), with biblical allusions ("lucifer ... abraham and isaac" from "father's day"; "I am your prodigal freedom" from "To My Father"), and mythological references ("daedalus," "Icarus' old man"), seem to lend to the figure of the father who is the emotional and social centre, a larger-than-life stature. In di Michele's "Mimosa," the speaking "I" looks to the parent with compassion, "Even more than a tired man, Vito is a sad man" for whom "[t]here is only one heaven, the heaven of the home./ There was only one paradise, the garden" as "[h]e listens to an Italian tenor sing Mimosa/ and savours his banishment ... and holds back tears" because "[h]e remembers the choice he had to make." And yet his domineering force is not forgotten: "He never wanted the girls to grow up." The speaking "I" of "In My Backyard" reviews his boyish rejection of his unskilled father, "My youth was spent in shame of him. /My tiny face would blush, my eyes avert." But now, the boy become adult has regrets and his eyes "avert in shame" that he "ever was that boy." The poem that follows, "Din Don," speaks to the father figure when, after a quarter century, he revisits his town in Italy to the celebrating call of bells that "welcomed" him "back home" among those hills that have remained unchanged by time. The connection with the native soil is taken up also in "Il Macchione - Terra di mio Nonno," a land inheritance passed along family generations and in which each person can recognize his or her past, and the promise for the future. The filial homage that is paid to the father finds a counterpart in "What My Mother's Hands Smell Like," where the mother, traditional soulful centre of the hearth, is celebrated in the concluding verses, "But after dinner ... take her hands ... bring them to your face, breathe deeply/ and somewhere, worked into her red knuckles ... is the scent of one's soul in a dry dwelling-place."

These and other Italian Canadian writers who recognize in the past a basis for the present and a spiritual catalyst for the future, bring to mind the indelible image of an aged parent and adult child inscribed in the pages Western literature: the closing portrait of Book II of *The Aeneid* by Virgil describes Aeneas fleeing Troy, carrying his aged, lame father, Anchises, on his back and leading his son Iulus by the hand. Here, Aeneas bears his father, the weight of the past, upon his back, leading his son, the hope of Rome's future, forward by the hand. In this classic image of *pietas* that involves the proper regard for family obligations, the younger generation eloquently and courageously carries the past into the future progressing toward maturity and self-understanding. Perhaps anthologies, such as *Italian Canadian Voices*, are best suited for evidencing how Canada's literary and cultural heterogeneity encompasses voices with individual registers, but which at the same time project concerns reflecting broader contours of what it means to be human in today's complex global environments. Although the selections included in the five sections of *Italian Canadian Voices* address issues and concerns characteristic of the Italian-Canadian ethnos ("in the dull cities of steel/ we let ourselves be defeated, be exiled/ ... I too am one of you" from "Emigrant"), they also often reflect upon and mirror the very contemporary human fabrics that transcend traditional ideas of "culture" and "ethnos" as determined by national and racial boundaries.[26] With its recurring gaze toward the ancestral past, "Italian Canadiana is as much about resurrection as it is about death." [27] This can perhaps be said of much of the recent Canadian literature that articulates a communality and a commonality — as opposed to an undifferentiated universality — of human experience, since in today's reality the intervention of technology has rendered cultural and national borders and differences more than ever transparent.

In this way communities, whether in Canada or beyond its borders and its shores, are inescapably part of one another, embracing race, politics, language, economy, religion. If the image of the literary anthology as a "bridge" has been effectively applied before, that image is all the more alive and dynamic today at the beginning of a new millennium. A re-edited collection of *Italian Canadian Voices* can awaken new energies between writers and readers, opening windows for renewed critical and theoretical discourses. It can provide evidence of growth and change within the landscape of Italian Canadiana and Canadian literature. But it can also assist in confirming that the movement on that connective bridge is not one way (from root culture to adopted culture), but two-way, because the writers' creative imagination operates in association with and draws from broad cultural signifiers from the adopted, as well as from the root culture, as we have seen. By being a site for diverse voices which offer a panoramic sweep — a view from the bridge — *Italian Canadian Voices* functions as a "sacred" bridge because not only does it span daunting gaps between languages, between past, present and future, between genres, genders, and generations, between shores, but it also "consacrate[s] the writers quoted"[28] celebrating and cementing the interrelatedness between history, culture, and literary representation, contextualized as it is, within the human geography of contemporary Canadian as well as global experience.

END NOTES

1. de Carteau, Michel, 63.

2. See George Elliott Clarke's introduction. As is well known to most Canadians, in October 1971 the Canadian Prime Minister Pierre E. Trudeau introduced in the House of Commons the White Paper, the policy of multiculturalism. Later, the "Act for the preservation and enhancement of multiculturalism in Canada" was passed in 1988, just prior to Brian Mulroney's election as Conservative Prime Minister of Canada. The 1969 Canadian Official Language Act established French and English as the official languages of Canada. For a discussion on the effects of the policy of Multiculturalism and how it sponsored the teaching of heritage languages to grade school students see the English/Italian study by M. Kuitunen, *From Caboto to Multiculturalism* (Welland, ON: Soleil, 1997). For a discussion on the effects of the policy of Multiculturalism on promoting or slowing cultural pluralism in Canada see Smaro Kamboureli's "Introduction" to her edition *Making a Difference*.

3. Since the early stages of Confederation the Canadian Government has relentlessly resorted to the effectiveness of policies in order to exercise promotion and stewardship over immigrants welcomed to populate the nation's vast lands. In his *A Social History of Canada* (NY: Viking, 1988), George Woodcock points to Sir John A. Macdonald 's 1878 National Policy related to the settlement era: the building of the transcontinental railroad to connect distant centres, and "the populating of the prairies by immigrants from Europe. ... Even at the time of Confederation ... Canada was still a country of small towns. ... Less than 20 percent ... lived in urban centres, that is, places with one thousand inhabitants or more. There was far more variety among these mid-nineteenth century communities than there is among the Canadian towns of the late twentieth century" (302-303).

4. F. P. Grove's arrival to Manitoba in 1912 occurred, as H. Dahlie states, at a time in which "thousands of settlers ... landed in the Canadian West during the great wave of immigration that lasted from the 1890s to the eve of World War I. His choice, therefore, to depict in *Settlers of the Marsh* the life of a Swedish immigrant in Manitoba is not surprising, and his

dramatization of the standard responses of many immigrants—their sense of isolation, their experience of misunderstanding and hostility, their problem with the language, their varying degrees of accommodation to the new land — is convincingly handled" (14), *Isolation and Commitment: Frederick Philip Grove* (Toronto: ECW, 1993). Margaret R. Stobie also alludes to the striking plurality of ethnic cultures and languages characterizing central Canada at the time of Grove's arrival and writing: "At the time, Manitoba had an ambitious and idealistic bilingual school system, developing out of the French-English background of the province, but extended to bilingual schools for the settlements of Polish, Ruthenian, Swedish, Austrian, Icelandic, and German newcomers, to try to help them in the transition to their adopted country" (25), *Frederick Philip Grove* (New York: Twayne, 1973).

5. For a history of women writers of early Canada, see the study by Wendy J. Robbins, where she states that "Canadian literature in English begins in the pre-Confederation or colonial era (about a hundred years before Canada became an independent country in 1867), just after the British conquest of the French and their garrisoning of Quebec; it begins with the writing of a woman-novelist Frances Brooke (1723-1789) ... whose epistolary novel of manners *The History of Emily Montague*, set in Quebec, was published in London in 1769."

6. On the subject of the fiction of cultural purity and the "national model," see Linda Hutcheon.

7. It may be interesting for the reader and student of *Italian Canadian Voices* to consider that the literature formed on Italian soil through the centuries presents if not similar, some parallel considerations: Dante Alighieri composed his greatest work the *Divine Comedy* while in exile from Florence, his *patria*. Later, three of the most celebrated writers had family roots in other cultures and languages: Vittorio Alfieri in France, Ugo Foscolo in Greece, Italo Svevo (born Schmidt) in the Slavic culture adjacent to Trieste. For more extended theoretical discussions on di Michele as well as Di Cicco, see my "'Growing for the Flight: Mary di Michele's Reception in Canada." Mary di Michele: Essays on Her Work. Ed. Joseph Pivato, forthcoming 2006, and "Di Cicco's Elusive Virgin: Hunting the Universal Feminine." Pier Giorgio Di Cicco: Essays on His Works. Ed. Francesco Loriggio. Forthcoming 2006.

8.   This revised anthology carries the same title as the first, 1984 edition, *Italian Canadian Voices*. Over the past two decades, notions traditionally interpreting "voice" as the author's perspective, have been subject to radical questioning and shifts. Looking at some current critical problems associated with authorial "voice," Pauline Rosenau in her *Post-Modernism and the Social Sciences*, writes: "Post-modernists question the attribution of privilege or special status to any voice, authors, or a specific person or perspectives. The 'public' voice, however, is more acceptable to post-modernists because it democratizes rhetoric, makes discourse broadly understandable, and at the same time subverts 'its own expert culture'" (Princeton: Princeton U Press, 1992, xiv).

9.   Interesting examples of self-narration by Italian immigrants in southern Ontario are offered in *Ricordi*. Ed. G. A. Niccoli. (Welland, ON: Soleil, 2000).

10.   The subject of internment of ethnic Canadians during WWII has been variously studied in the 1970s and 1980s. Attention is given to the internment of Italian Canadians in Joseph F. Krauter & Morris Davis, *Minority Canadians: Ethnic Groups* (Toronto: Methuen, 1978) 60-120, and in Kenneth Bagnell, *Canadese: A Portrait of the Italian Canadians* (Toronto: Macmillan, 1989), 72-97. On this 60th anniversary of the end of World War II, one can find aspects of the war history of Italian Americans and of Italian Canadians recaptured and recreated on two interesting videos: "Barbed Wires and Mandolins" (48 mins., 00 secs., 1994, National Film Board of Canada) recreates in black and white the environment of the Canadian internment camps, and also provides interviews of several internees; "Prisoners in Paradise" (48 mins. 40 secs., 2001, directed by Camilla Calamandrei), shows the previously untold story of 51,000 Italian soldiers who were brought to the USA as prisoners of war during WWII. Featuring rare period footage of POW camps, the film follows 6 Italian POWs, and the women they met in America, on their extraordinary journey. (ItalianPOW@aol.com)

11.   Readers interested in relating Durliani's work to literary and philosophical trends of the times between the wars and after WWII, may wish to consult the thought of Emmanuel Levinas who was very concerned with issues of nationalism, community, "the same" and "the other." See

Encounters with Levinas, a special edition of *Yale French Studies*. Ed. T. Trezise, No. 104 (2004). In conjunction with Mario Duliani's *The City without Women*, the reader may wish to examine Primo Levi's *Se questo è un uomo* (1947, *Survival in Auschwitz*), where Levi, a scientist and an Italian Jew from Piedmont, wrote of his own internment experiences. As well, Carlo Levi's major novel *Cristo si è fermato a Eboli* (1945, *Christ Stopped at Eboli*), gives an account of his own confinement in the south Italian region of Lucania between 1935-36.

12. What Joy Kogawa said in 1989 of her war experiences could also be applied to Duliani: "We have within us the political person and at times I think that person is yanked out of silence to speak" (Kamboureli, 120). In structure and temper *The City without Women* and *Obasan* differ substantially. Nevertheless they are closely related thematically as fictionalized first-person accounts (City by a man, Obasan by a woman), of a profoundly grievous moment of Canadian history and identity. The introductory essay by Antonino Mazza is a very important historical and cultural contextualization of Duliani's work. Much has been written about *Obasan* and other works that chronicle the internment of Japanese Canadians. See for example, Marlene Goldman, "A Dangerous Circuit: Loss and the Boundaries of Racialized Subjectivity in Joy Kogawa's *Obasan* and Kerri Sakamoto's *The Electrical Field*," Modern Fiction Studies 48:2 (Summer 2002): 362-388.

13. Matthew Arnold's noted idea of "culture" articulated in the 1860s as the best of what has been thought and said, has undergone considerable revisioning, by Edward Said, for example, who states that "culture is a concept that includes a refining and elevating element, each society's reservoir of what has been known and thought. ... Arnold believed that culture palliates, if it does not altogether neutralize, the ravages of a modern, aggressive, mercantile, and brutalizing urban existence" (1994 xiii). Francesca L'Orfano examines some aspects of Italian Canadian culture in her cogent article, "Fragments of Memory: Mainstream Representation and Italian Canadian Film and Video," in the *Central European Journal of Canadian Studies* 3 (2003): 43-55.

14. To date, the Italian Canadian novels have received some critical attention in the framework of minority texts and ideological expressions of Canadianness they offer. Additional interpretations may emerge in

time, for example, from postmodern theoretical approaches that propose to interrogate entrenched concepts which the Italian Canadian novel at once valorizes and questions. In her celebrated study on postmodernism, Linda Hutcheon states, "Like much contemporary literary theory, the postmodernist novel puts into question that entire series of interconnected concepts that have come to be associated with what we conveniently label as liberal humanism: autonomy, transcendence, certainty, authority, unity, totalization, system, universalization, centre, continuity, teleology, closure, hierarchy, homogeneity, uniqueness, origin. ... To put these concepts into question is not to deny them—only to interrogate their relation to experience. ... It questions the very bases of any certainty (history, subjectivity, reference) and of any standards of judgement. Who sets them? When? Where? Why? Postmodernism marks ... a challenging of the very concept upon which we judge order and coherence" (1988, 57). In this context it may be worth noting Charles Taylor's observations regarding the culture of modernity; he considers that "The agent seeking significance ... has to exist in a horizon of important questions. ... Only if I exist in a world in which history, or the demands of nature, or the needs of my fellow human beings, or the duties of citizenship, or the call of God, or something else of this order *matters* crucially, can I define an identity for myself that is not trivial. Authenticity is not the enemy of demands that emanate from beyond the self; it supposes such demands" (1991, 40-41).

15. On the subject of the presence and function of Italian expressions within Italian Canadian literature see Licia Canton and Joseph Pivato (1999). On the subject of Italian Canadian literature in French in French Canada, look for some of the following titles: *Cross/cut: Contemporary English Quebec Poetry* (Montreal: Guernica, 1982); *Quêtes, Textes d'auteurs italo-québécois*, ed. F. Caccia and A. D'Alfonso (Montreal: Guernica, 1983); *Sous le signe du Phénix*, ed. F. Caccia (Montreal: Guernica, 1985); *Voix-off: Dix poètes anglophones du Québec* (Montreal: Le Castor Astral/Guernica, 1985).

16. Offering a "preliminary mapping of early Canadian maternity poetry," Wendy J. Robbins in her article titled, "'Breasting Body': the Beginnings of Maternity Poetry by Women in Canada," affirms that "Critical attention has not been directed to the evolution of Canada's maternity poetry." *Canadian Poetry* 49 (Fall/Winter 2001): 74-93.

FOOTNOTES

1 Porter, John, *The Vertical Mosaic* (Toronto: U Toronto Press, 1965) p. xiii.

2 Atwood, Margaret, *The Journals of Susanna Moodie* (Toronto: Oxford U Press, 1970) p. 62.

3 Pivato, Joseph, *The Anthology of Italian-Canadian Writing* (Toronto: Guernica, 1998) p. 10.

4 Whitman, Walt, *Complete Poetry and Collected Prose*. Ed. Justin Kaplan (New York: Library of America, 1982) p. 5.

5 Bhabha, Homi K., "Introduction: Narrating the Nation." *Nation and Narration*. Ed. Homi Bhabha (New York: Routledge, 1990) p. 3.

6 Valdés, Mario J. , "Rethinking the History of Literary History." *Rethinking Literary History*. Ed. L. Hutcheon and Valdés (Toronto: Oxford U Press, 2002) p.77.

7 Valdés, Mario J., "Conclusion: Concepts of Fixed and Variable Identity." *Identity of the Literary Text*. Ed. Valdés and Owen Miller (Toronto: U Toronto Press, 1985) p. 299.

8 Duliani, Mario, *The City without Women*. Trans. Antonino Mazza (Oakville, ON: Mosaic Press, 1994) p. 156.

9 Mazza, Antonino, "The War on the Home Front: A Duplicitous Legacy." Introduction to the English edition of Mario Duliani. *The City without Women*. Trans. Antonino Mazza (Oakville, ON: Mosaic Press, 1994) p. ix.

10 Taylor, Charles, *The Malaise of Modernity* (The Massey Lectures Series , Toronto: Anansi, 1991) p. 211.

[11] Eco, Umberto, *On Literature*. Trans. Martin McLaughlin (New York: Harcourt, 2004) pp. 2,3.

[12] Makolkin, Anna, *A History of Odessa, the Last Italian Black Sea Colony* (New York: Mellen Press, 2004) p.78.

[13] Paré, François, *Exiguity: Reflections on the Margins of Literature*. Trans. L. Burman. (Waterloo, ON: Wilfrid Laurier U Press, 1997) p. 77.

[14] Paci, Frank G., "Tasks of the Canadian Novelist Writing on Immigrant Themes." *Contrasts: Comparative Essays on Italian-Canadian Writing*. Ed. Joseph Pivato.(Montreal: Guernica, 1991) p. 38.

[15] Ibid. p. 46.

[16] Ibid. p. 59.

[17] Tuzi, Marino, *The Power of Allegiances: Identity, Culture, and Representational Strategies* (Toronto: Guernica, 1997) p. 75.

[18] Taylor, op.cit., p. 121.

[19] Di Cicco, Pier Giorgio, "Mediterranea: Notes toward a Poetic Manifesto." *Writers in Transition: The Proceedings of the First National Conference of Italian-Canadian Writers*. Ed. C. Dino Minni and A. Foschi Ciampolini (Toronto: Guernica, 1990) pp. 111,114.

[20] Lee, Dennis, "Di Cicco's Paradise: An Afterword." *Living in Paradise* By Pier Giorgio Di Cicco (Toronto: Mansfield Press, 2001) p. 158.

[21] Ibid., p. 163.

[22] Cixous, Hélène, "Castration or Decapitation?" Trans. A. Kuhn, *Signs* 7: 1(1981) p. 53.

[23] Goldman, Marlene, "Mapping the Door of No Return: Deterritorialization and the Work of Dionne Brand." *Canadian Literature* 182 (Autumn 2004) p. 24.

[24] De Franceschi, Marisa, "The Immigrant Writer's Dilemma: Duality of Experience." *Palimpesti culturali: Gli apporti delle immigrazioni alla letteratura del Canada.* Ed. Anna Pia De Luca, Jean-Paul Dufiet, Alessandra Ferraro (Udine: Ed. Universitaria Udinese, 1999) p. 17.

[25] Hall, Stuart, Old and New Identities, Old and New Ethnicities." *Culture, Globalization and the World-System: Contemporary Conditions for the Representation of Identity.* Ed. Anthony D. King (Minneapolis: U Minnesota Press, 1997) p. 58.

[26] Verdicchio, Pasquale, *Devils in Paradise: Writing on Post-Emigrant Cultures* (Toronto: Guernica, 1997) p. 16.

[27] Loriggio, Francesco, "Italian-Canadian Literature: Recapitulating." *Italian Canadiana* 14 (2000) p. 82.

[28] Pare, op.cit., p. 79.

Sources

This is a listing of the original publications from which the selections in this anthology were taken. A wealth of information about the writers and their publications can be found by searching internet websites.

Selections which were included previously in the volume *Italian Canadian Voices: An Anthology of Poetry and Prose, 1946-1983* (Mosaic Press, Oakville, 1984) will be identified by the notation *Voices* ,1984.

George Amabile, "Generation Gap" and "Ancestors" from *The Presence of Fire*, McClelland and Stewart: Toronto, 1982. Permission granted by author, 2004. *Voices,*1984.

Alexandre Amprimoz, "Roman Return" from *Roman Candles*, Hounslow Press: Toronto, 1978. Permission granted by The Dundurn Group, 2005. "Preludes" from *In Rome,* Three Trees Press: Toronto, 1980. "10/r" and "s/10" from *10/11,* Prise de Parole: Sudbury, 1980 ."la réalité est le cancer de l'âme" from *Changements de Tons,* Les Editions des Plaines: Saint-Boniface: 1981. "To a Country without Nostalgia" and "Deraciné" from *Fragments of Dreams,* Three Trees Press: Toronto, 1982.Permission granted by the author. *Voices,*1984.

Isabella Colalillo Katz, "Dzikir of Love" and "Washing Day II" from *Journal for the Association for Research on Mothering*, Vol. 4, No. 2 :Fall/Winter, 2002. "A Woman's Identity" from *Journal for the Association for Research on Mothering*, Vol. 5, No. 1: Spring/Summer, 2003. Permission granted by author.

Saro D'Agostino, "The Wake" from *Roman Candles,* 1978; The Dundurn Group, 2005. *Voices,* 1984.

Celestino De Iuliis, "In my Backyard" and "Din Don" from *Love's Sinning Song,* Centro Scuola:Toronto,1981. Permission granted by author. *Voices,* 1984.

Pier Giorgio Di Cicco, "The Man Called Beppino" and "Italy, 1974" from *Roman Candles,* 1978; The Dundurn Group, 2005. *Voices,*1984. "The Happy Time" from *Virgin Science* McClelland and Stewart:Toronto,

1986. "Flying Deeper into the Century", "Country Priest", "Singing in my Skin", and "Something out of Nothing" from *Living in Paradise* The Mansfield Press: Toronto, 2001. "Some Self-Reflection" from *The Honeymoon Wilderness* The Mansfield Press: Toronto, 2002. Permission granted by publishers and by author.

Bruna Di Giuseppe-Bertoni, "Il Macchione-Terra di mio Nonno" from *Sentieri D'Italia* Lyrical Myrical Handmade Book:Toronto, 2004.English translation provided for this anthology. "I Remember...Pier 21" from The Valigia D'Oro Project, 2002. Permission granted by author.

Mary Di Michele, "Tree of August" and "Enigmatico" from *Roman Candles,* 1978. Permission granted by The Dundurn Group, 2005. "Mimosa", "Marta's Monologue" and "Lucia's Monologue" from *Mimosa and Other Poems* Mosaic Press/Valley Editions: Oakville, 1981. Permission granted by author. *Voices,*1984.

Mario Duliani, "Nocturne" section of *La Ville sans Femme* (Montreal, 1945) English translation for *Voices,* 1984. Permission granted by publisher.

Caterina Edwards, "Assimilation", 2003, permission granted by the author. Excerpt from *A Whiter Shade of Pale*, NeWest Publishers Ltd.: Edmonton,1992. Permission granted by the author.

Len Gasparini, "I Was a Poet for the Mafia" and "Il Sangue" from *Roman Candles* 1978. Permission granted by The Dundurn Group, 2005. "To my Father" from *Breaking and Entering* Mosaic Press/Valley Editions: Oakville,1980, and *Voices,*1984. Revised for this anthology. Short story "Laura" first published in *Accenti* Vol. 2, no. 1, Jan.-March, 2004. Permission granted by the author.

Gianni Grohovaz, "A Bruno" from *Parole, parole e granelli di sabbia* Privately printed: Toronto, 1980. *Voices,*1984.

Darlene Madott, Short story "Vivi's Florentine Scarf" from *Joy, Joy, Why Do I Sing?* Women's Press, an imprint of Canadian Scholar's Press Inc.: Toronto, 2004. Permission granted by publisher and by author.

Joseph Maviglia, "Father's Day", "Michael" and "Monologue I" from *freakin' Palomino Blue* Mosaic Press: Oakville, 2002. Permission granted by publisher and by author.

Antonino Mazza, "Our House Is in a Cosmic Ear" and "Canadese" from *Roman Candles*, 1978. Permission granted by The Dundurn Group, 2005. "Viaggio" in *Italia-America*,Vol. 4, nos. 1&2 , 1979; "Ossobuco" in *Anthos* Vol. 1, Winter, 1978; and "Release the Sun" in *Anthos* Vol. 2, nos. 1&2, 1980. *Voices*, 1984. Short story "Urban Harvest = Raccolta urbana" first published by Trans-Verse Productions: Ottawa, 2004. Permission granted by author.

Frank G. Paci, Excerpt from *Black Madonna* Oberon Press: Ottawa, 1982. Permission granted by publisher and by author. *Voices*,1984.

Corrado Paina, "Open Collage" and "Italian Saturday" from *Hoarse Legend* The Mansfield Press: Toronto, 2000. Permission granted by publisher and by author.

Romano Perticarini, "Emigrante-Emigrant", "Bella Vancouver-Beautiful Vancouver", and "Richezza di un sogno- The Preciousness of a Dream" from *Quelli della Fionda /The Sling-shot Kids* Azzi Publishing Co.: Vancouver, 1981. English translations by Antonino Mazza prepared for *Voices*, 1984.

Tony Pignataro, "The Immigrant" from *Roman Candles*, 1978. Permission granted by The Dundurn Group, 2005, and by author. *Voices*, 1984.

Giuseppe Ricci, Excerpt from *L'Orfano di Padre* Printed privately: Toronto, 1981. English translation by Vilma Ricci prepared for *Voices*, 1984. Permission granted by Vilma Ricci.

Nino Ricci, Excerpt from *Lives of the Saints* Cormorant Books Inc.: Toronto, first printing 1990. Permission granted by publisher for 2002 edition, 19th printing. ISBN 1-896951-43-0.

Matt Santateresa, "A freeze-dried notion of beauty", "Rhythm and Archeology" and "Ovid by the Black Sea" from *Icarus Redux* Mansfield Press: Toronto, 2003. Permission granted by publisher and by author.

Carmine Starnino, ""Credo", "What My Mother's Hands Smell Like" and "A Father's Love" from *Credo* McGill-Queen's University Press: Montreal & Kingston, 2000. Permission granted by publisher and by author.

Matilde Gentile Torres, Excerpt from *La Dottoressa di Cappadocia* Edizioni Dell'Urbe:Roma, 1982. English translation by Ann Cameron prepared for *Voices*, 1984. Permission granted by author.

MEMBER OF SCABRINI GROUP

Québec, Canada
2006